Also by Dan Bongino

*Protecting the President: An Inside Account of the Troubled
Secret Service in an Era of Evolving Threats*

*The Fight: A Secret Service Agent's Inside Account of
Security Failings and the Political Machine*

*Life Inside the Bubble: Why a Top-Ranked Secret Service
Agent Walked Away from It All*

SPYGATE

THE ATTEMPTED SABOTAGE OF DONALD J. TRUMP

DAN BONGINO
AND D.C. MCALLISTER
WITH MATT PALUMBO

Post Hill
PRESS

A POST HILL PRESS BOOK

Spygate:
The Attempted Sabotage of Donald J. Trump
© 2020 by Dan Bongino
All Rights Reserved
First Post Hill Press Hardcover Edition: October 2018

ISBN: 978-1-64293-537-0

Cover design by Cody Corcoran

Post Hill Press
New York • Nashville
posthillpress.com

Published in the United States of America

Dedication

This book is dedicated to all of the police-state Liberals, swamp-rat Republicans, and delusional Never-Trumpers who showed us what can happen when your claim on power is challenged. Without you, this book exposing your grotesque abuses of power wouldn't have been possible.

CONTENTS

INTRODUCTION

Imagine if every night a group of suited men in shades came to your door, asking you to join them in a spectacular new business venture. Maybe some other people stopped by later, selling products and dropping hints that they're part of the business plan as well. The men in shades return, asking you again to sign up. If they pressed you enough, you might agree to join them so they'd leave you alone. But once you accept, they reveal they're undercover FBI agents, and you've just conspired to take part in a Ponzi scheme, not a business venture.

Unethical, right? A so-called crime was orchestrated out of nothing. While police officers and federal agents approaching suspects in an undercover capacity is a tried-and-true investigative technique for gathering information, the order of events is critical. Typically, we would expect some basic evidence of a crime or a pressing intelligence need *before* asking officers, agents, and intelligence operators to approach a subject in an undercover or clandestine manner, not the other way around. When the same officers and agents contact innocent persons— with no factual information or evidence of a predicate crime to justify the allocation of resources—it's an abuse of power, a violation of the trust given to law enforcement by the American people. It's a setup.

We believe this is what happened to the Trump team during the presidential campaign. As reported by investigative journalist Sara Carter, "Senior Obama officials used unsubstantiated evidence to launch allegations in the media that the Trump campaign was colluding with Russia during the run-up to the 2016 presidential election, according to newly discovered documents and communications obtained by Congress."[1] Representative Mark Meadows, a member of the House Oversight and Government Reform Committee, told Carter, "It appears there was a coordination between the White House, CIA, and FBI at the onset of this investigation and it's troubling... What we're finding is the more we dig the more we realize that there appeared to be a willful coordination between multiple groups outside the Department of Justice and FBI."[2]

This scandal is complicated and messy, involving intersections among the Clinton campaign, the Obama administration, intelligence agencies, and foreign operatives. The streams twist across the political landscape, but each flows into the same river. There's no simple story here, no conspiracy theory—that's something we're not interested in pursuing. We don't think all the actors in this scandal gathered in a smoke-filled room and hatched a plot. There's no Doctor Evil at the helm. We do believe, however, that each entity, driven by its own motivation, played a role in creating a false narrative that almost caused Donald Trump to lose the election and continues to hound him in his presidency. It's a narrative that has disrupted the US democratic system, lessened the credibility of American law-enforcement agencies, and sown contention in civil society. For the sake of truth, justice, and, yes, the American way, we need to expose what really happened in the 2016 presidential election—and beyond.

PART I

MAKING OF THE TRUMP-RUSSIA COLLUSION NARRATIVE

IN EARLY SPRING 2016, Donald Trump was rising to unbeatable status in the Republican primary. As GOP candidates braced for defeat, the Democrats prepared for attack. Nothing Republican opponents had done stuck to Trump. His supporters remained by his side, with numbers growing by the day. Something more needed to be done. The following is an account of how various pieces came together to create and perpetuate the belief that Trump was conspiring with the Kremlin to undermine the American democratic system and defeat Hillary Clinton.

When trying to prove wrongdoing, experienced investigators have a good tip: *remember the names.* Just keep in mind the names of significant subjects and note their reappearance at critical junctures. By doing this, the smoke will begin to clear, and the true culprits, tactics, and motives will come into focus. You will see the real scandal for what it was: an effort to cast a cloud of Russian collusion over Donald J. Trump to sabotage his campaign and delegitimize his victory.

PAUL MANAFORT

Paul Manafort couldn't have imagined the train wreck heading his way when he joined the Trump presidential campaign in the spring of 2016. If he had, the experienced political consultant and controversial lobbyist would have chugged along in the opposite direction. Instead, Manafort reentered the fray of American politics, carrying with him a history of questionable foreign interests and Russian entanglements that brought his campaign work to a screeching halt and shored up speculation that Trump was in cahoots with the Russians.

Manafort had a history of working on presidential campaigns, having advised those of Gerald Ford, Ronald Reagan, George H. W. Bush, and Bob Dole. In the 2008 presidential race, Senator John McCain considered hiring Manafort to manage the Republican convention. The political consultant, however, became too much of a liability when he and McCain's top adviser, Rick Davis, arranged a meeting between the senator and Russian billionaire Oleg Deripaska, who was pals with Russian president Vladimir Putin and had recently been denied a US visa due to suspicions of being connected to organized crime. At first, Deripaska's shaky status didn't deter Manafort and Davis from setting up a meeting with the senator at a swanky ski chalet in Switzerland, but when the association between the McCain team and Deripaska came to light, ties with Manafort were severed.

During this time, between 2006 and 2010, Manafort worked as an adviser to Ukrainian president Viktor Yanukovych. Controversial and pro-Russian, Yanukovych won the fourth election after Ukraine's independence from Russia; his opponent, however, claimed the 2004 election runoff was rigged. The questionable results incited a series of protests culminating in the Orange Revolution, where protesters wore orange against the frigid backdrop of the Ukrainian winter in support of Yanukovych's rival, Viktor Yushchenko. The peaceful demonstrations had their desired effect: the Supreme Court of Ukraine overturned the election and ordered a repeat of the second-round ballot. Yushchenko won 52 to 44 percent. As a result, Yanukovych's political image was in shambles, and his clout among foreign governments, such as the United States, took a heavy blow. It was Manafort's job to rehabilitate his image and the reputation of Yanukovych's Party of Regions.

Manafort wasn't the only American working on behalf of the pro-Kremlin political party. According to documents from the State Department, the Podesta Group, headed by Tony Podesta, "a Clinton bundler and brother of Clinton's 2016 campaign chairman John Podesta, represented the Party of Regions."[1] As reported by Judicial Watch, which obtained the documents in a Freedom of Information Act lawsuit, "the Podesta Group had to retroactively file Foreign Agent Registration Act disclosures with the Justice Department for Ukrainian-related work."[2] The Judicial Watch press release continued:

> *The filing states that the Podesta group provided for the nonprofit European Centre for a Modern Ukraine "government relations and public relations services within the United States and Europe to promote political and economic cooperation between Ukraine and the West. The [Podesta Group] conducted outreach to congressional and executive branch offices, members of the media, nongovernmental organizations and think tanks."[3]*

But, as Judicial Watch points out, Robert Mueller's special counsel investigation into Russian interference and collusion with a foreign government "hasn't indicted anyone from the Podesta Group."[4] In addition, documents show that Bill Clinton's right-hand man, John Podesta, lobbied on behalf of his brother's firm. The connections to the Party of Regions and the lobby work on its behalf are problematic, but nothing has been done about it. According to Judicial Watch,

"By the standards of the Mueller special counsel operation, these emails alone would have been enough for the Podestas to have been hauled before a grand jury or worse," said Judicial Watch President Tom Fitton. "These emails are a stark reminder that the Mueller's special counsel operation seems more interested in the alleged foreign ties of the Trump team, rather than Hillary Clinton's (and Barack Obama's) associates."[5]

To date, the Podestas haven't been held accountable for failing to register as a foreign agent—a stark difference from Manafort, who was indicted for the very violation the Podestas committed. A double standard couldn't be more obvious.

During the Ukrainian campaign, Manafort lobbied American politicians to treat Yanukovych on par with his rival, something that helped change the Party of Regions' image "from that of a haven for mobsters into that of a legitimate political party," as ambassador John Herbst wrote at the time.[6] Manafort's efforts were a success, and Yanukovych defeated one of the leaders of the Orange Revolution and his fiercest rival to win the presidency in 2010. Yanukovych's victory made Manafort an enemy of pro-democracy, pro-Western Ukrainians, and his lobbying on behalf of Yanukovych would later come back to haunt him, as Manafort would be charged with violating the US Foreign Agents Registration Act for failure to reveal the nature of his work in Washington on behalf of foreign entities.

In 2014, after four years under Yanukovych's reign, Ukrainians once again took to the streets, protesting his decision to back out of a European Union trade deal linked to anti-corruption reforms. If Ukraine had agreed to the European Union pact, Russia would have had less influence in the country. Instead of choosing the West, Yanukovych accepted a multibillion-dollar bailout from Russia, angering those who wanted to be free of their shadowed Russian overlords and the corruption that festered in the Ukrainian government. The conflict led to police shooting citizens in the streets and the deaths of dozens of protestors. The demonstrations that ended in bloodshed forced Yanukovych to flee to Russia for asylum, thus ending Manafort's working relationship with the former president.

This exit from Yanukovych's sphere, however, wasn't the end of Manafort's work in Ukraine. When the new president, Petro Poroshenko, called for immediate parliamentary elections in the fall of 2014, Manafort returned to Ukraine to reinvigorate Yanukovych's Party of Regions and establish the broad-sweeping Opposition Bloc faction that included anyone opposed to the new pro-Western government. His efforts—once again—were a success, and the pro-Russian party retained power in parliament. Manafort then decided to leave Ukraine and get back in the saddle of American politics, oddly assuming no one would mind a lobbyist with Russian contacts jumping aboard the Trump train that was bulldozing through the Republican primaries.

In February 2016, Manafort reached out to Trump through a letter, asking to be part of the campaign. Despite dominating the Republican field, Trump was rough around the edges and would need help wrapping up the nomination and defeating Hillary Clinton. No one knew how to polish a candidate's image like Manafort, but he would have to make a strong case to be hired. Contrary to rumors that he was close to Trump, Manafort had only brushed shoulders with him through business dealings in the 1980s, so the bridge to Trump was a mutual friend, real estate investor Thomas Barrack Jr.

Barrack met with Manafort and looked over his memo of selling points, adding bold language to charm Trump. In his letter, Manafort set himself apart from the Washington establishment, citing his work overseas, which freed him from insider baggage. This claim might have been true to some extent, but he was still carrying baggage—just the Ukrainian and Russian kind. After Yanukovych was deposed, Manafort became a subject of an FBI investigation focusing on work done by Washington consulting firms for the former pro-Russian ruling party of Ukraine. Ukraine was also engaged in investigations, probing corruption and illegal transactions during Yanukovych's presidency. As part of the FBI probe, a Foreign Intelligence Surveillance Act (FISA) request was granted to wiretap Manafort—surveillance that continued through his work on the Trump campaign. According to *Fortune* magazine, "It is unclear whether the President [Trump] was recorded as part of the investigation."[7]

Unaware of his precarious legal position, Manafort sold himself to the Trump campaign as a man without skeletons in his closet. "I have managed Presidential campaigns around the world," Manafort wrote to Trump. "I have had no client relationships dealing with Washington since around 2005. I have avoided the political establishment in Washington since 2005. I will not bring Washington baggage."[8] Manafort also said he wanted to work for free and added that he lived in Trump Tower—something that would have appealed to Trump's ego.

After finishing going over the letter, Manafort gave the envelope to his friend Barrack, who delivered it to Ivanka Trump and her husband, Jared Kushner. They, in turn, passed it along to Donald Trump. Trusting his advisers and lacking other choices of experienced election operatives because of shunning by the Never-Trump movement, Trump brought Manafort onto the campaign in March 2016. After a short time, Manafort was elevated to the position of campaign manager, replacing Corey Lewandowski.

Manafort's hiring on March 29, 2016, was immediately questioned in the media due to his business connections with Russian billionaires and Ukrainian politicians close to Putin. His addition only fueled whispered speculation that Russian forces controlled the Trump campaign. NBC News charged that Manafort was helping to shape the foreign policy of the "most pro-Russian political campaign in modern American history."[9] Some questioned how much Manafort's lucrative business transactions with Russian oligarchs influenced Trump's apparent Putin sympathies. "It's just extraordinary," Michael McFaul, US ambassador to Russia under Obama, told NBC News. "This is not a Republican or Democratic thing. Almost nobody agrees with Trump on this stuff."[10]

David Kramer, a former State Department official in the George W. Bush administration and McCain associate who worked on Marco Rubio's campaign, told NBC News that the connections between Trump advisers and Russia "are deeply disturbing.... Trump's attitude on Russia is not in line with most Republican foreign-policy thinking.... Trump has staked out views that are really on the fringe."[11] Kramer would later serve as a liaison between McCain and former British spy Christopher Steele to collect his DNC-funded fictionalized dossier on Trump and hand it over to the FBI. Kramer's involvement in the dossier delivery would later lead him to invoke the Fifth Amendment to avoid incriminating himself when interviewed by the House Intelligence Committee.

Alexandra Chalupa

Allegations of Trump-Russia collusion began to gain steam after Manafort joined the team. A driving force behind that narrative was Ukrainian-American Alexandra Chalupa, a DNC consultant with a long history of working for Democrats and former Clinton campaign officials, as well as serving in the White House Office of Public Liaison during the Clinton administration. The DNC paid her 412,000 dollars from 2004 to June 2016 for consulting work, after which she left to research Manafort full time. Chalupa had Manafort in her sights since 2014 when his boss, Yanukovych, had protesters gunned down in the streets during the Ukrainian Revolution. A pro-Western Ukrainian activist and lawyer who supported the pact with the European Union, Chalupa hated Russia's role in destabilizing her home country. She was concerned Russia would do the same in America through Donald Trump, and she planned to do everything in her power to stop it.

The moment Manafort joined the Trump team, Chalupa alerted the DNC of the "threat" of Russian influence. Chalupa's sister, Andrea, spread the word on a Ukrainian television show, calling Manafort's hiring a "huge deal" and describing him as the "puppet master of some of the most vile dictators around the world."[12] His hiring, she said, sent a "very, very, very, very, very serious warning bell going off."[13] This fear was rooted in the belief that Manafort was the mastermind behind Yanukovych's corruption.

Not everyone believed he controlled Yanukovych to that extent. Julia Ioffe wrote in *The Atlantic* that Manafort's lobbying efforts for the benefit of Russia and Ukraine were not that unusual. Manafort wasn't a puppet master but "fancy window dressing meant to signal to the West that the Russians were legit and on par with the countries of the West."[14] The problem, Ioffe argued, wasn't Manafort's work on Russia's behalf, but that he joined a campaign seemingly enamored with Putin during an election fraught with rumors of Russian meddling. Nothing Manafort did, she explained, was "out of the ordinary" because many Westerners do business with the Russians—an enterprise in which Americans aren't always conforming to Western values.[15]

Manafort might not have been the puppet master, but Ukrainians who fought against Yanukovych's regime and members of the current government believed he was a Russian tool being used to strengthen ties between Trump and Putin. Pro-democracy activists in Ukraine found the thought terrifying, especially if Trump won, thereby turning a great ally in the West away from Ukraine and toward its foe to the east.

Spurred on by this conviction, Chalupa began her information campaign through a network of journalists, particularly Michael Isikoff of Yahoo News. Interestingly enough, Isikoff played another role in spreading the Trump-Russia collusion narrative by publishing leaked information from the Steele dossier later that year. That article was used by the FBI—in nonsensical circular fashion—as supporting "evidence" of the dossier's credibility in a FISA request to spy on a former member of the Trump campaign, Carter Page.

In the spring and summer of 2016, Chalupa's goal was to start the dominoes falling in the Trump campaign by getting the scoop on Manafort and the Russians into the public realm. She also "floated the idea of getting damaging information from the Ukrainian embassy."[16] Isikoff appeared to follow her lead and began reporting information that was damaging to Manafort and the campaign. In April 2016, he published an article about

Manafort's lobby work, writing that in the past his "role as an adviser to Ukraine's then prime minister, Viktor Yanukovych, an ally of Russian President Vladimir Putin, prompted concerns within the Bush White House that he was undermining US foreign policy."[17]

In another article, Isikoff highlighted a court case in which officials in the Cayman Islands questioned Manafort about his connection to a twenty-six million-dollar investment by his partner Deripaska in a failed telecommunications development in Ukraine. "[T]he court documents shed new light on a trail of complicated offshore business dealings (many of them through firms registered in the Cayman Islands, Cyprus and elsewhere) that Manafort engaged in with wealthy Russian and Ukrainian oligarchs," Isikoff wrote. "These ties could prove problematic for Manafort."[18]

In an email to a DNC colleague dated May 3, 2016, Chalupa wrote that there's "a lot more coming down the pipe":[19]

> *I spoke to a delegation of 68 investigative journalists from Ukraine last Wednesday at the Library of Congress...they put me on the program to speak specifically about Paul Manafort and I invited Michael Isikoff whom I've been working with for the past few weeks and connected him to the Ukrainians. More offline tomorrow since there is a big Trump component you and Lauren need to be aware of that will hit in the next few weeks.*[20]

After the event, Chalupa and Isikoff headed over to the Ukrainian embassy for a reception.

In just a few months, Chalupa and her band of journalists achieved their goal of getting Manafort ousted, but they never proved Trump was colluding with the Russians. On August 19, 2016, Manafort resigned from the Trump campaign after more came down the pipe. *The New York Times* reported that Ukraine's Anti-Corruption Bureau found a black ledger in a bank vault abandoned by Yanukovych showing twelve million dollars in cash payments earmarked for Manafort by Yanukovych's political party. "Investigators assert that the disbursements were part of an illegal off-the-books system whose recipients also included election officials," the *Times* reported. "In addition, criminal prosecutors are investigating a group of offshore shell companies that helped members of Mr. Yanukovych's inner circle finance their lavish lifestyles."[21]

Manafort's financial interests in Russia and Ukraine had already been reported in the press, but Manafort's job with the Trump campaign and the supposed hacking of the DNC emails by the Russians put them under the microscope. This examination revealed "new details of how he mixed politics and business out of public view and benefited from powerful interests now under scrutiny by the new government in Kiev."[22]

By the next year, with the campaign well behind him, Manafort found himself at the center of another investigation by several government agencies, including the CIA, NSA, FBI, DNI (Director of National Intelligence), and the financial crimes unit of the Treasury Department, based on "intercepted Russian communications as well as financial transactions."[23] A report in *The New York Times* on January 19, 2017, disclosed the investigation to the public.[24] Special Counsel Robert Mueller took over the probe on May 17, 2017, and just a few months later, FBI agents conducted a no-knock raid on Manafort's home and seized documents.

Manafort surrendered to the FBI after being indicted by a federal grand jury in October 2017. He has since been jailed, facing decades of imprisonment if convicted on all charges.

These include failure to register as a foreign agent, conspiracy against the United States (not related to the Trump campaign), and money laundering. Like every indictment resulting from Mueller's special counsel investigation, the crimes Manafort allegedly committed have absolutely nothing to do with Trump or his campaign, nor do they confirm any ties to the Kremlin on Manafort's part.

Chalupa and others, however, were positive the Manafort hiring would be the key to proving Trump's collusion with Russia. It wasn't, but it did reveal possible collusion of a different sort—that between Ukraine and the DNC in a media campaign against Manafort and, by extension, Trump. There's a reason White House deputy press secretary Sarah Huckabee Sanders said in 2017, "If you're looking for an example of a campaign coordinating with a foreign country or a foreign source, look no further than the DNC, who actually coordinated opposition research with the Ukrainian Embassy."[25]

In a *Politico* article on Ukraine's role in the election, Kenneth Vogel and David Stern make the case that the Ukrainian government worked to bolster the Clinton campaign.[26] The article focuses on Chalupa, who told *Politico* that Ukrainian government officials gave her information to pass along to the DNC—an admission she has since denied.

Ukraine would have been interested in affecting the outcome of the election, considering Manafort's work for Yanukovych and Trump's supposed affinity for Putin. Ukrainians believed these connections could potentially set the United States against Ukrainian interests. These were the same fears that compelled Chalupa—fears she reportedly shared with Ukraine's ambassador to the United States, Valeriy Chaly, and a top aide, Oksana Shulyar, in early 2016. *Politico* reports that

Chalupa asked for an interview with President Poroshenko, but the embassy turned her down; they wouldn't get directly involved, though they would provide guidance.[27]

Embassy officials have insisted they didn't work with Chalupa's network of reporters, including Isikoff, whom she put in direct contact with Ukrainians. Shulyar claims she never worked with Chalupa on the campaign, but a source in Shulyar's office told *Politico* there was coordination with Chalupa and the Clinton campaign regarding the investigation of Manafort.[28]

Chalupa also contacted Democratic congresswoman Marcy Kaptur of Ohio, co-chair of the Congressional Ukrainian Caucus, to discuss initiating a congressional investigation on Manafort and his ties to Russia before the end of summer.[29] That plan never came to fruition, but Chalupa reportedly continued to work with both American journalists and Ukrainian contacts to bring down Manafort and expose collusion between Trump and Russia.

The DNC has insisted that Chalupa did her research on her own and not for the committee, but she communicated with DNC officials and promised to give them sensitive materials offline while she was still working for them in May. Chalupa had to provide the information in person because her Yahoo account had been breached by a state-sponsored actor (which she concluded was Russia), and she couldn't trust online communications.[30]

After *Politico* published its investigative report, the Foundation for Accountability and Civic Trust filed a complaint with the Federal Election Commission (FEC) against the DNC and Chalupa for "soliciting, accepting, and receiving contributions from foreign nationals in violation of the Federal Election Campaign Act."[31] Providing anything of value, including information and leads, to a political committee is an "in-kind contribution."[32]

Republican senator Chuck Grassley of Iowa also raised concerns over Chalupa's activities. Writing to Deputy Attorney General Rod Rosenstein in July 2017, Grassley said, "Chalupa's actions appear to show that she was simultaneously working on behalf of a foreign government, Ukraine, and on behalf of the DNC and Clinton campaign, in an effort to influence not only the US voting population but US government officials."[33] He continues,

> Aside from the apparent evidence of collusion between the DNC, Clinton campaign, and Ukrainian government, Chalupa's actions implicate the Foreign Agents Registration Act (FARA). As you know, the Committee is planning a hearing on FARA enforcement. Given the public reporting of these activities in support of a foreign government, it is imperative that the Justice Department explain why she has not been required to register under FARA.[34]

These are the same federal charges Special Counsel Mueller brought against Manafort. Rosenstein, however, has done nothing with the Chalupa case, a point Grassley made in a follow-up statement in October. He writes,

> As always, it's important to let our legal system run its course. While we don't have any more information regarding the current status of the special counsel's investigation other than what has already been made public, it's good to see the Justice Department taking seriously its responsibility to enforce the Foreign Agents Registration Act. I've been raising concerns about lackluster enforcement of this foreign influence disclosure law for years now, regardless of administration or political party. It should be enforced fairly and consistently,

regardless of politics or any other factor. The dirty little secret is that lots of people across the political spectrum in Washington have skirted their FARA registration obligations for years with little to no accountability. I've been working on legislation to improve the Justice Department's enforcement of FARA, and expect to introduce it very soon.

The Judiciary Committee is continuing its work to ensure that the Justice Department and FBI are functioning free from inappropriate influence, consistent with our constitutional oversight responsibility.[35]

Grassley questioned the DOJ "about possible FARA violations by Clinton confidantes Sidney Blumenthal and John Kornblum for their reported work on behalf of a political party in the nation of Georgia, Fusion GPS and various individuals working to undermine the Magnitsky Act, Lt. Gen. Michael Flynn's retroactive registration under FARA and Democratic National Committee consultant Alexandra Chalupa's reported work with Ukrainian officials to undermine the Trump Campaign."[36] No charges have been brought against those related to the Clinton campaign.

Serhiy Leshchenko

One of the most effective pieces of information that showed up in US media during the election came from a Ukrainian parliamentarian and former investigative journalist. Serhiy Leshchenko revealed documents that supposedly proved Manafort had received a cash payment of 12.7 million dollars from Yanukovych's pro-Russia party. The Clinton campaign used this report to pound away at the Trump team, further advancing the narrative that they were working with the Russians to win the election.

Manafort denied receiving the money, but curiously, elements of this same story showed up in memos compiled by Clinton operative Christopher Steele, partially confirming the legitimacy of the report. According to BuzzFeed, Steele's memo claims that "Ex-Ukrainian President Yanukovych" confided "directly to Putin" that he had "authorised kick-back payments to Manafort, as alleged in western media."[37] According to Steele, Yanukovych assured Putin that there was no "documentary evidence/trail" of the transactions. So if there were actual payments, and the mysterious ledger is legitimate, Yanukovych lied to Putin about there being evidence.[38] But it's inexplicable that Yanukovych would leave such an important document in an empty bank vault for his enemies to find, so maybe he was telling Putin the truth—or all of it is fabricated. We don't know because, like many things in Steele's fake dossier, this conversation has never been verified.

The revelation of the black ledger listing a cash payment to Manafort had its desired effect—it led to his resignation. Leshchenko told *The Financial Times* why he made the information public: "A Trump presidency would change the pro-Ukrainian agenda in American foreign policy. For me it was important to show not only the corruption aspect, but that he is [a] pro-Russian candidate who can break the geopolitical balance in the world."[39] According to Leshchenko, most of Ukraine's politicians are "on Hillary Clinton's side."[40] Leshchenko later changed his tune when speaking to *Politico*, saying he wasn't interested in who won the election. He simply made the alleged payoff to Manafort public because he wanted make people aware of the investigation and its political importance.[41]

Adrian Karatnycky, a senior fellow at Washington's Atlantic Council, a think tank active in Ukraine, told *The Financial Times* that Ukrainians were upset over "the Trump team's alleged role in removing a reference to providing arms to Kiev from the Republican platform at its July convention."[42] Given this kind of anti-Ukrainian policy from the Trump campaign, Karatnycky said, it's "no wonder that some key Ukrainian political figures are *getting involved to an unprecedented degree* [emphasis added] in trying to weaken the Trump bandwagon."[43] When Trump would later tweet that the Ukrainians had interfered in the US elections to boost Clinton, it was Karatnycky who shot back with the argument that it didn't matter because nothing Ukraine did could be compared to Russia's interference. The information released from Ukraine "were related solely to Manafort's activities on Ukrainian soil and were limited to his relationship with Yanukovych and the Party of Regions."[44]

Those materials, Karatnycky argued, were provided by a disaffected former deputy head of Ukraine's Security Service, not Ukraine's president. Poroshenko has insisted that no one in the Ukrainian government had anything to do with Leshchenko's actions or influencing the election. But, according to Vogel and Stern of *Politico*, a former adviser to Poroshenko found it unlikely that he or someone close to him didn't approve in some way.[45]

Victor Pinchuk

While Chalupa and Leshchenko were on their crusades to bring down Manafort, they were not the only Ukrainians with a finger in the election pie. Victor Pinchuk, Ukrainian oligarch and longtime contributor to the Clinton Foundation, arranged meetings between US journalists and Ukrainian lawmakers in April, the same month Chalupa was gathering journalists for a media blitz on Manafort. One of those Ukrainians was Olga

Bielkova, a member of the Poroshenko Bloc faction in parliament and deputy head of the Committee on Fuel and Energy Complex, Nuclear Policy, and Nuclear Safety. Bielkova traveled to the United States to meet with individuals in the media and government, including *New York Times* reporters Judy Miller and David Sanger, *Washington Post* reporter David Ignatius, *Washington Post* editorial page editor Fred Hiatt, and David Kramer, senior director for Human Rights and Democracy at the McCain Institute.

The stated purpose of the meetings was to discuss "energy reform and energy independence."[46] The meeting with Kramer (John McCain's go-between in obtaining the Steele documents), however, included another person whose presence brings into question the purpose of the meeting on April 12, 2016. That individual was Ukrainian lawmaker Pavlo Rizanenko, who works in banking, not energy. From 1999 to 2005, Rizanenko lived in Moscow and worked in investment banking, then later moved to Ukraine. After becoming a member of parliament, he joined a special commission to investigate privatizations during the 2000s. In May 2016, Rizanenko was nominated to a special investigative commission to look into government corruption and offshore financial dealings.

Leshchenko, the rabid investigator who released dirt on Manafort in the midst of Russian collusion allegations against the Trump team, was also considered to be on the same commission. He was denied a seat, however, because he had spread negative reports about an official in the Poroshenko administration, an act of disloyalty the president didn't appreciate. Leshchenko told the *Kyiv Post* "that even if he doesn't end up on the commission, he will try to visit its meetings to share his knowledge of the political corruption with the members."[47]

Rizanenko and Leshchenko are both members of the Euro-optimists, a pro-democratic parliamentary group in Ukraine, and they share an association with Pinchuk.[48] Rizanenko has participated in Pinchuk's Yalta European Strategy conference and, as part of the commission to probe privatizations in Ukraine, he investigated a highly explosive case involving Pinchuk and two other oligarchs. The three men entered a business deal in the sale of an iron ore factory that ended in a vicious feud. Pinchuk claimed he had been cheated out of billions of dollars by the two business tycoons. The case was fraught with accusations of violent attacks and multiple murders on both sides. An investigation by Rizanenko's commission led to the prosecutor general's office looking into the possibility that the state sale had been illegal. The matter ended, however, just before it went to trial in early 2016 when Pinchuk and the two oligarchs came to a secret settlement in London.[49]

Leshchenko's history with Pinchuk involves payments from his foundation in 2016—information that was reported in the press when the lawmaker's tax returns were leaked. Leshchenko told the *Kyiv Post* that the payments were "for his participation in events organized by Pinchuk during the World Economic Forum in Davos"[50] in January 2016. The money, however, didn't come from Pinchuk: "The Victor Pinchuk Foundation had received money from George Soros's International Renaissance Foundation to finance his participation and that of other Ukrainian lawmakers in the Davos Economic Forum."[51]

So, two Ukrainian officials—both involved in some fashion with investigations into government corruption in Ukraine, both with ties to Pinchuk, and one who has received funding from liberal political activist George Soros—make an appearance in the United States during its highly contested presidential election in which the presumptive Republican nominee is supposedly in lockstep with Moscow. Why was Leshchenko so hell-bent on releasing financial documents about Manafort, even though their authenticity was questionable? Was it, as he initially said, to bring down Trump? Why did Rizanenko and Bielkova meet with Kramer of the McCain Institute? If contacts between Trump advisers and foreigners should be examined in this "meddling environment," these should be as well.

A lobbyist working for Pinchuk arranged the meeting, but when questioned about this, Bielkova tried to distance herself from Pinchuk's role and financial support. Bielkova has worked with the Ukrainian oligarch for several years, and she told a *Kyiv Post* reporter that the "Victor Pinchuk Foundation paid neither for this trip nor for any others."[52] Bielkova added that the lobbyist who made the arrangements "gets monthly payments for his services, regardless of my presence."[53] She insisted she made the trip after being invited by the Atlantic Council. But this doesn't put much distance between her and the Ukrainian billionaire—Pinchuk sits on the International Advisory Board of the Atlantic Council.

The Washington-based think tank is connected to Ukrainian interests through its Ukraine in Europe Initiative, which "is designed to galvanize international support for an independent Ukraine within secure borders whose people will determine their own future."[54] Pinchuk has helped fund the Atlantic Council, as has George Soros' Open Society Initiative for Europe. Serving on the International Advisory Board with Pinchuk is Obama's director of national intelligence, James Clapper. Obama's assistant secretary of state for European and Eurasian affairs, Victoria Nuland, who claims to have received the Steele dossier at the State Department and then passed it on to the FBI before the investigation started, has spoken at the Atlantic Council.[55] And Dmitri Alperovitch, the CTO of the only company that investigated the hacking of the DNC's servers and quickly determined it was the Russians, is a nonresident senior fellow in cybersecurity at the think tank.[56]

The Atlantic Council came under scrutiny in 2014 by *The New York Times* for being one of several "prominent Washington research groups" that "have received tens of millions of dollars from foreign governments in recent years while pushing United States government officials to adopt policies that often reflect the donors' priorities."[57] Research firms have been transformed into "a muscular arm of foreign governments" lobbying in Washington. Some scholars say they have been pressured to reach conclusions friendly to the government financing the research."[58] *Times* reporter Eric Lipton continues,

> *The think tanks do not disclose the terms of the agreements they have reached with foreign governments. And they have not registered with the United States government as representatives of the donor countries, an omission that appears, in some cases, to be a violation of federal law, according to several legal specialists who examined the agreements at the request of* The Times.
>
> *Some scholars say the donations have led to implicit agreements that the research groups would refrain from criticizing the donor governments.*[59]

According to the *Times*, the Atlantic Council "is a major recipient of overseas funds, producing policy papers, hosting forums and organizing private briefings for senior United States government officials that typically align with the foreign governments' agendas."[60] The Atlantic Council told the newspaper that they have no conflicts of interest because most governments realize they're not lobbyists. Their "contracts and internal documents," however, seem to say otherwise. The *Times* discovered in its investigation that "foreign governments are often explicit about what they expect from the research groups they finance."[61]

It's not surprising, therefore, that Pinchuk and the Atlantic Council would want Bielkova to meet with US media and officials as Chalupa was firing warning shots about Manafort and Trump's collusion with Russia. Bielkova's history as an activist is a long one, not just for energy independence but for freedom from Russian influence. During the presidential elections, she opposed Yanukovych and has been a watchdog on Putin's activities in the country. A blogger at *Huffington Post*, Bielkova wrote in 2014 that Ukraine must continue its crusade against corruption and Russian influence with help from the West. The money flow from Russian plutocrats to Western banks needs to stop, she said. "The violent separatist movement in eastern Ukraine, which has increasingly resorted to terrorist tactics, as it is unable to muster popular support, is widely understood to be financed by Yanukovych and his henchmen."[62] Ukraine, she wrote in another blog, "will no longer tolerate irresponsible government, and this is how I know our nation will not be defeated."[63]

A Harvard graduate, Bielkova served as the former international projects director and financial administrative director for Pinchuk's foundation and is associated with the Atlantic Council, having spoken in forums and published with one of its fellows. More significantly, she is connected to the Clinton Foundation, having managed the WorldWideStudies program of the Clinton Global Initiative and the Victor Pinchuk

Foundation.[64] The program helps talented Ukrainian students pursue their master's degree in universities outside Ukraine. As reported in *The Wall Street Journal* in 2015,

> *In 2008, Mr. Pinchuk made a five-year, $29 million commitment to the Clinton Global Initiative, a wing of the foundation that coordinates charitable projects and funding for them but doesn't handle the money. The pledge was to fund a program to train future Ukrainian leaders and professionals "to modernize Ukraine," according to the Clinton Foundation. Several alumni are current members of the Ukrainian Parliament.*[65]

Bielkova's trip to the United States happened shortly after Yanukovych's former adviser, Manafort, had been added to the Trump campaign. The meetings were arranged by Democratic lobbyist and former pollster for Bill Clinton, Douglas Schoen, who was working on behalf of his longtime employer, Victor Pinchuk. Schoen has a long history of either advising or lobbying for Pinchuk, dating back to 2000. It was Schoen who first introduced the steel tycoon to the Clintons in 2004. When Hillary Clinton was secretary of state in the Obama administration, Schoen lobbied on behalf of Pinchuk "in the dissemination" of his "views on democratization in Ukraine and European integration."[66]

Schoen's work for Pinchuk occurred before the Ukrainian Revolution in 2014 when Manafort's boss, Yanukovych, fled from Ukraine to Russia. At the time, Pinchuk was "one of Ukraine's only oligarchs to have deep ties to Washington," the *Times* reported in 2014. "Many of the country's richest businessmen are suspected of having links to organized crime and do not have visas to the United States, much less a relationship with a former and potentially future president."[67] Not so with

Pinchuk. The oligarch, with connections to the Clintons and interests in steel that sometimes put him at odds with steel-workers in the United States, seemed to have an open door to the United States and its halls of power.

According to *The New York Times*, Pinchuk was in "frequent contact with Mrs. Clinton's State Department, at meetings arranged by a Clinton political operative turned lobbyist, Douglas E. Schoen."[68] Schoen insisted that they only talked about democratization in Ukraine, but suspicions were piqued in the media because during this same period Pinchuk and his company Inter-pipe Ltd. were embroiled in trade disputes and allegedly making illegal steel dumps in the United States, which angered local steel-workers. As Pinchuk visited the State Department and lobbied in the United States between 2006 and 2013, he donated 13.1 million dollars to the Clinton Foundation. Schoen's lobbying on behalf of Pinchuk on pro-democracy issues ended the same year Clinton left her position as secretary of state.

Pinchuk's company could have also benefited from his relationship with Clinton when in 2011 to 2012, a series of shipments were sent from Interpipe to Iran. "Among a number of high-value invoices for products related to rail or oil and gas, one shipment for $1.8m (1.7m) in May 2012 was for 'seamless hot-worked steel pipes for pipelines' and destined for a city near the Caspian Sea," *Newsweek* reported. "Both the rail and oil and gas sectors are sanctioned by the US, which specifically prohibits any single invoice to the Iranian petrochemical industry worth more than $1m."[69] It's likely that Interpipe qualified for penalties because of its subsidiary on American soil, but the company received no penalties. And who was the US official responsible for overseeing non-US companies during this time? Hillary Clinton.

Pinchuk's relationship with the Clintons has always been favorable. According to the *Washington Post*, the Clintons "have attended meetings and private events with Victor Pinchuk," despite his facing "formal complaints in the United States for unfair trade practices."[70] Pinchuk said he supported the Clinton Foundation because of the "unique capacity of its principals to promote the modernization of Ukraine."[71] Bill Clinton has spoken at Pinchuk's Yalta European Strategy conference, which aims to move Ukraine away from Russia and toward the West. At one of these conferences in September 2013, Pinchuk told Bill Clinton, "Mr. President, you are really a superstar, but Secretary Clinton, she is a real, real megastar."[72] While Hillary Clinton was secretary of state, she invited Pinchuk to a private gathering in her home—a fact revealed in an undisclosed email obtained by Citizens United—despite Clinton denying she met with him while she worked in the Obama administration.[73] Pinchuk also supported her 2008 election campaign and donated 8.6 million dollars through his foundation to the Clinton Foundation while she was secretary of state.

One would think that with this history, the American public would have heard Pinchuk's name in association with the Clinton campaign in the 2016 presidential race, but that's not the case. Instead, it was when the Mueller investigation began questioning a 150,000-dollar donation from Pinchuk to Trump's charity that the Ukrainian billionaire made headlines. After donating to the Clintons for years, Pinchuk suddenly seemed to "switch sides" by giving to Trump and causing questions to be raised by investigators about whether this was actually a campaign donation in violation of election rules.

When we probe a little deeper, we see that Pinchuk didn't switch sides, and the money he gave was to the Trump charity for a twenty-minute video on behalf of the Ukrainian people and not a donation to the Trump campaign. The allegation is that it might have gone to the charity, but the payment of 150,000 dollars was too much for such a short video clip, so it must have been a political donation. Some have even said Pinchuk would have happily supported Trump because Pinchuk once said Ukraine could not be successful without Russia.[74]

Supporting Trump in this context might make sense if Pinchuk were a pro-Russian political activist, but he's not, despite the comment—and his family ties. He's a Ukrainian of Jewish descent who took a steel company and turned it into a billion-dollar asset, making him one of the wealthiest men in the world—something many entrepreneurs tried to do in post-Soviet capitalist Ukraine. Most have done it by breaking the law, but Pinchuk claimed that he has always played by the rules in an admittedly legally fluid environment.

Pinchuk dived into the middle of politics when he married the daughter of former Ukraine president Leonid Kuchma, a pro-Russian robber baron who was accused of murdering a journalist. Despite Kuchma's shady reputation, in 1994, President Bill Clinton praised the Ukrainian president for his wisdom and courage as he sought to "build a peaceful and prosperous Ukraine."[75] Kuchma's protégé was Yanukovych, who hired Manafort to clean up his image. Given this connection, it would seem that Pinchuk would have a natural affiliation with Manafort, making his donation to the Trump "campaign" likely.

The problem is that despite supporting Yanukovych in the 2004 election, Pinchuk was sympathetic to the protestors in the Orange Revolution. His change in political loyalties, along with his love of capitalism, moved him toward the democratization of Ukraine and away from an affinity with Moscow. The future of Ukraine was freedom, capitalism, and democracy. When the revolution of 2014 happened, and fellow citizens were being gunned down in the streets, Pinchuk identified with the people. "We were in shock," he told *Forbes*. "To see death as it happens, live on the air, is horrible.... We were on the phone constantly—with businessmen, with politicians, with our Western and Eastern friends, discussing what all of us could do."[76] With his thoughts fixed on the struggles of his countrymen, Pinchuk arranged for medical supplies to be delivered to the wounded in the central square.

Pinchuk supported the revolutionaries, but as a businessman, he knew stabilizing his country would require bringing many actors to the table, and his comments about the future of Ukraine reflect this complexity. "The goal of a businessman is to do everything to avoid bloodshed and to bring about peace and compromise," he told *Forbes*. "It's not necessary to be a member of the European Union, but European values will solve a great number of Ukraine's problems."[77] But, "Ukraine cannot be successful without Russia." Such a comment makes sense, given that Pinchuk's business is affected by Russia's damaging tariffs. He has to do business with Moscow, after all. But, when all is said and done, Pinchuk believes, "Ukraine is Ukraine in its current borders—and we must not give up any part of it."[78]

Given this mix of concerns and motivations, it's understandable that Pinchuk would seek out any Western leaders who would speak on Ukraine's behalf, which is exactly what he did as the US presidential election was getting started in 2015. During this time, Pinchuk asked several leaders to voice their support at his Yalta conference. He was particularly persistent to meet with Hillary Clinton, and if she wasn't available, then he wanted her husband to participate. In John Podesta's leaked emails, officials from the Clinton campaign discuss whether Bill should meet with Pinchuk to show his support for Ukraine. "Victor Pinchuk is relentless following up about a meeting with WJC in London or anywhere in Europe," the staffer wrote. "Ideally he wants to bring together a few western leaders to show support for Ukraine with WJC probably their most important participant.... I sense this is so important because Pinchuk is under Putin's heel right now, feeling a great degree of pressure and pain for his many years of nurturing stronger ties with the West."[79]

Neither Hillary nor Bill met with Pinchuk during this time, having expressed "downsides" about the meeting.[80] These concerns weren't detailed in the email, but it could have been that Pinchuk had already been connected to Clinton in one campaign and had given her charity millions while she was secretary of state. Donations to the Clinton Foundation had been a focal point of criticism in the media, and Clinton didn't need any more bad press about the foundation and its questionable cash flow. Pinchuk then turned to Trump, who was revving up his campaign and clear of Russian allegations that would come later. Trump agreed and provided a video sharing his support of Ukraine. Pinchuk offered no money in exchange, but being the New York businessman he is, Trump asked through his lawyer, Michael Cohen (or Cohen did it on his own), for a donation to his foundation. Pinchuk agreed and gave a meager 150,000 dollars (by comparison) to Trump's charity.

Pinchuk, in other words, never intended to give a dime to Trump. He was working on nurturing stronger ties with the West, which apparently was his concern. It's not surprising, therefore, that Pinchuk would pay Schoen to lobby on his behalf and connect a Ukrainian parliamentarian with politicians and journalists in the United States in the midst of a presidential campaign. The meetings might very well have been about energy, as stated, but the Ukrainians were worried that their march toward the West would be halted if Trump became president—and he had just hired one of the greatest threats to that goal, Paul Manafort. They didn't want their biggest ally to be tied to the fingers of Vladimir Putin. This potential threat is why, as Leshchenko said, the majority of Ukraine's politicians were "on Hillary Clinton's side." Trump's trek to the White House had to be stopped.

GEORGE PAPADOPOULOS

George Papadopoulos is an ambitious young man who, without significant experience working on political campaigns, pulled strings to become a foreign policy adviser to the Trump team. His contacts with shady individuals during the election instigated an FBI investigation into Russian interference, and this resulted in Papadopoulos being charged with making false statements to the FBI during an interview on January 27, 2017—a minor charge that has led to no indictment relating to collusion. Papadopoulos, however, is a pivotal actor in the Trump-Russia collusion narrative, as investigators have claimed his actions gave the FBI the factual basis it needed to open a full counterintelligence investigation of the Trump campaign, allowing it to use the most invasive techniques available to gather information on American citizens.

Joseph Mifsud

Papadopoulos's story began in March 2016 when he was named a foreign policy adviser to the Trump campaign with a supposed emphasis on improving US relations with Russia. During this time, Papadopoulos traveled to Italy and met Joseph Mifsud, a Maltese professor of diplomacy based in London, where Papadopoulos was also living. On April 26, 2016, Mifsud met with Papadopoulos in London and told him he had damaging information from the Russians on Hillary Clinton. Mifsud is a shadowy character who seems to have connections with government officials throughout the world, even though these associations often appear exaggerated on Mifsud's part.

One contact he claimed to know well was Russian foreign minister Sergey Lavrov. According to Mifsud's fiancée, identified as Anna by Alberto Nardelli of BuzzFeed, Mifsud said Lavrov was a friend, and he showed her a picture of the two of them together as "proof."[81] Lavrov most likely crossed paths with Mifsud through the Valdai Discussion Club, which presents itself as a vehicle to "promote dialogue of Russian and international intellectual elites and to deliver independent objective scholarly analysis of political, economic, and social developments in Russia and the world,"[82] though there could be more to it. Russian president Vladimir Putin attends the club's annual meeting every year, as does Lavrov, and this could have been Mifsud's point of contact. From Mifsud's comments on the Valdai Discussion Club's website, he seemed to be a Putin fanboy, exuberantly praising the Russian president for his foreign policy in areas such as Syria and Saudi Arabia.[83]

Mifsud's other Russian connections include Alexander Yakovenko, the Russian ambassador to Britain, as well as two others: Aleksei Klishin and Ivan Timofeev. Klishin, a former Russian parliamentarian and professor at a Russian university run by the Foreign Ministry, was invited to speak at Mifsud's now-shuttered London Academy of Diplomacy. Timofeev is the program director of both the Valdai Discussion Club and the Russian International Affairs Council, a Russian government-backed think tank that works with Russian and foreign diplomats, experts, businessmen, and government officials. Mifsud introduced Timofeev to Papadopoulos, and they often corresponded through email reportedly to establish relations on foreign policy.

The FBI has focused on Timofeev as a Russian spy, but his contacts with a US organization that provides international policy solutions cast some doubt on the validity of this concern. On April 25, 2016, just one day before Mifsud met with Papadopoulos in London, Timofeev participated in a seminar with a well-respected bipartisan think tank in Washington, D.C., the Center for Strategic and International Studies (CSIS),[84] and has worked with its officials to develop a report on US-Russia relations (published in August 2017).[85] If the FBI was concerned that Timofeev threatened US national security, why didn't they warn CSIS? Instead they said nothing, and CSIS continued its publication with significant help from Timofeev on the development of policy proposals for better relations between Russia and the United States—the very focus of Papadopoulos's email communications, which were arranged by Mifsud.

Mifsud's connection with Russian academics like Timofeev and his loose dalliances with Russian officials and diplomats didn't provide Papadopoulos anything of substance, calling into question Mifsud's actual sphere of influence. Mifsud's former assistant, Natalia Kutepova-Jamom, told Karla Adam of the *Washington Post* that the professor sought out contacts to get in touch with important people, and he even claimed to have had a private meeting with Vladimir Putin. But she didn't believe him because he was "a too 'small-time'" person.[86]

Another associate, Nabil Ayad, who gave Mifsud the director position at the London Academy of Diplomacy, told the *Post* he didn't think the professor "has any special connections or relationships. If a meeting took place between a Russian official or he introduced someone, it must have been by chance, not by design."[87]

Still, because of Mifsud's contacts with the Russian government and his ongoing secrecy, he is suspected to be a Russian spy,[88] an allegation Mifsud flatly denies. He insists his role in foreign affairs is to "facilitate contacts between official and unofficial sources to resolve a crisis. It is usual business everywhere. I put think tanks in contact, groups of experts with other groups of experts."[89] Mifsud could be lying, of course, and he has now dropped out of sight with some of his website bios and contacts scrubbed, so we can't currently gather any information from him directly. We do know, however, that he never delivered on any of his promises to Papadopoulos about setting up foreign policy meetings with the Russian government, and he even lied about the actual identity of at least one individual he introduced to Papadopoulos—a woman he said was "Putin's niece." Mifsud appears to have been merely spinning wheels around Papadopoulos as he put him in contact with "Russian operatives." The question is why? If he wasn't being directed by Russians, who was Mifsud working for when he contacted Papadopoulos?

The assumption that Mifsud is a Russian agent has been a common piece of media lore, but other connections paint him in a different light. In 2012, he worked with Claire Smith, a member of the UK Joint Intelligence Committee, on a training program for the Italian military and law enforcement at the Link Campus University in Rome, where Mifsud headed the international relations department. The program was managed by the London Academy of Diplomacy, where Mifsud was the director.[90] According to Smith's LinkedIn profile, they worked together in Italy while she was a member of the UK Security Vetting Appeals Panel.[91] The website for Geodiplomatics, which provides diplomatic practice and training, posted a picture of Smith and Mifsud that was taken during the training program in Rome.

The photo is notable, not because it's proof of familiarity, but as a member of the Joint Intelligence Committee, Smith participated in overseeing all British intelligence agencies. The committee is part of the Cabinet Office that reports directly to the prime minister, so this puts Smith in a high-ranking position in British intelligence. Given her extensive experience in vetting UK intelligence personnel, she would be wise enough not to work with a Russian spy. The Security Vetting Appeals Panel is tasked with investigating those who have already failed to pass or had their security clearance revoked.

The assumption that Mifsud was a Russian spy rather than a possible resource for either the CIA or MI6—or both—is based on little evidence, particularly since most of his work to that point had been with friendly nations. As Lee Smith wrote, there's simply no evidence that he was a Russian spy:

> *Although Mifsud has traveled many times to Russia and has contacts with Russian academics, his closest public ties are to Western governments, politicians, and institutions, including the CIA, FBI and British intelligence services. One of Mifsud's jobs has been to train diplomats, police officers, and intelligence officers at schools in London and Rome, where he lived and worked over the last dozen years.[92]*

A UK political analyst focusing on international relations and security also has his doubts about Mifsud being in bed with the Russians. Chris Blackburn contacted journalist Elizabeth Lea Vos and told her of his own examination of Mifsud based on his work as an analyst and involvement in counterintelligence investigations. Blackburn explained that in counterintelligence investigations, FBI agents "look into a person of interest's family, friends, colleagues, debts, holidays, neighbors, romances, hobbies...they go through a person's biography with a fine-tooth comb to look for patterns and trends."[93] Given this process, Blackburn said, "Peter Strzok, the FBI's former counter-intelligence chief who was running the Mifsud case, should have found a few major red flags that would bring his motives into question."[94]

If Strzok had done his job, he would have discovered that Mifsud's law firm, which has been accused of being a Russian front group, engaged in activity that countered this claim. Additionally, according to Blackburn, Mifsud's London Academy of Diplomacy wasn't the shady operation the press made it out to be. Blackburn explained his point to Vos:

> British diplomats and Foreign Office ministers often visited LAD. Sir Tony Baldry, Alok Sharma MP and former Foreign Secretary William Hague all visited LAD or spoke at their conferences.
>
> The Commonwealth and various governments, including Saudi Arabia and Kuwait, sent their diplomats to train there. Nabil Ayad, the founding director of LAD, had built up the academy as a respectable powerhouse in London's diplomatic community. Counter-intelligence investigators would only be concentrating on Mifsud's high-frequency contacts and associations. They would be examining people he worked with on a regular basis. As an academic working in diplomacy,

Mifsud would have thousands of contacts. FBI investigators would be looking for intelligence ties.

Mifsud worked with diplomats and NATO allies, so they would need to know the potential damage he had caused. I found that two of Joseph Mifsud's closest colleagues, who the FBI would have designated as high-frequency, were Claire Smith and Gianni Pittella [Italian politician and European member of Parliament]. They had followed him between LAD, Stirling University and LINK Campus in Rome. Claire Smith was a former member of Britain's Joint Intelligence Committee (JIC). As a team, Smith and Mifsud trained Italian law enforcement on intelligence at LINK Campus in Rome. LINK Campus' ties to the Italian Foreign Ministry and intelligence agencies had been quickly skimmed over by the Washington Post, The New York Times, BuzzFeed and The Guardian.

Gianni Pittella has known Mifsud for a while. They met at the European Parliament and have collaborated on numerous projects together. In July 2016, Pittella gave a rousing speech at Hillary Clinton's presidential campaign launch in Philadelphia, calling Donald Trump "a virus" which needed to be stopped, while his close collaborator Mifsud was supposedly helping Trump's campaign to conspire with Russia. If the FBI had been doing a proper investigation into Joseph Mifsud, these two connections should have raised red flags immediately.[95]

These connections with Western intelligence would be "rather pertinent in an espionage scandal," Blackburn said—if only the FBI cared to look. Mifsud's association with Link Campus in Rome would have also raised red flags because the CIA "has a long history of working there."[96] David Ignatius of the *Washington Post* described one such gathering in Rome:

*Last week I attended a CIA-sponsored conference here that
was described as an "experiment" with these disruptive ideas.
The conference, "New Frontiers of Intelligence Analysis,"
brought together officials from intelligence and police agencies
of nearly 30 countries. The sessions were all unclassified, and
I was one of several journalists and a dozen or so academics
who were invited.[97]*

The conference organizer was Carol Dumaine, who worked
with the Link Campus of the University of Malta in Rome. She
and her team also organized "similar seminars at Harvard, Stan-
ford and other leading American universities," Ignatius wrote.[98]

According to Blackburn, the FBI has also worked with the
Rome campus:

*The FBI's Legat [legal attaché office] in Rome also sends its
agents to train Italian and Maltese law enforcement at the
small private campus. Mifsud had worked at LINK Campus
for quite some time. Before the story broke in August last year,
Mifsud had been working with CNN's Freedom Project to host
a televised debate on modern slavery. After Mifsud had been
named, CNN continued with the event. Richard Quest hosted
while one of Mifsud's colleagues, Franco Frattini, acted as one
of the panelists.[99]*

Clearly, the investigators and the media seem to have
failed to exercise due diligence in their examination of Mifsud.
"If Mifsud is a genuine Russian asset, he has been enabled by
the United States' most trusted allies," Blackburn said. "His
relationship with senior intelligence and political leaders in
Europe should constitute one of the greatest security breaches
in decades. He had access to diplomats in training, sanctions
targets and counter-terrorism strategy in the Middle East and
South Asia. However, government reactions don't show that.

The FBI doesn't appear to have warned their closest allies."[100] Blackburn's criticism of the FBI and media is harsh. He tells Vos,

> *There are too many contradictions and blatant omissions concerning Joseph Mifsud, in the media and the judicial system, to ignore. The NSA would have been monitoring Mifsud's communications with the production crew that worked on the CNN Freedom Project before the George Papadopoulos indictment was made public. Why didn't CNN Europe's producers come out and say anything? It's one of the greatest scandals in US history. Does CNN's European division not read the news?*
>
> *After Mifsud allegedly engaged George Papadopoulos in trying to set him up with allegedly stolen data, he went on to host conferences with US Treasury officials, ex-CIA agents, congressmen and State Department officials in numerous venues. If the investigation were genuine, US authorities would have alerted the British government and the Italian Ministry of Foreign Affairs. Mifsud would not have been able to get into a position to be photographed with the British Foreign Secretary Boris Johnson if he was a security threat or an agent of influence.*
>
> *Mifsud still hasn't been named by Special Counsel Robert Mueller or indicted by his team. The first time an official named him was when Rep. Adam Schiff (D), the minority chairman of the House Permanent Select Committee on Intelligence (HPSCI), mentioned him in a rebuttal to the majority memo on FISA abuses in the FBI and Department of Justice (DOJ).*
>
> *There are enough red flags here to suggest that Mifsud was potentially tied to efforts to kick-start a phony investigation that was designed to be leaked to the American press. Peter Strzok, the counter-intelligence official that started the Joseph Mifsud investigation, has been demoted and removed from*

Mueller's investigative team. Mifsud is a mystery to people that can't be bothered to look, but many journalists are aware of his links.[101]

Considering the many links between the British and the Trump-Russia narrative, Mifsud's Western connections should be taken just as seriously as his overblown Russia associations. The same can be said for his association with the Clinton Foundation.

After traveling to Moscow, Mifsud told an Italian newspaper that he understood the Russians to be skeptical of "changing the status quo, under the presidency either of Clinton or Trump."[102] As reported in *Repubblica,*

I talked about this topic also with Russian Foreign Ministry Sergej [sic] Lavrov, when the European Union elected a new president of the European Commission.... I suggested Foundations to keep talking and the bypass was still Timofeev. I am not a secret agent. I never got any money from the Russians: my conscience is clear.[103]

We don't know which "Foundations" Mifsud was talking about in this comment, but we do know he claimed to be connected to only one: the Clinton Foundation. "I am a member of the European Council on Foreign Relations," he told the Italian newspaper, "and you know which is the only foundation I am member of? The Clinton Foundation. Between you and me, my thinking is left-leaning."[104] While there doesn't appear to be any evidence of Mifsud being a "member," according to an investigation by Chuck Ross at the Daily Caller, "A search of the charity's online donor database found two donations of $250 from a 'Joseph Mifsud' and a 'Joseph J. Mifsud.'"[105]

It appears that Mifsud was a fan not only of Putin but of Clinton. He was also friends with Clinton supporter and member of European Parliament (MEP) Gianni Pittella, who worked with him at the London Centre of International Law Practice and was a visiting professor at the London Academy of Diplomacy. In the summer of 2016, Pittella traveled to America to enter the fray of a US election usually reserved for US citizens. "I have taken the unprecedented step of endorsing and campaigning for Clinton because the risk of Donald Trump is too high," the Italian MEP told Jay Newton-Small of *Time* magazine.[106] Interestingly, Pittella played a part in the Papadopoulos story by introducing Mifsud to Simona Mangiante, an Italian associate who subsequently worked for the professor in his law practice, where Papadopoulos also worked.[107] After discovering the two shared a common employer, Papadopoulos connected with Mangiante through LinkedIn. The Italian beauty with connections to Mifsud and the Clinton-supporting MEP soon began dating Papadopoulos, and they eventually married. After the FBI charged Papadopoulos, Mangiante became an outspoken critic of the Trump campaign.

As you can see, the connections to Mifsud are a tangled web, and most don't point to Trump sympathies. Instead, he's a left-leaning donor to the Clinton Foundation with a close friend who went out of his way to support Clinton. Why, then, would Mifsud home in on Papadopoulos to offer his humble services in Trump's favor? Was he simply introducing "important" people to one another out of the goodness of his heart, as he once claimed?

When Mifsud first met Papadopoulos in March, he didn't seem very interested in him, especially since Mifsud's modus operandi appears to have been pushing his foot into the door of powerful and influential people. Papadopoulos probably didn't seem beneficial to Mifsud until he learned that Papadopoulos had joined the Trump campaign as a foreign policy adviser. Once Mifsud discovered Papadopoulos's new position, he began to have "great interest" in him. He became a tasty morsel on Mifsud's menu, with the professor pumping Papadopoulos full of promises about his "extensive" Russian connections. Papadopoulos, of course, was instantly receptive since his supposed job was to help build bridges with Russia. And, at least at this point in time, they were discussing only meetings between Trump and Russian officials.

Later that month in 2016, Papadopoulos met with Mifsud in London to discuss setting up meetings between the Trump campaign and the Russian Federation. At this meeting, the professor brought along a woman reportedly named Olga Polonskaya, who Mifsud claimed was Vladimir Putin's niece. In reality, as we've mentioned, Polonskaya wasn't related to Putin at all. She was merely the manager of a Russian wine company, and her real relatives say she wasn't involved in politics.

Polonskaya's brother told *The New York Times* "she has never worked for the Russian government and was introduced to Papadopoulos while discussing an internship with Mifsud. She didn't speak English well enough to fully follow the conversation between Papadopoulos and Mifsud."[108] Her brother also said her involvement in any collusion scheme is "totally ridiculous. She's not interested in politics. She can barely tell the difference between Lenin and Stalin."[109] Mifsud later echoed the same line, claiming she was just a student who didn't know anything. Papadopoulos, however, was none the wiser. He believed Polonskaya was what Mifsud told him at the time— someone with connections to high-level Russian officials who could help him set up a foreign policy trip to Russia.

Others Mifsud introduced to Papadopoulos included the Russian Ambassador in London and, of course, Timofeev. Papadopoulos corresponded with Timofeev in much the same manner as he did with Polonskaya—working to set up contacts to promote foreign relations. Timofeev reportedly talked with an elder Russian statesman about a possible meeting, but nothing ever came of the discussions.

Undoubtedly excited by the prospect of forming such connections, and probably hoping to make a big splash in the Trump campaign with an eye to work in his administration, Papadopoulos contacted the Trump team. He told them he was in the process of making arrangements for "a meeting between us and the Russian leadership to discuss US-Russia ties under President Trump."[110] The campaign supervisor he talked to said the campaign would discuss it, adding that Papadopoulos had done "great work."

During the weeks that followed, Papadopoulos worked to make these meetings happen. He even forwarded a foreign policy speech to his contacts to show that Trump was willing to work with Russia. Polonskaya emailed him in response, saying she was glad Trump had a "softer position" toward Russia than other candidates, though this hasn't turned out to be the case. Papadopoulos contacted her several times, with her responding at one point, "We are all very excited by the possibility of a good relationship with Mr. Trump. The Russian Federation would love to welcome him once his candidature would be officially announced."[111] If Olga couldn't speak English very well, her emails didn't reflect that, though we don't know who was actually writing emails.

Papadopoulos also emailed an official at the Russian Ministry of Foreign Affairs (MFA)—the department headed by Lavrov, who worked closely with Secretary of State Hillary Clinton on the reset of relations between the United States and Russia. This reset, as we now know, proved to be a farce because Russia subsequently invaded Ukraine. The individual at the MFA, who is cited in Papadopoulos's court documents as being "unknown," is presumed to be Timofeev. According to a statement by the Russian International Affairs Council, of which Timofeev is the program director, Papadopoulos did indeed communicate with the council, putting "forth the idea of a possible visit to Russia by Mr. Trump or his team."[112] As reported in the *Washington Post*,

> *"Given the RIAC's established practice of hosting public meetings with prominent politicians and public figures from the US and other countries, the US initiative was a matter of routine for the Council," the statement said, pointing out that among the council's guest speakers was former US ambassador Michael McFaul.*[113]

According to the *Post*, Timofeev told them "that the idea of a meeting with Trump officials was dropped after he received no official request from the Trump campaign for a meeting."[114] Even though Papadopoulos was promised meetings between Putin and Trump, Mifsud's contacts never succeeded in arranging any meetings.

In late April 2016, Papadopoulos met Mifsud for breakfast at a hotel in London after Mifsud returned from a trip to Moscow, where he claimed to have met with high-level Russian officials. Papadopoulos told the FBI many months later, after the investigation into Russian interference had already started, that Mifsud claimed to have learned about the Russians having "dirt" on Hillary Clinton from "thousands of emails."[115] There is no evidence, however, that Papadopoulos talked to the campaign about the supposed dirt on Clinton, though he did continue to speak with the foreign affairs contact in Russia about setting up a possible meeting between Trump and Putin.

During this time, Papadopoulos emailed a Trump campaign official, telling him he "had been receiving a lot of calls over the last month about Putin wanting to host him and the team when the time is right."[116] This back and forth about a meeting continued into the summer. At one point, Papadopoulos told the campaign he would meet with Putin if Trump didn't want to make the trip, but this never occurred. A campaign adviser responded by saying, if he wanted to make a trip, it would have to be "as a private citizen." The adviser drove the point home by saying, "You're not authorized to meet with him [Putin] by the campaign, nor can you reflect the views of the campaign on security issues in that meeting."[117]

When the FBI eventually began to question Papadopoulos and his meetings with the professor were reported in the press, Mifsud went MIA. Retired CIA veteran Steven Hall, who managed Russian operations for three decades, alleges that Mifsud's behavior is more like that of a spy than a professor. "The Papadopoulos indictment tells a story containing several elements consistent with how Russian intelligence (and in this case, most likely the Russian Foreign Intelligence Service, the SVR) operates," he wrote in the *Washington Post*.[118] The use of a professor rather than a Russian government official as an intermediary to Russia "makes operational sense from the perspective of Russian intelligence."[119]

There's a reason Mifsud never supplied the information he claimed to possess—because he wasn't trying to spread dirt on Clinton. It's more likely he was trying to gather intelligence on the Trump team. Hall continues,

Next, the professor offered Papadopoulos concrete contacts in Moscow, specifically with the Russian Ministry of Foreign Affairs (MFA), as well as with an unidentified woman with senior contacts in the Kremlin. This is consistent with the incremental approach to a relationship like this that Russian intelligence typically favors.[120]

It's common for the Russian government to use the MFA as cover for their intelligence work, and it would be in keeping with his actions that Mifsud was trying to gather intelligence when contacting Papadopoulos. But we still don't know his purposes or even his actual associations in Britain or Russia, given that no real connections ever materialized. The only significant information communicated to Papadopoulos supposedly had to do with Clinton's emails, which Papadopoulos reportedly never received or passed on to the campaign—and, which, as we will explain in the following section, the FBI could not have known about, at least in the way they claimed.

While no facts about collusion can be gleaned from Papadopoulos's contact with Mifsud, it did accomplish one thing of significance—the impression that someone in the Trump campaign was "working with the Russians"—a perfect opening paragraph to the fabricated media narrative that Trump was colluding with the Russians.

Alexander Downer

In May, after Mifsud gave Papadopoulos false information about the Russians having dirt on Clinton—something Mifsud now claims he never said—Papadopoulos went to the Kensington Wine Rooms in London to meet with Australia's top diplomat in the United Kingdom, Alexander Downer. The two had previously met through an Israeli embassy official, and the meeting was arranged at Downer's request.[121] During their discussion, Papadopoulos told Downer about the Russians having material that would damage Clinton.

After reports of this meeting surfaced, *The New York Times* commented, "It is unclear whether Mr. Downer was fishing for that information that night in May 2016."[122] His motivations were indeed unclear at the time. Downer, however, told Jacquelin Magnay of *The Australian* in 2018 that his interest in Papadopoulos was piqued when the Trump adviser publicly demanded that British prime minister David Cameron apologize for saying Trump was "divisive, stupid, and wrong."[123]

According to Downer, he and Papadopoulos "had a drink and [Papadopoulos] talked about what Trump's foreign policy would be like if Trump won the election.... During that conversation [Papadopoulos] mentioned the Russians might use material that they have on Hillary Clinton in the lead-up to the election."[124] By all indications from Downer's account, Papadopoulos wasn't drunk, as has been widely reported. Downer added, regarding Papadopoulos's comments about the emails, "He didn't say dirt, he said material that could be damaging to her. No, he said it would be damaging. He didn't say it was."[125] In other words, no emails were mentioned to Downer.

This acknowledgment by Downer draws into question the whole investigation's premise that Russian spies approached Papadopoulos with hacked emails on Clinton—an indication of espionage. When the FBI opened its counterintelligence investigation, the only information it received about Papadopoulos was from the Australians, and if Downer is correct and Papadopoulos never mentioned emails, then the FBI's "factual basis" for opening the investigation on July 31, 2016, falls apart. It wasn't until months later, after the investigation began, that Papadopoulos told FBI investigators that Mifsud had mentioned "thousands of emails."

For Downer, however, it didn't matter whether it was emails or not. He still found Papadopoulos's claim that the Russians supposedly had material on Clinton "intriguing." In a proactive step, he said he reported it to Australia the next day.[126] According to *The Australian* newspaper,

> *Downer's conversation with Papadopoulos then apparently drifted into other areas, such as what Trump as president would be like on foreign policy. Australia's interests were firmly focused on the Trans-Pacific Partnership, with the aim of easing any trade protectionism with the US, as well as promoting a steady US policy towards China, where any deviation could have a big effect on Australia's economic prospects.*
>
> *"We didn't know anything about Trump and Russia and we had no particular focus on that," Downer says of the Papadopoulos meeting.*
>
> *"For us we were more interested in what Trump would do in Asia. By the way, nothing he (Papadopoulos) said in that conversation indicated Trump himself had been conspiring with the Russians to collect information on Hillary Clinton. It was just that this guy (Papadopoulos) clearly knew that the Russians did have material on Hillary Clinton—but whether Trump knew or not? He didn't say Trump knew or that Trump was in any way involved in this. He said it was about Russians and Hillary Clinton; it wasn't about Trump."[127]*

Two months after that meeting, Australian officials informed the FBI of Papadopoulos's comments to Downer. It's not clear, however, how exactly the FBI received this information. Downer said he sent it back to Australia, and the Australian newspaper he spoke to later added that "after a period of time, Australia's ambassador to the US, Joe Hockey, passed the information on to Washington."[128] But according to an investigative report in *The Wall Street Journal* by Kimberley Strassel, a diplomatic source told her, "Mr. Hockey neither transmitted any information to the FBI nor was approached by the US about the tip. Rather, it was Mr. Downer who at some point decided to convey his information—to the US Embassy in London."[129] This delivery is problematic because passing information in this way is not standard procedure. Material of this nature is supposed to be shared by intelligence networks between the five English-speaking countries, dubbed the "Five Eyes." According to Strassel, Australian intelligence didn't alert the FBI; the material the FBI used to start the investigation into Russian meddling didn't contain any intelligence.[130]

The information from Downer seems to have first made its way to the Obama State Department. "The Downer details landed with the embassy's then-chargé d'affaires, Elizabeth Dibble," Strassel writes, "who previously served as a principal deputy assistant secretary in Mrs. Clinton's State Department."[131] Downer's information didn't go through intelligence channels, but back channels, and even then he offered no information that Papadopoulos knew about supposedly stolen emails a month before the claim of a DNC hack by the Russians was made public.

The FBI has reported that the tip on Papadopoulos and the damaging "material" came directly after WikiLeaks dumped hacked emails online. On this basis the FBI concluded it had enough "facts" to open an investigation into collusion by the Trump team. The basis of this investigation, however, seems to be founded on very little: no official intelligence, no evidence of a Russian spy, and no evidence of emails—just someone with connections to Russia, the CIA, and MI6 talking to a low-level

Trump adviser about mysterious information on Clinton provided by the Russians.

With Downer being such a pivotal character in the Russian meddling investigation, it's important to follow the dots to that infamous meeting at the London bar. His story begins years earlier with uranium deals and donations to the Clinton Foundation. Like Hillary Clinton in 2010, Downer was instrumental in making a deal that transferred uranium from his home country of Australia, which holds about 40 percent of the world's uranium reserves, to Russia. The agreement, which Downer publicly supported in 2007, allowed Australia to export at least one billion dollars' worth of uranium annually to the Kremlin.[132] This deal came just a year after Downer played a central role in the transfer of money from the Australian government to the Clinton Foundation. In total, the Clinton Foundation received over eighty-eight million dollars from the Australian treasury between 2006 and 2014.[133]

A retired Australian police detective named Michael Smith alleged in August 2016 that the Clinton Foundation had mishandled those Australian government funds. He told Mark Tapscott of LifeZette in early 2018 that he was asked to provide the FBI with additional details surrounding the allegations.[134] Smith handed over materials to the FBI that focused on a 2006 memorandum about an understanding between the Australian government and the Clinton Foundation's HIV/AIDS initiative. Smith claimed the Clinton Foundation received a "$25M financial advantage dishonestly obtained by deception."[135] Downer was Australia's minister of foreign affairs at this time and apparently well known to the Clintons.

Smith also claimed to have evidence proving a "corrupt October 2006 backdating of false tender advertisements purporting to advertise the availability of a $15 million contract to provide HIV/AIDS services in Papua, New Guinea on behalf of the Australian government after an agreement was already in place to pay the Clinton Foundation and/or associates."[136] There's also a third complaint alleging ten million dollars obtained by fraud in a separate scheme.

In addition to playing a part in the transfer of money to the Clinton Foundation during this time, in 2008, Downer joined the advisory board of London-based Hakluyt & Company. Hakluyt was founded by former MI6 agents to provide investigative research for governments and large corporations, much like the work at Fusion GPS (more on them below). One of the founders, Mike Reynolds, previously of the British foreign service, is reportedly a close friend of Sir Richard Dearlove, an associate of Christopher Steele.[137]

Hakluyt has many associations with government agencies and other intelligence and consulting firms. One of those firms was Kissinger McLarty Associates, an international strategic advisory firm that has now separated into two groups, Kissinger Associates and McLarty Associates. Henry Kissinger was former secretary of state, and Thomas McLarty was White House chief of staff under Bill Clinton. Kissinger formed a partnership with Hakluyt "to facilitate introductions, refer clients and cooperate on projects,"[138] though Hakluyt is known for doing much more than this.[139] In a Czech commercial case in 2002, Hakluyt allegedly delivered bullet points of opposition research through a UK ambassador to Prague to give the "untrue" information validity. This information "contained a number of allegations which were undoubtedly grave and implicated the claimants in corruption and in one instance in murder."[140]

Kissinger Associates is of particular interest due to its connections to Hakluyt and individuals or entities associated with the Clintons. One that is especially noteworthy is the partnership between Kissinger Associates and APCO Worldwide,[141] which has lobbied on behalf of Russia's state-owned nuclear company and has donated hundreds of thousands of dollars to the Clinton Global Initiative between 2008 and 2016, with the Clinton Foundation underreporting the extent of those donations.[142] These two clients, APCO and Hakluyt,[143] were apparently partnered with Kissinger Associates during the same period.

According to *The Financial Times*, Hakluyt has more than a hundred "associates," with "some based in London [and] others at stations worldwide, formed by personal contacts."[144] The article continues,

> *They might be investigative journalists, diplomats' wives, senior business people, former diplomats or consultants. They are "intuitive, determined, highly intelligent" and have intimate knowledge of the country in which they operate. Associates are free to turn down assignments and are expected to use their judgement about dangerous situations. When Hakluyt receives an assignment, it calls up to five associates back to London to be briefed and then "deploys" them. The work essentially involves "talking to the right people. It's all about people, following up contacts," says Mr. James. Each associate is given different questions and works independently.*[145]

The Bureau of Investigative Journalism's Henry Williams describes Hakluyt as "one of the more secretive firms within the corporate investigations world," LifeZette reports.[146] He added that the firm's "style appears to be much more in the mold of the Steele dossier. Clients pay for pages of well-sourced prose from Hakluyt's contacts across the globe."[147] According to an Australian news report, in 2001, Hakluyt was caught "funding a former German spy to infiltrate environmental groups in Europe allegedly on behalf of oil company clients. Most recently in 2012, it hit the headlines when one of its part-time investigators was murdered in a Chinese hotel room under mysterious circumstances involving a high-level Communist Party figure and claims of espionage."[148]

As reported at LifeZette, several of Hakluyt's US representatives made substantial contributions to Clinton's 2016 presidential campaign. While Downer had resigned from the board in 2014, "his information connections continued uninterrupted."[149] In early 2016, News Corp Australia reported,

> *It can be revealed Mr. Downer has still been attending client conferences and gatherings of the group, including a client cocktail soirée at the Orangery at Kensington Palace a few months ago. His attendance at that event is understood to have come days after he also attended a two-day country retreat at the invitation of the group, which has been involved in a number of corporate spy scandals in recent times.*[150]

So, Downer, an Australian diplomat who had been involved in donations to the Clinton Foundation amid uranium deals and is connected to a secretive firm that has ties to the Clinton campaign, shows up in London to talk to George Papadopoulos—a volunteer for the Trump campaign who had been told by Mifsud that the Russians had damaging material on Clinton. Then, when Democratic Committee emails start appearing online in an assumed Russian hack, the Australians spill that information to the FBI—information that to this day hasn't led to any criminality, except Papadopoulos's lying to the FBI.

TRUMP TOWER MEETING

On June 3, 2016, Donald Trump Jr. received an email from British publicist and former tabloid reporter Rob Goldstone that he thought would help his father's presidential bid. It didn't turn out that way. Instead, the email led to an infamous meeting that would solidify suspicions that the Trump team was indeed colluding with the Russians.

> *Good morning. Emin [Agalarov] just called and asked me to contact you with something very interesting.*
>
> *The Crown prosecutor of Russia[151] met with [Emin's] father Aras this morning and in their meeting offered to provide the Trump campaign with some official documents and information that would incriminate Hillary and her dealings with Russia and would be very useful to your father. This is obviously very high level and sensitive information but is part of Russia and its government's support for Mr. Trump—helped along by Aras and Emin.*

Trump Jr. seemed to give little thought to the stated source of the information—the prosecutor general of Russia, which is the equivalent of the US attorney general. It would have been wise to contact the FBI about an email that claimed the Russian government had compromising information on the former secretary of state, but it came in the midst of a campaign with law enforcement working for the opposition party. No one could be trusted. Trump Jr. could have ignored it, and a more experienced campaign probably would have. But politics took priority over judgment, and Trump Jr. naively thought it would serve his father to at least check it out. When he was later criticized for agreeing to the meeting, he tweeted a message laced with sarcasm. "Obviously, I'm the first person on a campaign to ever take a meeting to hear about an opponent," Trump Jr. said, adding that the meeting "went nowhere but [I] had to listen."[152]

Anxious to help his father's campaign, Trump Jr. told Goldstone, "If it's what you say, I love it especially later in the summer. Could we do a call first thing next week when I am back?"[153] Goldstone emailed Trump Jr. on June 7 promising that a "Russian government attorney" would deliver the "ultra sensitive" information at a meeting two days later. That attorney was Natalia Veselnitskaya, who had ties to both the Russian prosecutor general Yuri Chaika and Aras Agalarov, but more significantly, she was working with Fusion GPS, the research firm creating the narrative for the DNC that Trump was in league with the Russians.

The Backstory

Goldstone and his client, Azerbaijani-Russian pop star Emin Agalarov, were the perfect vehicles to lure Trump Jr. into a meeting. Years before in 2013, Goldstone and Agalarov were introduced to Trump through the Miss Universe Organization when they were recording a music video and wanted to have the reigning Miss Universe make an appearance. Discussions about the video morphed into a plan to have the Miss Universe pageant in Moscow where Agalarov would perform, giving him much-needed international hype.

Agalarov and Goldstone met with Trump, owner of the Miss Universe Organization at the time, to discuss the possibility of Moscow hosting the event. They knew the proposal would appeal to Trump because of his ambitions to build a hotel in Moscow. As expected, he loved the idea, and in November he traveled to Moscow to make arrangements with billionaire businessman and property developer Aras Agalarov, who also had connections to Vladimir Putin and is friendly with the prosecutor general. The success of the pageant confirmed in Trump's mind that Goldstone and the Agalarovs were trusted associates, something not easily found in business relationships at home or abroad, particularly in Russia.[154]

In an ironic twist of fate, the trip to Russia—a positive event that benefited Trump in so many respects—would become a point of contention in his campaign for president. It was during his Moscow visit that Trump stopped off at the Ritz-Carlton, which would become the alleged scene of the golden showers fiction that showed up in Christopher Steele's dossier. Steele listed the source of that story as Belarusian businessman Sergei Millian, who received the information second- or third-hand. The origin of the story, however, was likely the Agalarovs, who—unlike Millian—were present at the time. Emin was the one who offered to send prostitutes to Trump's room that night,[155] but according to Trump's bodyguard, Keith Schiller, Trump laughed it off and went to bed alone.[156]

Three years later in the summer of 2016, Goldstone and Agalarov stepped into the limelight once again with promises of compromising information on Hillary Clinton from the Russian government. The actual source of the information, however, wasn't prosecutor general Chaika, as Goldstone wrote in his email—he later admitted he was guilty of "hyping the message and going the extra mile for my clients. Using hot-button language to puff up the information I had been given."[157] The real source was the Russian lawyer, Veselnitskaya, who was in Washington lobbying against sanctions imposed by the Magnitsky Act and representing a Russian oligarch whose Cyprus-based company, Prevezon Holdings Ltd., was accused of laundering millions of dollars into the Manhattan real estate market.

The Magnitsky Act is named after Sergei Magnitsky, a Russian tax accountant hired by the CEO of Hermitage Capital Management, William Browder, to investigate fraud against his firm, formerly the largest foreign investor in Russia. In those investigations, Magnitsky unearthed a money-laundering scheme involving a Russian criminal network that worked with tax officials and Russian police to launder 230 million dollars of fraudulent tax refunds by stealing the corporate identity of companies from Hermitage's investment portfolio. When Browder presented the findings to the Russian government, they countered by starting a criminal investigation into Magnitsky for committing fraud himself and colluding with Hermitage against Russia.

Magnitsky was arrested in 2009 and later died under suspicious circumstances while in Russian custody. The diary he kept in prison tells how guards tried to convince him to drop his accusations against the police and tax authorities. Each time Magnitsky refused, they would move him to a smaller cell in increasingly worse parts of the prison. They also denied necessary medical treatment for a blocked gall bladder and pancreatitis. The Russian authorities listed "heart attack" as the cause of death on Magnitsky's death certificate, but even a Kremlin-led investigation found that he had been severely beaten.

Magnitsky's death incited an international outcry by human rights activists, demanding justice and assurance that the torture of prisoners would never happen again. In response, Obama signed the Sergei Magnitsky Rule of Accountability Act in 2012. The law imposed sanctions on those involved in the Magnitsky case and any Russian credibly charged with human rights violations. Russia retaliated by banning American adoption of Russian children.

The US Justice Department later accused Prevezon Holdings of using millions of dollars funneled from the 230 million dollars in laundered money to buy real estate in New York. In 2013, the DOJ seized the company's US assets, and in response, Prevezon and the Russian government began a campaign to overturn the Magnitsky Act.

Natalia Veselnitskaya

Veselnitskaya was hired by the head of Prevezon, Denis Katsyv, to argue the case in federal court. She and her team of lobbyists contacted congressional staffers and spread negative press about those supporting the sanctions, particularly Browder, whom Veselnitskaya accused of stealing the 230 million dollars of laundered money and then blaming the Russians. The conflict between the two sides intensified with accusations against Browder of murder and criminal activity, and Browder accusing Veselnitskaya of being a henchman for the Russian government, not a simple lawyer for an embattled company as she pretended to be.

Prevezon, through Veselnitskaya and its American law firm, BakerHostetler, hired Fusion GPS and cofounder Glenn Simpson to find anything that would smear Browder and strengthen Prevezon's legal case, as well as help repeal sanctions against Russian individuals. According to testimony by Browder before the House Intelligence Committee, Veselnitskaya "hired a number of lobbyists, public relations executives, lawyers and investigators to assist her in this task."[158] One of those lobbyists was Rinat Akhmetshin, a former Russian spy who worked on the Prevezon case with Fusion GPS and accompanied Veselnitskaya to the meeting in Trump Tower. Simpson has stated in congressional hearings that Akhmetshin used Fusion GPS research to lobby on the Hill. According to Browder,

> *[Veselnitskaya's] first step was to set up a fake NGO that would ostensibly promote Russian adoptions, although it quickly became clear that the NGO's sole purpose was to repeal the Magnitsky Act. This NGO was called the Human Rights Accountability Global Initiative Foundation (HRAGI). It was registered as a corporation in Delaware with two employees on February 18, 2016. HRAGI was used to pay Washington lobbyists and other agents for the anti-Magnitsky campaign. (HRAGI now seems to be defunct, with taxes due.)*
>
> *Through HRAGI, Rinat Akhmetshin, a former Soviet intelligence officer naturalised as an American citizen, was hired to lead the Magnitsky repeal effort. Mr Akhmetshin has been involved in a number of similar campaigns where he's been accused of various unethical and potentially illegal actions like computer hacking.*
>
> *[Simpson] contacted a number of major newspapers and other publications to spread false information that Sergei Magnitsky was not murdered, was not a whistle-blower and was instead a criminal. They also spread false information that my presentations to lawmakers around the world were untrue.*[159]

In another hearing, when US lawmakers questioned Simpson about Fusion GPS passing information to the media, he avoided answering the question, leaving open the possibility that he didn't have any problem bleeding intelligence from one project to another.

The documents Veselnitskaya took with her to Trump Tower that warm summer day came out of the research Fusion

GPS had done for Prevezon. This fact, of course, had to be kept secret. Better for the Trump campaign to think the information came from Chaika, thus fueling the narrative that Trump's team was colluding with the Russians. Goldstone's email citing the Russian prosecutor general as the source might have been what Goldstone said it was—hyped language—or it could have been what he was directed to write. What better proof of collusion than an email explicitly saying the information was coming from the Russian government and it wants to help Trump win?

According to Veselnitskaya, however, the meeting with Trump Jr. didn't involve the prosecutor general in any way. She told NBC News that she didn't discuss the New York meeting with him "or with any of the officials of the prosecutor general's office."[160] Aras Agalarov also maintains that Chaika didn't arrange the meeting. As reported in *The Wall Street Journal*,

> "Natalia has done some real estate-related legal work for Mr. Agalarov's company over the years," said Scott Balber, an attorney representing the Agalarov family. He denied the elder Mr. Agalarov met with Mr. Chaika, the prosecutor general, as described in the email. Mr. Agalarov, speaking on Russian radio Wednesday, called the content of the correspondence "some kind of fiction."[161]

The prosecutor general's office echoed Agalarov and Veselnitskaya's claim. In a statement to *The Wall Street Journal*, the office said it "does not exchange information and does not conduct any meetings at the international level outside the framework regulated by international legal agreements and Russian procedural legislation."[162]

Veselnitskaya also tried to distance herself from the Agalarovs and the details of the email to Trump Jr. She told NBC News that the meeting came about as a result of her spreading information to friends and their friends, rallying them to the cause and seeking help to get Congress to repeal the Magnitsky Act. "I never asked anybody for a particular meeting with Mr. Donald Trump Jr., or with anybody else," she said.[163] The report continues,

> *In describing how the meeting came about, Veselnitskaya didn't name the person who set it up over the phone while she was in New York for work.*
>
> *She added that she now knows that it was arranged in part by pop-star Emin Agalarov.... She said she has never met Agalarov.*[164]

Whether she had ever met Emin Agalarov or not, she knew his father, and according to *The Wall Street Journal*, Veselnitskaya "asked the elder Mr. Agalarov for help in arranging a meeting with the Trump campaign but denies it was about Mrs. Clinton."[165] So she wanted to meet with someone for some reason, no matter how many different ways she wants to put it. She might not have asked for a meeting with Trump Jr. in particular, but that's eventually what happened. It's possible the first contact might even have been with Trump's campaign manager, Paul Manafort, who also attended the meeting in Trump Tower. In a report on the raid of Manafort's home in connection with the special counsel investigation into Russian interference in the US election, reports reveal that federal investigators "were looking for 'communication, records, documents and other files' surrounding the June 2016 Trump Tower meeting. They were also looking for any communication with 'Aras and Amin [sic] Agalarov.'"[166]

Was it possible that the Agalarovs first tried to contact Manafort but then were redirected to Trump Jr.? It would make sense that Manafort would be a point of contact to lure Trump's team into a meeting with Russians under the pretense of communicating intelligence from the Russian government. He wasn't exactly known for having clean hands, and Simpson had a history of investigating him. A big part of the Steele dossier was about Manafort, and he would need to be front and center in a setup.

The meeting didn't produce what either Manafort or Trump Jr. hoped. The information Veselnitskaya shared with Trump Jr. about Clinton was part of the presentation, but it was nestled in research relating to the Magnitsky Act—and it wasn't much. The information Simpson had gathered showed how the American company Ziff Brothers Investments had made illegal purchases of shares in a Russian company and then committed tax evasion both in the United States and Russia amounting to tens of millions of dollars. Two of the brothers were major donors to Democratic candidates, including Clinton. When Trump Jr. asked Veselnitskaya for proof of a connection to Clinton, she said she didn't "have any financial records of that time—there was no chance that I could somehow, anyhow, have such records."[167]

Those who attended the meeting with Trump Jr. weren't impressed. There was no "there" there. Trump's son-in-law, Jared Kushner, left after ten minutes and didn't come back. Manafort twiddled his thumbs and, according to Veselnitskaya, looked bored. Trump Jr. finally interrupted her and said, "Well, the story that you've told us, it sounds very interesting but unfortunately at the moment, there is nothing that we, we can help you with about it. But maybe if we come to power, maybe one day, we will get back to you on that, because it really sounds interesting."[168] When he realized Veselnitskaya had nothing of worth on Clinton, the meeting ended. It lasted only twenty to thirty minutes.

Glenn Simpson

While it's possible Veselnitskaya was working for the Russian government to collude with Trump and not playing a part in creating evidence of that collusion for Fusion GPS, her contacts before and after weren't with the Russians, but with Simpson. He created the pro-Russian opposition research, he met with Veselnitskaya hours before the Trump Tower meeting, he met with her afterward, and he was working on an anti-Trump dossier at the same time. It is reasonable to assume Simpson would have known there was at least a hint of dirt on Clinton in the documents—something the Trump campaign would want—and he would have known that the mere appearance of providing that information to the team could give the impression that intelligence was flowing from the Kremlin to the Trump campaign, as recorded in Steele's unverified dossier.

According to Browder, who had been targeted by Fusion GPS in the Prevezon case and the Russian government because of his efforts to expose corruption in Russian companies, Simpson is a master of spreading false information and manipulating narratives. He has done it "on behalf of people connected to the Russian government to try to protect Russian torturers and murderers from consequences," Browder told Chuck Ross of the Daily Caller. "Glenn Simpson's job was to knowingly and dishonestly change the narrative of how Sergei Magnitsky came to die from murder to natural causes, and to change the narrative that Sergei Magnitsky was a criminal and not a whistleblower."[169] Browder told US lawmakers in an intelligence hearing that Simpson was paid by the Russian government, even if indirectly, which means he was paid by the Clinton campaign and the Russian government at the same time. Simpson has denied Browder's charge, maintaining that he and colleagues were never "working for the Russian government then or ever."[170]

Could it be that Simpson, through Veselnitskaya, was using anti–Magnitsky Act research, paid for by Russians, to shore up Steele's opposition research against Trump? Was the entire scenario created in the bowels of Fusion GPS to use their Russian contacts, including a former Russian spy, to generate "evidence" of collusion to put in a dossier funded by the DNC and Clinton campaign? Did someone (Veselnitskaya directly or through Chaika) contact the Agalarovs promising dirt on Clinton, much in the same way Joseph Mifsud promised Russian intelligence to George Papadopoulos? Does the sloppiness of the email promising information from the "Crown prosecutor," which doesn't exist, indicate fabrication? Fusion GPS certainly had an interest in establishing a flow of information from the Russians to Trump's team, just as it had an interest in getting information from the Russians to use against Trump.

Simpson, however, claims the two projects never intersected. In a House intelligence hearing, he said he didn't hear about the meeting with Trump Jr. until 2017:

> To be clear, I didn't know about this meeting before it happened, and I didn't know about it after it happened. And I found out about it, I think, you know, within a day of it being disclosed in The New York Times. Someone called me and said you heard about this meeting? And I said no. So anyway, that was the first I had heard about it.[171]

Yet, Simpson had met Veselnitskaya right before the Trump Tower meeting at the Manhattan federal courthouse and the following day at dinner. He claims they never discussed the meeting or her effort to lobby the Trump campaign using his research materials, but a member of the House Intelligence Committee found this hard to believe:

> *I mean, we have talked a lot about coincidences and interesting connections, but, I mean, it's quite something that you would have been investigating Trump for 8 months, and one of your colleagues from this other litigation who you were with shortly before and after the meeting had, in fact, met with Trump Jr. and other high ranking Trump associates on a related topic in the same time period.*[172]

Veselnitskaya and Simpson had been working together for two years, yet her meeting with the Republican nominee's son was kept secret from him? Like the lawmaker said—that's "quite something." Regardless, an attorney for Fusion GPS told NBC News, "No one from Fusion GPS had any idea Ms. Veselnitskaya would be meeting with anyone from the Trump campaign. Nor did anyone from Fusion GPS know she would be sharing anything she learned from either the company or the Prevezon matter with the Trump campaign. This whole episode came as a complete surprise to Fusion when the news broke this summer."[173]

In the Senate Judiciary Committee hearing, investigators grilled Simpson on how much information was leaked to different parties, particularly the press. Simpson said, "It's a general strict prohibition on sharing information about the nature of the work you're doing, your findings, with anyone outside of, you know—we're the client in this case. So they're not allowed to share information with anyone outside the case,"[174] yet Simpson shared information about Prevezon with journalists. He responded that this was part of the job, that when journalists asked questions, they gave them "facts" about the case or corrected mistakes. One of the investigators, however, pointed out that disinformation had been disseminated to the press regarding Browder. When pressed on this point, Simpson basically agreed that this happens. He also admitted to talking to reporters regarding the Steele dossier, saying, "Some of what we discussed [with reporters] was informed by Chris's reporting."[175] So, it seems, there's not a "general strict prohibition" on sharing information with anyone outside the case.

The claim that there could be no intersection between Steele's dossier and the anti-Magnitsky research doesn't hold up in light of other instances of crossover between Simpson's projects. Lee Smith of *Tablet* magazine reported in late 2017 that work Simpson had done as a reporter for *The Wall Street Journal* was apparently the source of sections in the dossier related to Manafort. As a journalist, Simpson had reported on Manafort extensively, particularly during John McCain's presidential run in 2008 when the senator was cozying up to Manafort and "inadvertently" reaching out for Russian donations.[176] Significantly, Fusion GPS was hired by the DNC just after Manafort joined the Trump campaign. Smith explains,

> *Once you understand that Simpson knew exactly who Paul Manafort was, it's impossible not to spot the former journalist's creative wit sprinkled throughout the dossier, which uses the tantalizing figure of "PUTIN" to draw attention to corruption that Glenn Simpson knew was entirely real from his own reporting. "Ex-Ukrainian President YANUKOVYCH confides directly to PUTIN that he authorised (sic) kick-back payments to MANAFORT, as alleged in western media," the dossier relates. "Assures Russian President however there is no documentary evidence/trail."[177]*

Simpson, Smith writes, seems to confirm this in testimony to Congress that "he was at least a co-contributor to the Manafort sections":[178]

> *A congressional investigator asks Simpson if it's "fair to characterize the research" he was doing "as kind of a separate track of research on the same topic" Steele was researching.*
>
> *"I wouldn't say it was completely separate," says Simpson, "because, for instance, on some subjects I knew more than Chris. So when it comes to Paul Manafort, he's a long-time US political figure about whom I know a lot. But his reporting— you know, so there may have been some bleed between things I told him about someone like Manafort."*[179]

So, as Smith observes, "If there was 'bleeding' on the subject of Manafort, it is reasonable to conclude that there was 'bleeding' elsewhere, too."[180] It could very well be that the prosecutor general heard from Veselnitskaya that she and her cohorts at Fusion GPS wanted dirt on Trump. Chaika supplied her with the information from Aras that some prostitutes went to Trump's hotel in 2013. "In other words," Smith writes, "the dirt in the Steele Dossier was put there by Russia, for the purpose of ridiculing and undermining Donald Trump, at the same time as Russians sought to embarrass Hillary Clinton by distributing emails stolen from her campaign."[181] He continues,

> *Simpson's testimony shows that the Senate Judiciary Committee is alert to the likelihood that information on Fusion's two Russia-related jobs may have flowed in both directions. "Was there any overlap," asked one investigator, "between the employees from Fusion who were working on the Trump investigation and the Prevezon case?" Simpson answers: "I can't tell you that there was a Chinese wall of separation.*

*Various people specialize in certain things and can contribute
ad hoc to something." In other words, yes.*[182]

Simpson also told the investigators that he had hired a
subcontractor, Edward Baumgartner, who worked on the
Prevezon case and opposition research on Trump at the same
time. "At the end of the Prevezon case," Simpson said, "we asked
him to help."[183] According to Smith,

*The issue isn't just that there are two Fusion GPS employees
working on both dossiers. It is that one of their employers
worked closely with the Russian government who played a
prominent role in both the anti-Magnitsky campaign and the
Trump-Russia collusion story.*[184]

Veselnitskaya was the linchpin in the Trump Tower setup
scenario. She had the research from Fusion GPS that could be
used to lure Trump Jr. into a meeting. She had the contacts with
high-level Russian officials and former Russian spies to create
the impression of collusion. In a US Senate hearing, Simpson
tried to perpetuate this narrative. While ignoring how he had
worked with Russians to overturn the Magnitsky Act without
even registering as a foreign agent in compliance with the
Foreign Agents Registration Act, he piled on to the collusion
narrative. Simpson knew the information he had gathered for
Veselnitskaya had no real compromising material on Clinton,
but he would have known Trump Jr.'s mere acceptance of taking
the carrot would look bad for the Trump team—the perfect
scenario to bolster a fake dossier. During the Senate hearing,
Simpson set up his argument that Trump Jr. was colluding with
the Russians by citing the Steele dossier: "I mean, one of the key
lines here in the second paragraph says, 'However, he and his
inner circle have accepted a regular flow of intelligence from

the Kremlin, including on his Democratic and other political rivals.'"[185] Simpson then goes on to describe the Trump Tower meeting as evidence:

> *So the issue with the Trump Tower meeting, as I understand it, is that the Trump people were eager to accept intelligence from a foreign government about their political rivals and that is, you know, I would say, a form of interference. If you're getting help from a foreign government and your help is intelligence, then the foreign government's interfering. I mean, you know, I think that also—of course, in retrospect we now know this was pretty right on target in terms [of] what [the dossier] says...it depicts them as accepting information. What we have seen to date with the disclosures this year is they were at a minimum super interested in getting information.*[186]

Simpson tried to legitimize the fake Steele dossier by using the Trump meeting as "proof" of "regular flow of intelligence from the Kremlin." It's possible this "flow of intelligence" was the Russians working, not with the Trump team, but with Simpson to spread and recycle information created by Fusion GPS in the first place.

Rinat Akhmetshin

Another variable in the Trump Tower scheme is Rinat Akhmetshin, a former Russian spy turned lobbyist who is suspected of having ongoing ties with Russian intelligence, though he denies it. Akhmetshin accompanied Veselnitskaya to the Trump Tower meeting and showed up at dinner with her the next day, the same one attended by Simpson. Who better to strengthen the Russian collusion narrative than a former Russian spy bearing dirt on Clinton, especially one with as many ties to the Kremlin as Akhmetshin? According to *The New York Times*,

> He has an association with a former deputy head of a Russian spy service, the F.S.B., and a history of working for close allies of President Vladimir V. Putin. Twice, he has worked on legal battles for Russian tycoons whose opponents suffered sophisticated hacking attacks, arousing allegations of computer espionage. He helped federal prosecutors bring corruption charges against an American businessman in the former Soviet Union who turned out to be working for the C.I.A.[187]

The *Times* also reports that Akhmetshin made his way from Russian spy to Washington lobbyist through "Edward Lieberman, a lawyer with corporate and political clients in former Soviet countries who was married to President Bill Clinton's former deputy chief of staff, Evelyn S. Lieberman, who died in 2015."[188] Edward Lieberman worked for BakerHostetler, the law firm that hired Fusion GPS for Prevezon and likely had access to research done by Fusion. According to the *Times*, Lieberman and Akhmetshin started the Eurasian Institute for Economic and Political Research. The *Times* reports, "Supposedly set up to promote democratic reforms in former Soviet states, it was essentially a vehicle to burnish the reputation of one client, Akezhan Kazhegeldin, an ex-K.G.B. officer and the former prime minister of Kazakhstan."[189] When the *Times* tried to contact Lieberman, he couldn't be reached for comment.

Akhmetshin has also been entangled in hacking accusations, which includes, as first reported by the *Times*, "a financier close to Mr. Putin in a commercial and political dispute with a Russian competitor, Ashot Egiazaryan."[190] The other occurred when Akhmetshin "worked as a consultant to a law firm representing EuroChem, a fertilizer and mining company controlled by another Russian billionaire close to Mr. Putin—Andrey Melnichenko. Mr. Akhmetshin's target was a rival mining company, International Mineral Resources."[191]

So a Russian with links to the Kremlin and a shady past in hacking was working with Fusion GPS when he just happened to show up at the Trump meeting (not to mention when the DNC servers were supposedly hacked before this). Akhmetshin says he was having lunch with Veselnitskaya when she asked him to come along with her to meet with Trump Jr. The *Times* reports that Akhmetshin said he didn't know why she wanted him there, and Veselnitskaya has maintained that he was there only as a fellow lobbyist against the Magnitsky Act—work Akhmetshin had done on behalf of a foreign entity without registering as a foreign agent.

This fact brought Akhmetshin to Senator Charles Grassley's attention after Browder filed a formal FARA complaint regarding the lobby work by both Fusion GPS and Akhmetshin. Grassley's claim of a FARA violation is reminiscent of the complaint brought against the DNC consultant Alexandra Chalupa during the election. In a letter to Deputy Attorney General Dana Boente, Grassley wrote, "Despite the reported evidence of their work on behalf of Russian interests, neither Fusion GPS nor Akhmetshin is registered as a foreign agent under [FARA]."[192] Because of this failure to register, "it is unclear whether the FBI was aware of the company's pro-Russia activities and its connection with Akhmetshin when evaluating the credibility of the dossier the company helped create."[193] Citing from press reports, Grassley writes,

> It is particularly disturbing that Mr. Akhmetshin and Fusion GPS were working together on this pro-Russia lobbying effort in 2016 in light of Mr. Akhmetshin's history and reputation.

Mr. Akhmetshin is a Russian immigrant to the US who has admitted having been a "Soviet counterintelligence officer." In fact, it has been reported that he worked for the GRU and allegedly specializes in "active measures campaigns," i.e., subversive political influence operations often involving disinformation and propaganda. According to press accounts, Mr. Akhmetshin "is known in foreign policy circles as a key pro-Russian operator," and Radio Free Europe described him as a "Russian 'gun-for-hire' [who] lurks in the shadows of Washington's lobbying world." He was even accused in a lawsuit of organizing a scheme to hack the computers of one [of] his client's adversaries.

The actions of Mr. Akhmetshin, Fusion GPS, and the others described in Mr. Browder's complaint appear to show that they acted on behalf of a foreign principal. This is exactly the type of activity Congress intended to reach with FARA. When properly enforced, FARA provides important transparency. However, in this case, because none of the parties involved in the anti-Magnitsky lobbying had properly registered under FARA, these suspicious connections were not appropriately documented and brought to public light.[194]

Akhmetshin shows up again months later in another connection with the Steele dossier. In November, he participated in a Canadian conference also attended by Senator John McCain and the senator's associate David Kramer. At this conference, McCain and Kramer were briefed by the British ambassador Sir Andrew Wood about making contact with Steele regarding the dossier. Kramer would later obtain the materials from Steele and deliver it to McCain. In January 2017, McCain's office told Catherine Herridge of Fox News that he had no contact with Akhmetshin at that conference. The senator said, "Late last year, I received sensitive information that has since been made public. Upon examination of the contents, and unable to make a judgment about their accuracy, I delivered the information to the Director of the FBI. That has been the extent of my contact with the FBI or any other government agency regarding this issue." Later, Herridge reported, "it's not known whether Akhmetshin had any contact with Kramer" and "Fusion GPS and Kramer did not respond to requests for comment."[195] As mentioned before, Kramer took the Fifth when questioned about his role in the dossier exchange.

Could Akhmetshin have known about the Steele dossier? He would have been the perfect actor to play a part in creating a narrative that intelligence was flowing to the Trump campaign from the Russian government, which found its way into the dossier. Were he and Veselnitskaya instructed by Fusion GPS to meet with Don Trump Jr. and other members of the Trump team to advance the "collusion narrative" and not to exchange information about Clinton? Or maybe, Akhmetshin and Veselnitskaya were simply tools of the DNC to sabotage the Trump team.

Whatever the case, the real collusion seems to be between the DNC and the Russians through Fusion GPS to smear a political opponent, not the Trump campaign and the Russians to win an election.

THE STEELE DOSSIER

Donald Trump wasn't supposed to be a serious candidate in the Republican primaries. In the beginning, many people didn't even think he would formally file with the Federal Election Commission, that he was just talking big and marketing himself, as usual. But as 2015 progressed and the number of rabid voters swelled at Trump's rallies, the other Republican candidates began to worry. Trump was legit, and something had to be done. Who best to beat a billionaire businessman than another with opposing political proclivities?

Paul Singer, a hedge-fund manager and supporter of Republican candidate Marco Rubio,[196] is a wealthy GOP donor who provides financial support to various Republican entities, including the conservative outlet *The Washington Free Beacon*. To stop the Trump train from gaining any more steam, Singer gave money to the news site to gather opposition research on Trump and other rivals. The *Free Beacon* then hired one of the best in the business—Glenn Simpson and Fusion GPS, an intelligence-gathering firm well known for its opposition research on political candidates, particularly for Democrats. In 2012, Fusion GPS had worked for Barack Obama during his campaign against Mitt Romney. In that deal, the campaign's payments to Fusion GPS were never publicly disclosed—a tactic the Clinton campaign would imitate in 2016.

According to Simpson, his research for the *Free Beacon* mainly focused on Trump's commercial enterprises. Initially, Russia was never part of the picture. Simpson told the Senate Judiciary Committee his objective was "sort of an unlimited look at his, you know, his business and finances and that sort of thing."[197] Russia inadvertently showed up on Simpson's radar when he "found various references to [Trump] having connections to Italian organized crime and later to a Russian organized crime figure named Felix Sater."[198] Simpson said the information wasn't hard to find, "but as someone who has done a lot of Russian organized crime investigations as a journalist, originally that caught my attention and became something that, you know, I focused on while other people looked at other things."[199] Trump has denied a close association with Sater, but Simpson believed there was more to it. The questionable ties to Sater, coupled with a flow of money from Kazakhstan to Trump businesses, piqued Simpson's curiosity. Some of the money trails, he said, "you just couldn't account for."[200]

Simpson's opposition research, however, didn't stop Trump—not his business dealings, taxes, or his past political views. There was no damaging "47 percent" moment as there was with Mitt Romney in 2012. With the primary season coming to a close, the inevitable became apparent—nothing surfaced to save Rubio or the other Republican candidates. Trump was going to become the Republican nominee.

In an unspoken admission of failure, the *Free Beacon* released Fusion GPS in the spring of 2016. Simpson, however, didn't want his investigation to end. He had a new angle, one that could help the Democrats. His research "wasn't really a Russia-focused investigation for the *first half of it* [emphasis added],"[201] but that would change, especially with Paul Manafort joining the Trump team and Alexandra Chalupa and her Ukrainian cohorts crusading to expose Manafort as a Russia-linked puppet master. In Simpson's mind, Trump had to be stopped. The seeds of a scandal were being sown—Russia was interfering with the election to help Trump. That was a sales pitch the Clinton campaign couldn't refuse.

So one spring day in April, Simpson contacted Marc Elias of Perkins Coie, the law firm with a host of connections to Barack Obama and counsel to the DNC. Simpson offered to continue his investigation of Trump for the Clinton campaign, and Elias heartily agreed. A deal was made, and Fusion GPS became the dirt digger for the DNC, with Russia quickly becoming the primary focus. As the Democrats saw it, they needed Simpson because Manafort's recent hire was an indicator that something was amiss in the Trump campaign—Chalupa's warning had been heeded.

Just a few weeks earlier, Manafort had pushed himself into the Trump orbit of his own accord, wanting to revive his political career in the States after years of working in the controversial world of Ukrainian elections. Manafort's addition to the Trump campaign gave the Russian collusion narrative legs. He had a history of pro-Russia politics in the midst of corruption and intrigue. He had been a business partner with Putin's favorite oligarch, Oleg Deripaska, even though their partnership had soured. Deripaska was breathing down Manafort's neck in the Cayman Islands for a business deal gone wrong.

With so much baggage from overseas, why would Manafort join the Trump campaign? One reason could have been to get into Deripaska's good graces by using his work on the Trump campaign to his advantage.[202] Potentially having the next president of the United States sympathetic to a Russian oligarch who was banned from the country, not to mention buddies with Putin, might have been just the olive branch to extend to Deripaska— and one that could prove financially beneficial to Manafort.

This possible motivation sheds light on Manafort's request to Deripaska for "private briefings" during the campaign. According to the *Washington Post*, Manafort sent an email on July 7, 2016, to an "overseas intermediary" in which he asked, "If he [Deripaska] needs private briefings we can accommodate."[203] Manafort looked like he was milking his new position for all it was worth. He was getting "positive press" at the time and had a "growing reputation." Musing on how best to take advantage of this, Manafort asked his contact in Kiev, "How do we use [this opportunity] to get whole?" As reported in the *Washington Post*,

> *The notes appear to be written in deliberately vague terms, with Manafort and his longtime employee, Konstantin Kilimnik, never explicitly mentioning Deripaska by name. But investigators believe that key passages refer to Deripaska, who is referenced in some places by his initials, "OVD," according to people familiar with the emails. One email uses "black caviar," a Russian delicacy, in what investigators believe is a veiled reference to payments Manafort hoped to receive from former clients.*[204]

Manafort has denied any nefarious intentions in his communications, and there's no evidence that anything came of the offer, but it did give the impression that he was willing "to profit from his prominent role alongside Trump."[205]

Manafort might have joined the Trump campaign to get back into American politics with the bonus of using his position to charm Deripaska. But his presence and actions only added fuel to a growing fire. Had it been any other election year, Manafort's controversial political background in Ukraine and business dealings with a Russian oligarch might have had a negligible impact on the campaign, sort of like when Senator John McCain had associations with Manafort and the same oligarch in 2008. It was problematic but didn't lead to a grand Russian conspiracy. In 2016, however, several things were happening that stirred the pot: the FBI had already wiretapped Manafort in an investigation into possible corruption; Trump's associations with Russians had become a focus of interest in Simpson's ongoing opposition research; Trump's ascendancy in the Republican field and his brash, antiestablishment rhetoric threatened political insiders in both parties; the United Kingdom and Ukraine bristled at campaign rhetoric that, if implemented, could destabilize their relationship with the United States; and the DNC reported its computers had been hacked.

DNC Servers and CrowdStrike

On April 29, 2016, an emergency meeting was called by DNC chairwoman Debbie Wasserman Schultz, chief executive of the DNC Amy Dacey, DNC technology director Andrew Brown, and Michael Sussmann, a lawyer for Perkins Coie who specializes in cybercrimes and was counsel to the DNC. They claimed someone had infiltrated the DNC servers and stolen data, including all emails. Something had to be done immediately. Sussmann took the lead and told the anxious DNC officials that the "three most important questions" at that time were "1) What data was accessed? 2) How was it done? 3) How do we stop it?"[206] Strange that Sussmann didn't ask, "Who has done this?" Since a *crime* had been committed, wouldn't that be an important question to ask? Stopping the hack was a top priority, of course, but knowing who did it would be essential to holding the criminals to account.

Perkins Coie, however, didn't call the FBI to investigate the crime; instead, they hired CrowdStrike, a cybersecurity firm that received one hundred million dollars in an investment round led by Google Capital (now known as CapitalG).[207] This is of interest because CapitalG is owned by Alphabet Inc., which was formerly chaired by Eric Schmidt, an ambitious Clinton supporter who tried to land an active role in the 2016 campaign. As reported by Jack Nicas in *The Wall Street Journal*, Schmidt "sent a Clinton campaign official a lengthy memo with advice on running the campaign. He told campaign officials he was 'ready to fund, advise recruit talent,' and 'clearly wants to be head outside advisor,' according to a 2014 email from Clinton campaign Chairman John Podesta to campaign manager Robby Mook."[208]

CrowdStrike is also associated with the Atlantic Council and Victor Pinchuk. CrowdStrike's chief technology officer, Dmitri Alperovitch, is a senior fellow at the Atlantic Council where Pinchuk sits on its international advisory board. Even more significantly, CrowdStrike is connected to the Obama administration: the company's chief risk officer, Steven Chabinsky, was appointed to Obama's Commission on Enhancing National Cybersecurity in April 2016—the very same month the DNC computers were reported to have been hacked.[209] Quite proud of the appointment, CrowdStrike wrote on April 18,

> *Under the Commission, Chabinsky and 11 other industry leaders have been directed by the White House to recommend "bold, actionable steps that the government, private sector, and the nation as a whole can take to bolster cybersecurity in today's digital world."[210]*

> *President Obama, in an official statement, commended the members for bringing "a wealth of experience and talent to this important role," and charged the Commission with "the critically-important task of identifying the steps that our nation must take to ensure our cybersecurity in an increasingly digital world."[211]*

Chabinsky was also deputy assistant director of the FBI in the Obama administration until he joined CrowdStrike in 2012.

According to Jason Leopold of BuzzFeed, the DNC "had hired CrowdStrike essentially in place of the FBI":[212]

> *DNC officials said they made the eyebrow-raising choice to go with a private firm because they were worried they'd lose control of their operations right in the middle of the campaign. Not only that, but the FBI was investigating Hillary Clinton's*

use of a private email server. Better, the DNC figured, to handle things privately.[213]

After examining the servers for a mere day, CrowdStrike concluded two Russian groups named Cozy Bear and Fancy Bear were responsible for the cyberattack. Cozy Bear had been meddling in the DNC computers for a year, but Fancy Bear was new to the scene in late April. The White House said Fancy Bear was known for receiving orders from top officials in the Russian government, but cyber experts admitted they knew very little about them. According to Sheera Frenkel of BuzzFeed, "No one knows, for instance, how many hackers are working regularly within Fancy Bear, or how they organize their hacking squads. They don't know if they are based in one city or scattered in various locations across Russia. They don't even know what they call themselves."[214]

The New York Times described the process of discovering who's behind a cyberattack as "more art than science."[215] CrowdStrike's Alperovitch said there was absolutely no way to know who did it. It's mainly a process of elimination. By ruling out other possibilities, CrowdStrike concluded only two cyberattackers could be responsible: Cozy Bear or Fancy Bear. The two groups weren't even acting in concert. According to the *Times*, "Fancy Bear, apparently not knowing that Cozy Bear had been rummaging in DNC files for months, took many of the same documents."[216]

The bulk of those documents had to do with opposition research on Trump. Makes you wonder whether the two hacks were different in more ways than timing and purpose. Did CrowdStrike examine and eliminate all possibilities? The company had been reportedly wrong before—and about the very same group they identified in the DNC breach, Fancy Bear.

In an investigation into the hacking of a Ukrainian artillery app, CrowdStrike blamed the Russians, but the International Institute for Strategic Studies says CrowdStrike erroneously used their data to come to that conclusion. As reported by Voice of America,

> *"The CrowdStrike report uses our data, but the inferences and analysis drawn from that data belong solely to the report's authors," the IISS said. "The inference they make that reductions in Ukrainian D-30 artillery holdings between 2013 and 2016 were primarily the result of combat losses is not a conclusion that we have ever suggested ourselves, nor one we believe to be accurate."*
>
> *In early January, the Ukrainian Ministry of Defense issued a statement saying artillery losses from the ongoing fighting with separatists are "several times smaller than the number reported by [CrowdStrike] and are not associated with the specified cause" of Russian hacking.*[217]

To put it bluntly, CrowdStrike has reportedly made mistakes in their process of elimination, wrongly using *assumptions* of Russian hacking as *proof* of Russian hacking. Postulating is exactly what Alperovitch was doing when he compared both the Ukrainian incident and the DNC hacking: "When you think about, well, who would be interested in targeting Ukraine artillerymen in eastern Ukraine? Who has interest in hacking the Democratic Party? [The] Russian government comes to mind."[218] Was it the Russian government? We don't know because only CrowdStrike examined the computers. The FBI was left out in the cold, and US government investigators were reliant on CrowdStrike's conclusions.

While meeting with the DNC, CrowdStrike said they were confident the Russians infiltrated the system, but not to worry because Russians don't share data they swipe from servers. DNC officials nervously asked Robert Johnston, CrowdStrike's cybersecurity expert who examined the servers, what would happen to all the emails that were stolen? As reported by Buzz-Feed, Johnston said, "I start[ed] thinking back to all of these previous hacks by Russia and other adversaries like China. I [thought] back to the Joint Chiefs hack. What did they do with this data? Nothing. They took the information for espionage purposes. They didn't leak it to WikiLeaks."[219]

So Johnston, who was convinced the Russians hacked the servers, assured the DNC that the Russians wouldn't do anything with the data. Yet, the emails were leaked. When WikiLeaks published the emails in the summer, CrowdStrike's expert was proven wrong. Isn't it odd that the Russians, who never share stolen data, deviated from standard behavior and handed over the emails to WikiLeaks? Could this be an indicator that maybe it wasn't the Russians, at least in the alleged April hack? Julian Assange, founder of WikiLeaks, has repeatedly claimed no state actors gave him the emails. "Our source is not the Russian government," he told Fox News host Sean Hannity.[220] Of course, Assange, a questionable character in his own right, could be lying. But again, we don't know for certain because the FBI wasn't on the case.

Not everyone in law enforcement was pleased with that decision. A senior law-enforcement official told CNN that it's important for the FBI to have access to servers when such a breach happens:

> *The FBI repeatedly stressed to DNC officials the necessity of obtaining direct access to servers and data, only to be rebuffed until well after the initial compromise had been mitigated. This left the FBI no choice but to rely upon a third party for*

information. These actions caused significant delays and inhibited the FBI from addressing the intrusion earlier.[221]

The DNC has said the FBI never asked to look at the servers,[222] but now former FBI director James Comey contradicted this claim in a Senate intelligence hearing when he said the bureau made "multiple requests at different levels."[223] Investigators at the FBI "always prefer to have access hands-on ourselves if that's possible," he said.[224] To this day, however, no one but CrowdStrike has examined the servers. No intelligence agency has ever investigated the scene of the crime.[225] Even when BuzzFeed subpoenaed the DNC's hacking information as part of the discovery process in a lawsuit, the DNC declined, forcing BuzzFeed to sue them "to force the DNC to follow the law and allow BuzzFeed to fully defend its First Amendment rights."[226]

The DNC also denied Obama's Homeland Security secretary, Jeh Johnson, access to the servers, saying they "did not feel it needed."[227] Johnson said he became aware of the hack sometime in 2016 and pressed his "staff to know whether DHS was sufficiently proactive, and on the scene helping the DNC identify the intruders and patch vulnerabilities."[228] Johnson said the answer "was not reassuring."[229] As reported by Austin Wright at *Politico*, "The FBI and the DNC had been in contact with each other months before about the intrusion," Johnson said, "and the DNC did not feel it needed DHS's assistance at that time."[230]

Inexplicably, DNC chairperson Debbie Wasserman Schultz denied the veracity of these officials' statements, saying,

It is astounding to me that the Chair of an organization like the DNC was never contacted by the FBI or any other agency concerned about these intrusions. As a member of Congress, I had the unique clearance to hear any classified briefing that

would be involved in such an intrusion, and the FBI clearly
should have come to me with that information. They did not.[231]

During the counterintelligence investigation, the Justice Department never issued a subpoena for the servers, "just like the Obama Justice Department decided not to issue subpoenas to demand the surrender of critical physical evidence in the Clinton e-mails investigation," former assistant US attorney for the Southern District of New York Andrew McCarthy observed. "Instead, the conclusion that Russia is responsible for the invasion of the DNC servers rests on the forensic analysis conducted by CrowdStrike. Rather than do its own investigation, the FBI relied on a contractor retained by the DNC's lawyers."[232]

The Obama administration assured the American people that the information from CrowdStrike was "rock solid." The US government was "100% certain" it was the Russians, so there was no need to examine it further.[233] But how could the Obama administration be 100 percent confident when CrowdStrike—the DNC contractor that looked at the servers firsthand—wouldn't even go that far?

Bottom line is the DNC didn't want their servers examined, and the Obama Justice Department complied without a hint of reservation. Did it have to do with Clinton's emails? Details about the hack? Donor information? Whatever the reason, the DNC servers became a closed door under lock and key, yet the DNC had no problem opening the floodgates of information about the hacking to the media. Once CrowdStrike made its report that the Russians were responsible, they were itching to go public. The DNC just needed the US government to give their claims teeth by parroting CrowdStrike's conclusions. The information had to be official, but the Obama administration was hesitant, and the FBI remained silent, for a time.

Even later, as word spread of a possible cybersecurity threat from the Russians, National Security Advisor Susan Rice put a lid on pursuing the matter. According to Michael Isikoff, she didn't want the issue to get out of Obama's control, and she was quite indignant about it, telling the White House cyber response team that wanted to do more aggressive investigating to stand down and "knock it off."[234] The stated reason for the shrill order was that Obama didn't want to be "boxed in" with questions from the press, and they didn't want to "provoke the Russians into materially affecting the outcome of the election."[235]

There was also the timing: the Obama administration didn't want to appear as if the Democratic president and his team were playing politics with an announcement that would cast doubt on the credibility of the election. Obama officials have said they were protecting the "integrity of the vote,"[236] but maybe there was more to it, having realized Russian interference was a two-edged sword. Alerting the public about the meddling might hurt Trump, but it would taint Clinton's win, calling into question its legitimacy. The Democrats couldn't have that. A better plan would be just to let it ride out until Clinton won in November and then it would all go away. No need to have her election called into question with news of Russian meddling—unless there was proof that Trump was colluding with the Russians. That would be worth investigating—and leaking—of course.

Folks at the DNC, however, couldn't contain themselves. In June, as Trump dominated the Republican field during the final lap before the convention, the DNC released the information to the media, even without backup from the FBI. On June 14,

2016, the *Washington Post* reported the cyberattack, explaining that the "intrusions are an example of Russia's interest in the US political system and its desire to understand the policies, strengths and weaknesses of a potential future president."[237] In the middle of the article, the *Post* homed in on a point the DNC wanted to be conveyed: "*Russian President Vladimir Putin has spoken favorably about Trump* [emphasis added], who has called for better relations with Russia and expressed skepticism about NATO. But unlike Clinton, whom the Russians probably have long had in their spy sights, Trump has not been a politician for very long, so foreign agencies are playing catch-up."[238] The seed of Russia favoring Trump had been planted in the context of a criminal act.

Three days later, the *Washington Post* ran another story. Its focus was on Trump's Russian business ties, his trip to Moscow for the Miss Universe pageant, and others in the Trump orbit with Russian associations. The article is significant regarding the push to get out the Trump-Russia collusion narrative because it references nearly all the people who would become the focus of the investigation—even fringe advisers who would later be examined for evidence of collusion, examinations that have not led to one charge relating to the Trump campaign conspiring with Russia.

In this June 17 article, before the Steele dossier was made public or anyone outside of the Justice Department supposedly knew about the counterintelligence inquiry, and before that investigation was fully opened, the following people were named in a *Washington Post* article regarding Trump's alleged ties to Russia: Emin and Aras Agalarov, Russian ambassador to the United States Sergey Kislyak, John McCain's associate David Kramer, former national security advisor Michael

Flynn, Donald Trump Jr., Paul Manafort, Carter Page, and Michael Caputo.[239] This last individual wasn't much of a blip on the radar at the time, but Caputo served as communications adviser to the Trump campaign for a short period. He also worked in Russia during the 1990s and developed associations with Kremlin officials. Because of these connections, the House Intelligence Committee interviewed him about collusion during the election, but as reported in *The New York Times*, Caputo "strongly denied that there was any collusion between him or anyone else on the campaign and Russian officials. He has also accused the committee of smearing him."[240] Caputo has not been charged, and the House Intelligence Committee has yet to find evidence of collusion, with the majority concluding there is none to be found.

The group of names included in a "narrative" of Trump ties to Russia reads like a report from an investigator—months later. But this article was published before the investigation even started. Congress wouldn't even know about the investigation until nearly eight months later, when James Comey spilled the beans in his congressional testimony. Yet, the reporters at the *Washington Post*—the same newspaper that published the first report about DNC hacking claims—put all these people together in one article. Who was their audience? Who was anxious that this troupe of actors be presented to the public sphere in the context of Russian interference, just as the contest between Trump and Clinton was intensifying? The article makes it look as if a narrative was being constructed to push the investigation forward and influence the public, just like the DNC wanted. A report of the Russians supposedly hacking the DNC led the way, and more in the same vein would follow as reporters would presuppose Trump collusion and turn a blind eye to any other possibility. The truth would be hidden in a flood of information.

The news of the hacking was unnerving to the American voter, but Wasserman Schultz assured the public that the Democratic Party had everything under control. She didn't want the narrative to get away from them. "When we discovered the intrusion, we treated this like the serious incident it is and reached out to CrowdStrike immediately," she said. "Our team moved as quickly as possible to kick out the intruders and secure our network."[241] CrowdStrike was on the case, so no one needed to worry. Perkins Coie made sure of that.

Perkins Coie

The law firm Perkins Coie was right in the middle of all the action, monitoring the flow of information and receiving monies from Democratic entities for opposition research and legal work. As reported by Sean Davis at *The Federalist*, Obama for America (OFA) paid thousands of dollars to Perkins Coie in late April 2016 for "legal services" after the firm had hired Fusion GPS. Obama's group paid Perkins Coie 98,047 dollars on April 25–26 and 700,000 dollars on September 29, 2016. Fusion GPS's contract with the firm ended in October 2016. By comparison, OFA paid Perkins Coie 174,725 dollars from January to August 2017.[242]

"Federal records show that Hillary Clinton's official campaign organization, Hillary For America, paid just under $5.1 million to Perkins Coie in 2016," Davis writes. "The DNC paid nearly $5.4 million to the law firm in 2016."[243] Fusion GPS was hired on April 12, and on April 25 OFA began paying the law firm for its "legal services." Payments from the Clinton campaign to Perkins Coie were also listed as legal fees in disclosure forms to the FEC.

In their book *Russian Roulette*, Michael Isikoff and David Corn confirmed that, just as OFA had done, the payments were "obscured on campaign disclosure reports filed with the Federal Election Commission":[244]

> *The payments to Fusion GPS were reported as legal fees to the law firm. Over time, more than $1 million in Hillary for America and DNC funds would be paid to Fusion GPS in fees and expenses. Yet many of the top officials at the Clinton campaign and the DNC were not aware of the arrangement and what Fusion GPS was up to. When, months later, Donna Brazile, then the interim DNC chair, picked up rumors about the firm's research in Russia, she confronted Elias and demanded an explanation. He brushed her off, according to Brazile, and said, "You don't want to know."*[245]

Wasserman Schultz and Clinton's campaign manager, John Podesta, said they had no idea Fusion GPS had been hired to dig up dirt on Trump. In a closed-door Senate Intelligence Committee hearing, Podesta was asked if the Clinton campaign had a contract with Fusion GPS. He said he didn't know of any agreement, yet sitting beside him during the interview was his attorney, Marc Elias, whose law firm hired Fusion GPS. Are we to believe Elias acted completely of his own accord, receiving reports from Simpson and Steele without communicating with Podesta and the DNC, or telling them where he got the reports?

The claim that no one at the DNC knew what Fusion GPS "was up to" fails the smell test in a big way. Elias was deeply connected to the DNC and Obama, having a history of working for both OFA and the DNC. "In *Shamblin v. Obama for America*, a 2013 case in federal court in Florida, federal court records list Elias as simultaneously serving as lead attorney for both OFA and the DNC," Davis writes.[246] These connections can't be ignored or shrugged off as mere coincidence. According to Davis,

> *The timing and nature of the payments to Perkins Coie by Obama's official campaign arm raise significant questions about whether OFA was funding Fusion GPS, how much Obama and his team knew about the contents and provenance of the dossier long before its contents were made public, and whether the president or his government lieutenants knowingly used a partisan political document to justify official government actions targeting the president's political opponents named in the dossier.[247]*

Money and attorneys, however, weren't the only connection between these entities. Davis explains,

> *At the same time that Clinton's campaign, Obama's campaign organization, and the DNC were simultaneously paying Perkins Coie, the spouse of one of Fusion GPS's key employees was working directly for Obama in the West Wing. Shailagh Murray, a former Washington Post reporter-turned-political operative, was serving as a top communications adviser to Obama while the Obama administration was reportedly using information from the dossier to justify secret surveillance of Trump campaign staff. Murray is married to Neil King, a former Wall Street Journal reporter who was hired by Fusion GPS in December of 2016. While at The Wall Street Journal, King worked alongside Fusion GPS's core team, even sharing bylines with Glenn Simpson, the Fusion GPS executive who personally hired Steele to probe Trump's alleged Russia connections.[248]*

Other connections include Bob Bauer, founder of Perkins Coie's political law practice, who served as Obama's personal attorney and general counsel to his presidential campaign before Bauer was appointed as White House counsel. Bauer had been a longtime adviser to the former president since Obama became a US senator in 2005. In 2013, Obama appointed Bauer to the co-chair of the Presidential Commission on Election Administration. Another Perkins Coie attorney, Judith Corley, became Obama's personal attorney when Bauer took on his new role. Bauer and Corley had known each other for decades. Elias's work for the Democrats was so extensive that a former FEC official told *Politico*, "There is no Democratic-side campaign finance lawyer who is more important than Marc Elias. That is without a doubt."[249] Needless to say, the ties between Obama, the DNC, and Perkins Coie are extensive and strong.

Christopher Steele

After Elias hired Fusion GPS and following the DNC claims of a cyberattack, Simpson brought on Christopher Steele, the ex-British spy who was a specialist in all things Russian, though he hadn't been there in years. Simpson claims the focus of Steele's job was Trump's business dealings, but the Russian connections were of particular interest, especially with the claim of a recent cyberattack by Russian hackers—information Simpson knew before it went public.[250] When Simpson met with Steele in early June, Russian interference was fresh on his mind. Simpson, however, emphasized to the Senate Judiciary Committee that he didn't tell Steele about the Russians supposedly hacking the DNC and that the shift to a Russian focus happened "organically." Fusion GPS had a lot of "general knowledge about Trump," Simpson explained, but they needed specifics. So they found a Russian specialist. Steele was "the leading Russianist at MI6 prior to leaving the government and an extremely well-regarded investigator."[251]

Simpson explained that Steele's assignment was triggered by all of Trump's trips to Russia, not by the claim of a Russian hack of the DNC. "[Trump's trips] struck me as a little bit odd and calling for explanation," he told the committee. "I'll just stress that we weren't looking for—at least it wasn't at the forefront of my mind there was going to be anything involving the Russian government per se, at least not that I recall."[252]

Steele seemed like a perfect fit to find Russian dirt on Trump. He had provided reliable research to the US government on Ukraine and corruption at the Fédération Internationale de Football Association. He had credibility. Simpson trusted his work on the mere basis of his reputation, not primarily the quality of his work.[253] Steele was a good guy, so his work would be good, Simpson thought. They were doing opposition research anyway, not national intelligence.

The ex-British spy also had connections to a network of Russians and people in London who could get him intel. According to former CIA deputy director Michael Morell, Steele got the information by paying liaisons. As reported by Chuck Ross at the Daily Caller, Morell said "the intermediaries paid the sources, and the intermediaries got the money from Chris. And that kind of worries me a little bit because if you're paying somebody, particularly former FSB officers, they are going to tell you truth and innuendo and rumor, and they're going to call you up and say, 'Hey, let's have another meeting, I have more information for you,' because they want to get paid some more."[254]

Steele received the money from the Clinton campaign, so essentially the campaign and the DNC paid Russian operatives for dirt on Trump. Steele's contacts were extensive, including at Cambridge, where he attended as a student and became president of the Cambridge Union. Reportedly, Steele was the first president of the debating society to invite someone from the Palestine Liberation Organization to speak. He also presided over "numerous high-profile political debates, including one [with the] proposition that President Ronald Reagan's foreign policies had hurt the UK."[255]

The British agent's connections with Cambridge remained strong and his reputation praiseworthy among many of his fellow spies. As reported by Jane Mayer in *The New Yorker*,

> *Richard Dearlove, who led M.I.6 from 1999 to 2004, has described his reputation as "superb." A former senior officer recalls him as "a Russia-area expert whose knowledge I and others respected—he was very careful, and very savvy." Another former M.I.6 officer described him as having a "Marmite" personality—a reference to the salty British spread, which people either love or hate.*[256]

In other words, Steele could be trusted to get information on Russia and any connections to Trump. He didn't even need to travel to Russia to gather the intel. His firm, Orbis Business Intelligence, had "many Russian contacts" who could be interviewed in other regions, "and London is the center of the post-Soviet Russian diaspora."[257] As we have already seen, the United Kingdom was the central hub of information flow in the creation of the Trump-Russia collusion narrative. Steele most likely contacted former and possibly current spies in British intelligence (because you never really stop being a spy) to gather some of the information on the Republican candidate. The fact that British intelligence was already accumulating material that involved Trump would have only helped the cause.

Steele made his contacts, gathered information, and regularly transmitted it to Simpson. Steele claims he didn't know he was working for the Clinton campaign and the DNC at the time, but it doesn't take much brainpower to put two and two together. If you're gathering opposition research on Trump while heading into the general election, who do you think your clients are? But Steele insists he didn't know, and he wouldn't have mentioned it to anyone anyway. His firm promises silence, but this doesn't mean there haven't been reports about some of its clientele—one of those names we've seen before and could call into question the origins of information in his dossier. According to *The New Yorker*,

> Some of [Orbis's] purported clients, such as a major Western oil company, are conventional corporations. Others are controversial, including a London law firm representing the interests of Oleg Deripaska, the billionaire victor of Russia's aluminum wars, a notoriously violent battle.[258]

The connection between Deripaska and Steele is Russian-linked Washington lobbyist Adam Waldman and a London-based lawyer named Paul Hauser, allegedly working with Orbis, though Hauser has refused to answer questions submitted to him by Senator Chuck Grassley. Both Waldman and Hauser reportedly represented Deripaska.

Grassley's inquiry into these connections stems from the release of Senator Mark Warner's texts—the ranking Democratic member of the Senate Intelligence Committee—that show Steele contacted the senator through Waldman in March 2017. In one of those texts, Waldman told Warner, "Chris Steele asked me to call you."[259] How was Steele connected to an attorney for Deripaska? The letter from Grassley gives a clue—Hauser, possibly a client of Orbis Business Intelligence, put him in touch with Waldman. So the chain was Steele contacted Hauser, who connected him to Waldman, who contacted Warner on Steele's behalf.

What are we to make of these connections between Clinton's opposition researcher and Deripaska, who had had conflicts with Manafort and was one of Putin's buddies? Grassley wrote to Hauser, posing the following questions:

1. Public reports and court documents indicate that you are an attorney for Mr. Oleg Deripaska. Do you serve, or have you served, as legal counsel for Mr. Deripaska or any business associated with him?

2. Have you ever hired or otherwise worked with Mr. Christopher Steele, Orbis Business Intelligence Limited, Orbis Business
International Limited, Walsingham Training Limited, or Walsingham Partners Limited? If so, when, and what was the nature of the arrangement?

3. Is it the case that Mr. Steele, through you, works or has worked on behalf of Mr. Deripaska or businesses associated with him?
If so, when has such work occurred?

4. Are you otherwise aware of any business or financial relationships between Mr. Steele and Russian government officials, Russian oligarchs, or Russian businesses?[260]

Concern about a possible relationship between Steele and a Russian oligarch was highly warranted. As former CIA director John Brennan said in a congressional hearing, "Russian intelligence agencies do not hesitate at all to use private companies and

Russian persons who are unaffiliated with the Russian government to support their objectives."[261] In the words of Lee Smith at
Tablet magazine, this puts the dossier "in a new light":[262]

> *If Steele worked for a Russian oligarch with close ties to Putin, it
> is likely to change prevailing views of the Russia investigations
> of the past year and a half. The three congressional inquiries
> (Senate Judiciary, Senate Intelligence, and House Intelligence),
> as well as special counsel Robert Mueller's probe, are based
> largely on allegations made in the dossier. Was Steele paid by
> Deripaska at the same time he was paid by the Washington,
> D.C., communications firm Fusion GPS for his work on
> behalf of the Clinton campaign and the Democratic National
> Committee? Did his work on behalf of Deripaska influence his
> investigations into the Trump team's possible ties to Russia?
> Was Deripaska one of Steele's Kremlin-insider sources—and
> what does that tell us about the contents and purpose of the
> Steele dossier?*[263]

Another connection between Steele and Deripaska is
through one of the sources in his dossier, "Source D," known
as Sergei Millian. Steele's "Source D" met with Deripaska at the
St. Petersburg International Economic Forum between June 16
and 18. As reported by Ross at the Daily Caller,

> *Two days after the forum ended, Christopher Steele, a former
> MI6 agent conducting research on Trump, wrote a memo
> based on information from an intermediary who spoke to a
> source later identified as Millian.*
>
> *Millian's appearance at the St. Petersburg expo, photos of
> which he posted on Facebook, establishes for the first time
> that he was in Russia at the time the dossier placed him there
> as a source. And if Millian did indeed discuss Trump at the
> conference, that means Steele's direct source was present at the
> conference.*[264]

The memo Steele wrote at that time cites Millian, who claimed that the Kremlin had a video of Trump engaging in lewd sexual behavior with prostitutes in Moscow to be used as blackmail. The contact between Millian and Deripaska at the forum brings up the possibility that Millian told Deripaska that story, and Deripaska passed it to Steele.

One of Steele's first contacts in gathering opposition research for Fusion GPS was with so-called Russian "collectors" who made contacts with sources in Russia.[265] A House report released in 2018 says Steele obtained information in the dossier second- and third-hand from "purported high-placed Russian sources, such as government officials with links to the Kremlin and intelligence services."[266] The House committee found that almost all the claims in the dossier are attributed to Russian-based sources, such as a "senior Russian government figure," a "senior Russian-leadership figure," an "official close to [the] Russian Presidential Administration," a "Kremlin insider," a "former top Russian officer," a "senior Russian financial official," a "senior Russian Foreign Ministry Figure," a "Kremlin official involved in US relations," and a "former top level Russian intelligence officer still active inside the Kremlin."[267] The House Committee communicated its concern "with the degree to which the Kremlin may have sought to influence information that was ultimately provided to Steele—through the potential provision of disinformation or otherwise—consistent with its ongoing efforts "to undermine public faith in the US democratic process."[268]

If the Russians knew Steele was gathering opposition research on a political candidate, they would have toyed with him, funneling information to him that would play well in the America media. As Leonid Bershidsky, a *Bloomberg View* columnist, observed,

If the F.S.B. and the Kremlin knew of Clinton's interest in putting together a dossier on Trump, all these people had an excellent reason to talk, and especially to provide nonsensical information—such as that Dmitry Peskov, Putin's press secretary, and not anyone in Russia's intelligence community, was the keeper of a top-secret file on Trump.[269]

Steele's Russian sources probably weren't acting in good faith but were engaged in an effort to sow chaos. Given the "quality" of information they relayed to him, it's hard to conclude that a seasoned intelligence operative such as Steele failed to uncover the misinformation. Although, based on Steele's feelings of animosity toward Trump, it's possible that he simply wanted the information to be true. Steele told DOJ associate attorney general Bruce Ohr that he "was desperate that Donald Trump not get elected and was passionate about him not being president."[270]

The "Dossier"

Steele's dossier narrates from a "fly on the wall" perspective, relying on "trusted compatriots," "former intelligence officers," and "ministry of foreign affairs officials."[271] These individuals, however, would have never relayed such information to Steele— if it were accurate (and we know for a fact it was not). According to an analysis of Steele's dossier by the Hoover Institution's Paul Roderick Gregory, the dossier "claims to know more than is knowable" and "the poor grammar and shaky spelling plus the author's use of KGB-style intelligence reporting, however, do not fit the image of a high-end London security company run by highly connected former British intelligence figures."[272] As Gregory explained in *Forbes* soon after BuzzFeed published the dossier, due to the secretive nature of the Kremlin, "outside researchers must grasp for flimsy straws to write their scholarly articles and books."[273] He continues,

> *As someone who has worked for more than a decade with the microfilm collection of Soviet documents in the Hoover Institution Archives, I can say that the dossier itself was compiled by a Russian, whose command of English is far from perfect and who follows the KGB (now FSB) practice of writing intelligence reports, in particular the practice of capitalizing all names for easy reference. The report includes Putin's inner circle—Peskov, Ivanov, Sechin, Lavrov. The anonymous author claims to have "trusted compatriots" who knew the roles that each Kremlin insider, including Putin himself, played in the Trump election saga and were prepared to tell him.[274]*

Gregory wonders if Steele even wrote most of the memos:

> *I have picked out just a few excerpts from the Orbis report. It was written, in my opinion, not by an ex British intelligence officer but by a Russian trained in the KGB tradition. It is full of names, dates, meetings, quarrels, and events that are hearsay (one an overheard conversation). It is a collection of "this important person" said this to "another important person." There is no record; no informant is identified by name or by more than a generic title. The report appears to fail the veracity test in the one instance of a purported meeting in which names, dates, and location are provided. Some of the stories are so bizarre (the Rosneft bribe) that they fail the laugh test.[275]*

A point many miss regarding the origins of the dossier, Gregory explains, is that "Steele did not have enough money to pay anyone with that much access to the inner circles of the Kremlin. They are all multi-millionaires. This means that either Steele made it all up or that inner-circle people really provided these reports to Steele. If the latter, it means that the dossier was written not by Steele but by the Kremlin."[276] In other words, it was Hillary Clinton's team that colluded with Russians, not Trump.

The intel Steele gathered read more like sleazy information pulled from the oily waters of gossip and rumor than well-verified research. The first memo he provided to Simpson on June 20 claimed the Kremlin had been supporting "Trump for at least five years and that he and his inner circle have accepted a regular flow of intelligence from the Kremlin, including on his Democratic and other political rivals."[277] Despite this close relationship with Russia, Trump was oddly reluctant to enter into any lucrative business deals. As Gregory says, "This story makes no sense":[278]

> In 2011, when the courtship purportedly begins, Trump was a TV personality and beauty pageant impresario. Neither in the US or Russia would anyone of authority anticipate that Trump would one day become the presidential candidate of a major US political party, making him the target of Russian intelligence.[279]

The memo also said Russian intelligence had compromising information on Trump, including perverted sex acts that could be used as blackmail against him. This, of course, is the "golden showers" fiction. As written in the dossier, the Russian authorities could "exploit Trump's personal obsessions and sexual perversion in order to obtain suitable 'kompromat' (compromising material) on him":[280]

> According to Source D, where s/he had been present, Trump's (perverted) conduct in Moscow included hiring the presidential suite of the Ritz Carlton Hotel, where he knew President and Mrs. Obama (whom he hated) had stayed on one of their official trips to Russia, and defiling the bed where

they had slept by employing a number of prostitutes to perform
a "golden showers" (urination) show in front of him. The hotel
was known to be under FSB control with microphones and
concealed cameras in all the main rooms to record anything
they wanted to.[281]

In a memo on July 19, Steele focused on Trump's adviser
Carter Page, asserting that he held secret meetings in Moscow
with Russian officials during a trip he took as a campaign
adviser. In those meetings, Page supposedly learned that the
Russian government had kompromat on both Clinton and
Trump, which a Kremlin official said Trump should "bear in
mind in his dealings with them."[282] Page was then allegedly
offered a 19 percent stake in a Russian oil company (Rosneft)
if Trump would lift Russian sanctions—if he became president.
Gregory quips, "This story is utter nonsense, not worthy of a
wacky conspiracy theory of an alien invasion":[283]

To offer [Carter Page] either the entirety of, or a brokerage
commission on, the market value of 19.5% of Rosneft shares—
even a 6 percent commission on $12 billion worth of Rosneft
shares would amount to an astonishing $720 million—would
deplete the cash that Putin desperately needed for military
spending and budget deficits, all in return for a promise to
lift sanctions if—and what a big "if"—Trump were elected.
Rosneft, as a public company, would have to conceal that the
US president was a party to this major transaction.[284]

Another memo claimed there was an "extensive conspiracy" between the Trump campaign and Moscow, and the
"highest levels" of the Kremlin were driving it. The thought of
the Russian government having compromising information
on a presidential candidate concerned Steele to the point that
he wanted to inform US authorities of what he found, even

though it was unverified, second- and third-hand, and in one case "pillow talk" shared by the lover of a Kremlin official.[285] Of course, the fact that Steele was "desperate" to make sure Trump wasn't elected can't be ruled out as a possible additional motivation.

First Contact

Steele met with Simpson and asked about giving the information over to the FBI because there was a "security issue about whether a presidential candidate was being blackmailed."[286] Simpson said he didn't agree or disagree with the suggestion: "I just put it off and said I needed to think about it. Then he raised it again with me. I don't remember the exact sequence of these events, but my recollection is that I questioned how we would do that because I don't know anyone there that I could report something like this to and be believed and I didn't really think it was necessarily appropriate for me to do that." Steele said he knew "the perfect person, they know who I am, I'll take care of it."[287]

While Fusion GPS usually doesn't share its research with anyone outside the case, Simpson said this situation was different—he believed espionage had taken place with the hacking of the DNC computers. A crime, he said, needed to be reported. To make sure that happened, Steele reached into his bag of contacts from the soccer corruption case and called Michael Gaeta at the FBI Rome office, asking him to fly to London to get the sensitive information.[288]

State Department and the FBI

According to Michael Isikoff and David Corn in *Russian Roulette*, Gaeta was intrigued, but he would have to get State

Department approval first, so the FBI called Assistant Secretary of State Victoria Nuland. She approved the meeting because, in the past, Steele had provided reliable research on Ukraine to the US government through State Department official Jonathan Winer.[289] Nuland didn't trust Trump, but she trusted Steele, so she gave Gaeta the "green light," and on July 5 he jumped on a plane to London to hear what was too sensitive to share over the phone. According to Isikoff, after reading the explosive details on Trump, Gaeta took the memos to FBI headquarters, turning them over to FBI agent Peter Strzok.[290]

Nuland's account of the State Department's role regarding the Steele dossier, however, is different from Isikoff's. In February 2018, she told *Face the Nation* that "in the middle of July, when [Steele] was doing this other work [on Trump] and became concerned...he passed two to four pages of short points of what he was finding and our immediate reaction to that was, this is not our purview. This needs to go to the FBI if there is any concern here that one candidate or the election as a whole might be influenced by the Russian Federation. That's something for the FBI to investigate. And that was our reaction when we saw this."[291]

Jonathan Winer has his own account of how the dossier ended up in the FBI's hands, and it differs from the two prior narratives. According to Winer in a *Washington Post* op-ed,

> *In the summer of 2016, Steele told me that he had learned of disturbing information regarding possible ties between Donald Trump, his campaign and senior Russian officials. He did not provide details but made clear the information involved "active measures," a Soviet intelligence term for propaganda and related activities to influence events in other countries.*

In September 2016, Steele and I met in Washington and discussed the information now known as the "dossier."

I was allowed to review, but not to keep, a copy of these reports to enable me to alert the State Department. I prepared a two-page summary and shared it with Nuland, who indicated that, like me, she felt that the Secretary of State [John Kerry] needed to be made aware of this material.[292]

Interestingly, Winer later admitted to doing pro bono work for the Clinton Global Initiative while he was working at the State Department and exchanging information with Steele. Winer also said he shared anti-Trump material with Steele that was passed to him by Clinton insider Sidney Blumenthal. That material came from Cody Shearer, a longtime fixer for the Clintons, who had created a dossier on Trump that sounded suspiciously similar to Steele's.

Shearer's involvement is significant because of the particular nature of his history with the Clintons and Blumenthal. According to *National Review*, his name "surfaced in connection with the so-called intelligence reports Sidney Blumenthal was channeling to Hillary Clinton during her time at the State Department."[293] This was during the Libyan uprising against Muammar Gaddafi in 2011 when Blumenthal authored around twenty-five memos that he emailed to Hillary Clinton in 2011 and 2012. Nearly a third of the emails Clinton received regarding the situation in Libya came from Blumenthal, who was not even employed by the State Department. She had tried to hire him in 2009 shortly after becoming secretary of state, but it was blocked by Obama's chief of staff Rahm Emanuel.[294]

Blumenthal's motive in this case was probably financial, given that at the time he was employed by Osprey, a Libyan start-up that aimed to profit off of medical and military contracts from the chaos of the uprising. Blumenthal denies exploiting the situation to further his business interests, even though he pushed for the hiring of military contractors in his emails.[295]

Regardless, the information presented in those memos was often bogus. In one email Blumenthal suggested that Libya's leadership wanted a positive relationship with Israel, a virtual impossibility to anyone who understands the region. His sources, without exception, were always anonymous. Aiding Blumenthal, however, was Shearer, a not-so-anonymous source. In one email, Blumenthal writes to Clinton about a conversation Cody had with one of "the key figures in the Libyan National Council that seeks to become an interim government."[296] Clinton writes back, "Good for Cody! I'll follow up."[297]

What are the odds that not one, but two, bogus dossiers can be tied to Hillary Clinton, and one written by a man with a history of making up information for Clinton? In a letter to DNC chair Tom Perez on January 25, 2018, regarding the then-recently confirmed revelation that the DNC and Clinton campaign had funded the dirty dossier, Senators Chuck Grassley and Lindsey Graham requested all communications from a number of figures, among them Fusion GPS, Christopher Steele, US Deputy Attorney General Sally Yates, Assistant Secretary of State for European and Eurasian Affairs Victoria Nuland, FBI Special Agent Peter Strzok, Cody Shearer, and Sidney Blumenthal.[298]

According to *The Guardian*, Steele passed the Shearer memo on to the FBI in October 2016, because it "corroborated" what he had learned from his independent sources. Garnering the same information from separate sources seems like a slam-dunk in verifying a claim, but Steele and Shearer had the same bogus information fed to them at the same time from different sources. What are the chances of that? In other words, we don't really know who contributed to the Steele dossier and where some of the information originated, but one thing is for sure—a lot of people wanted it in the hands of the FBI—and the FBI fell for it.

The opening of an official investigation into Trump smack dab in the middle of the election, as the FBI was clearing Clinton of any criminal wrongdoing in her own email scandal, was red meat for the Democrats. The FBI, trusting Steele's reputation, accepted the information as gospel, but as Kimberley Strassel at *The Wall Street Journal* said, "the FBI should have known better," if for no other reason than the tabloid nature of the memos and the speed at which Steele gathered the information from his location in London.[299]

From this point on, Steele and Fusion GPS used the FBI just like they used journalists—to promote their client's interests, i.e., the Hillary Clinton campaign. "Thanks to the FBI, Mr. Steele didn't have to present the media with crazy-sounding oppo research about sexual perversion," Strassel wrote, "he got to point to a full-on government investigation. The resulting stories were awesome for the Clinton campaign."[300]

John Brennan and GCHQ

Officials at the FBI and the State Department weren't the only ones pushing for an investigation. The CIA had a hand in it, too. According to CIA director John Brennan, he was the one who actually kick-started the counterintelligence investigation with information from British intelligence.

In the summer of 2016, British intelligence played a role in passing information to the CIA about contacts between Trump's campaign and "Russian intelligence operatives" (those conversations have never been made public). According to *The Guardian*,

> GCHQ (UK Government Communications Headquarters) *first became aware in late 2015 of suspicious "interactions" between figures connected to Trump and known or suspected Russian agents, a source close to UK intelligence said. This intelligence was passed to the US as part of a routine exchange of information, they added.*
>
> *Over the next six months, until summer 2016, a number of western agencies shared further information on contacts between Trump's inner circle and Russians, sources said.*
>
> *The European countries that passed on electronic intelligence—known as sigint—included Germany, Estonia and Poland. Australia, a member of the "Five Eyes" spying alliance that also includes the US, UK, Canada and New Zealand, also relayed material, one source said.*[301]

Sources have insisted that the British weren't spying on Trump or his team directly but "the alleged conversations were picked up by chance as part of routine surveillance of Russian intelligence assets."[302]

This news led Trump and his team to accuse British intelligence of spying on the campaign for the Obama administration. As *The American Spectator* put it, Brennan wanted to keep his position in the Clinton administration, so he "teamed up with British spies and Estonian spies to cripple Trump's candidacy. He used their phone intelligence as a pretext for a multi-agency investigation into Trump, which led the FBI to probe a computer server connected to Trump Tower and gave cover to Susan Rice, among other Hillary supporters, to spy on Trump and his people."[303]

Brennan is known as one of the most political CIA directors in US history. "An official in the intelligence community" told *The American Spectator* "that Brennan's retinue of political radicals didn't even bother to hide their activism, decorating offices with 'Hillary for president cups' and other campaign paraphernalia."[304] The report continues,

> *A supporter of the American Communist Party at the height of the Cold War, Brennan brought into the CIA a raft of subversives and gave them plum positions from which to gather and leak political espionage on Trump. He bastardized standards so that these left-wing activists could burrow in and take career positions. Under the patina of that phony professionalism, they could then present their politicized judgments as "non-partisan."*[305]

GCHQ and the CIA have denied collusion, but, as reported by The Guardian, "both US and UK intelligence sources acknowledge that GCHQ played an early, prominent role in kickstarting the FBI's Trump-Russia investigation, which began in late July 2016":[306]

> *According to one account, GCHQ's then head, Robert Hannigan, passed material in summer 2016 to the CIA chief, John Brennan. The matter was deemed so sensitive it was handled at "director level." After an initially slow start, Brennan used GCHQ information and intelligence from other partners to launch a major inter-agency investigation.*[307]

As reported by the BBC's Paul Wood, Brennan had also received information in April (the same month Fusion GPS was hired by the DNC and the DNC claimed it was hacked) from "an intelligence agency of one of the Baltic States" that was allegedly "a tape recording of a conversation about money from the Kremlin going into the US presidential campaign."[308]

Having received supposedly compromising information on Trump, Brennan contacted the FBI, urging them to start an investigation. "I was worried by a number of the contacts that the Russians had with US persons," Brennan said in testimony before the House Intelligence Committee. He didn't see any evidence of collusion between the Trump team and the Russians, "But I know that there was a sufficient basis of information and intelligence that required further investigation by the [FBI] to determine whether or not US persons were actively conspiring or colluding with Russian officials."[309] Brennan added in ominous tones, "People on a treasonous path...don't always realize they're on that path until it's too late."[310]

Brennan is no fan of Donald Trump, to say the least.[311] He was also a sharp critic of Trump's proposals to reinstate torture, or "waterboarding." This was a concern shared by British intelligence and would have motivated them to pass along information about the Republican candidate in the middle of an election. Trump's proposed policies threatened the "special relationship" between UK and US intelligence, and for the sake of national security and stability, they would have wanted him defeated.

While the media has reported that Australian intel about George Papadopoulos started the FBI investigation, Brennan has stated otherwise. It wasn't even Steele's memos that got the ball rolling, though one has to wonder if there wasn't some crossover between the British intelligence Hannigan gave Brennan and opposition research in ex-British spy Steele's memos. When *Meet the Press* host Chuck Todd asked the former CIA director—now MSNBC's new national security analyst—about

Papadopoulos's contacts with Russians during the election, Brennan slipped up about the actual flow of information.[312]

Todd asked Brennan if "the Papadopoulos thing came through the CIA, via the Five Eyes thing" (referring to intelligence-sharing between the five English-speaking states: the United States, United Kingdom, Canada, Australia, and New Zealand). Such sharing of intelligence would have been official, but Brennan's response didn't indicate this:

> Now I'm not going to get into details about how it was acquired. But the FBI has a very close relationship with its British counterparts. And so the FBI had visibility into a number of things that were going on involving some individuals who may have had some affiliation with the Trump campaign. And so the intelligence that we collected was pulsed against that. And I thought it would have been derelict if the FBI did not pull the threads, investigative threads, on American persons who might have been involved with Russia and working on their behalf either wittingly or unwittingly.[313]

In other words, Brennan got the information from British intelligence, not the "Five Eyes thing." Smith writes in *Tablet* magazine,

> Informed sources in Washington have been whispering for months that Britain's intelligence service, the Government Communications Headquarters, the UK's version of America's National Security Agency, was intercepting the emails and phone calls of Trump officials. "It's not impossible," a former high-ranking US intelligence officer told me, "that the information came from the Brits. Under certain circumstances, we can search their database, and they can search ours. Our intelligence-sharing relationship with the UK is much closer

than it is with anyone else, by far the closest we have. But
something like that wouldn't be routine in our relationship."[314]

This wouldn't be the first time intelligence agencies outsourced their spying to circumvent the system. In his 1994 book *Spyworld*, communications officer Mike Frost tells the story of his work with Canada's Communications Security Establishment (CSE), the Canadian equivalent of the NSA or GCHQ, in which he recounts several instances when he helped American intelligence bug agencies on their behalf. He even claims that the British had him do the same. In one passage from the book, he writes, "A request had come through GCHQ from [British Prime Minister] Margaret Thatcher asking if CSE could 'do something' to aid her in finding out if two of her Cabinet ministers were, to use her terms, 'on side.'"[315]

Frost tells of a colleague who was sent to London in 1983 to spy on two British politicians at Thatcher's request. The Canadian spy recorded conversations of the two politicians and handed them over to GCHQ. Frost continues,

> *The Thatcher episode certainly shows that GCHQ, like NSA, found ways to put itself above the law and did not hesitate to get directly involved in helping a specific politician for her personal political benefit.... [T]he decision to proceed with the London caper was probably not put forward for approval to many people up the bureaucratic ladder. It was something CSE figured they would get away with easily, so checking with the higher-ups would only complicate things unnecessarily.*[316]

The purpose of such missions, Frost explains, was so that the GCHQ could deny accusations of surveillance (if made public) since technically they weren't the ones who did the spying. Frost says he carried out similar missions for America's NSA, on targets in Norway and France. Both America and Britain have been outsourcing their spying for decades, so claims that this could have occurred during the election is nothing more than pointing out the obvious.[317]

Having received material from Hannigan, Brennan gave it to the FBI, which he said "served as the basis for the FBI investigation." During his testimony to Congress, Brennan admitted,

> *It was well beyond my mandate as director of CIA to follow on any of those leads that involved US persons. But I made sure that anything that was involving US persons, including anything involving the individuals involved in the Trump campaign, was shared with the bureau [FBI].... and we were uncovering information intelligence about interactions and contacts between US persons and the Russians. And as we came upon that, we would share it with the bureau.*[318]

Brennan told *Meet the Press*, "the CIA and the intelligence community had collected a fair amount of information in the summer of 2016 about what the Russians were doing on multiple fronts. And we wanted to make sure the FBI had full access to that."[319] Brennan was a dog with a bone, and he kept pushing despite having no legal ground for an investigation and no official intelligence.

Information was transferred from Hannigan to Brennan, but it wasn't sanctioned. As Devin Nunes told Fox News's Maria Bartiromo, the FBI opened a "counterintelligence investigation...at the height of a political campaign...using these intelligence services to spy on the other campaign." This, Nunes added, "is really serious stuff." Additionally, "there was no official intelligence to start this investigation."[320]

The lack of official intel or evidence didn't deter anyone hell-bent on defeating Trump with the Russia collusion narrative. Not Brennan, not Steele and Fusion GPS, not Perkins

Coie, and not the Clinton campaign. When WikiLeaks began its email dump, determination to get the word out intensified. The DNC and Clinton campaign had to push back with something compelling, and the best thing they had was convincing American voters that Trump was colluding with the Russians.

Robby Mook and the Media

According to Isikoff, not everyone in the Clinton campaign was ready to go with that narrative. Yes, the public had been made aware of the claim that the DNC had been hacked by the Russians, but it was another step altogether to say "the Russians were using WikiLeaks as part of a plot to elect Trump."[321] But Robby Mook, Clinton's campaign manager, believed it was true because he had seen Steele's research. "Mook—who by now had been briefed by campaign lawyer Marc Elias on some of the contents of the explosive Steele memos—wanted to go further," Isikoff wrote.[322]

On July 24, the day before the Democratic National Convention, Mook went on CNN and made an explosive claim:

> *What's disturbing to us is that we—experts are telling us that Russian state actors broke into the DNC, stole these e-mails. And other experts are now saying that the Russians are releasing these e-mails for the purpose of actually helping Donald Trump. I don't think it's coincidental that these e-mails were released on the eve of our convention here. And that's disturbing. And I think we need to be concerned about that. I think we need to be concerned that we also saw last week at the Republican Convention that Trump and his allies made changes to the Republican platform to make it more pro-Russian. And we saw him talking about how NATO shouldn't intervene to defend—necessarily should intervene to defend our Eastern European allies if they are attacked*

by Russia. So, I think, when you put all this together, it's a
disturbing picture. And I think voters need to reflect on that.[323]

Those "experts," of course, were the techs at CrowdStrike,
but Mook made a point to bring Trump into the narrative—and
that's precisely the message they wanted to make stick: Trump
was benefiting from Russian interference to defeat Clinton. If
the narrative worked, Trump would surely lose the election. If
somehow he won, his presidency would be delegitimized, and
it would only be a matter of time before impeachment proceedings were initiated. That was the plan, and the Democrats have
clung to it like spiders clinging to a broken web.

Russian interference had to remain front and center in
media coverage. The Clinton campaign was determined, in
Isikoff's words, "to keep the Russian intervention in the spot-
light."[324] To make that happen, Clinton operatives Jennifer
Palmieri and Jake Sullivan went on a media tour with one
purpose: "to convince the execs, editors, and anchors that they
should devote more attention to the Russian intervention."[325]

According to Isikoff, the Clinton campaign was met with
resistance at first—blaming everything on the Russians seemed
a weak effort to draw attention away from the Clinton email
scandal. But they kept pressing, and Democrats on the Hill
joined the effort by petitioning the White House to back up the
campaign's claims with an official statement about the Russians.
During the convention, Senator Dianne Feinstein and Representative Adam Schiff sent a letter to Obama, asking him to declassify
the intelligence on Russian meddling.[326] The White House didn't
act immediately, but eventually it did, as more "evidence" was
gathered that Trump was colluding with the Russians.

Steele's false memos, Carter Page's trivial jaunt to Moscow
prompting the FBI to spy on him, Trump Jr.'s meeting with a

Russian lawyer associated with Fusion GPS, and Papadopoulos rubbing elbows with shady characters in London were "glaring signs" that the Trump team had sold out to the Russians—at least that's how the Democrats saw it. The only problem was none of the reasons for starting an investigation carried weight. To this day, even Page has not been accused of a crime, though he has been the target of illegal leaks that have damaged his reputation. This personal assault led Page to write a letter to the House Select Committee on Intelligence in 2017, charging that the Obama administration used false evidence to obtain a Foreign Intelligence Surveillance Court warrant to spy on him. Page told Aaron Klein of Breitbart, "When the falsified FISA warrants against me are eventually revealed, the extent of illegal false evidence will show that there was never any probable cause but rather vindictive personal attacks used to justify the Clinton-Obama-Comey regime's domestic political intelligence operation."[327]

This claim proved valid when the FISA application to surveil Page was released in July 2018. Though highly redacted, the application revealed that the FBI used the unverified Steele dossier to obtain the warrant, despite statements within the application that the Bureau had verified the information. The application also showed that the FBI was not forthcoming about the nature of the information reported by Steele. Instead of saying one of its documentary sources was opposition research paid for by the Clinton campaign and DNC, the FBI vaguely said, "Source #1 [Christopher Steele] was approached by an identified US person, who indicated to [Steele] that a US-based law firm had hired the identified US person to conduct research regarding [Trump's] ties to Russia (the identified US person and [Steele] have a long-standing business relationship). The identified US person hired [Steele] to conduct this research. The identified US person never advised [Steele] as to the motivation behind the research into [Trump's] ties to Russia." The application then states that the FBI "speculated" that "the identified US person was likely looking for information that could be used to discredit [Trump's] campaign."[328] Speculated? It's the job of the FBI to know, not simply assume, and it defies credulity that they didn't. The information they were using was opposition research that had not been adequately verified. Yet, this highly significant information was not conveyed to the FISA court.

The application was released in 2018 only after Judicial Watch filed a Freedom of Information Act lawsuit. When the document was released, Judicial Watch president, Tom Fitton, said, "These documents are heavily redacted but seem to confirm the FBI and DOJ misled the courts in withholding the material information that Hillary Clinton's campaign and the DNC were behind the 'intelligence' used to persuade the courts to approve the FISA warrants that targeted the Trump team."[329]

PART 2

THE INVESTIGATIONS

LESS THAN A WEEK after Hillary Clinton defeated Bernie Sanders at the Democratic National Convention, the FBI opened a counterintelligence investigation into Russian interference in the US election and possible collusion between Trump's campaign and the Kremlin. In violation of protocol, the FBI did not inform Congress until March 2017. Inexplicably, FBI director James Comey said it was because the investigation was "too sensitive," but this is precisely why law enforcement informs Congress. The DOJ failed to do its duty and entered the fray of a presidential election with a case based on a house of cards. All the "evidence" leading up to the investigation was contrived, manipulated, and bundled into a fear-mongering scandal that would plague the Trump team through the election and beyond.

This investigation continued after the election until Deputy Attorney General Rod Rosenstein appointed a special counsel to oversee the inquiry. The following is an account of the nature of these investigations and the irregularities that have called into question their objectivity and goals.

COUNTERINTELLIGENCE

Did the Trump campaign collude with the Russian government to sway an election? Did Trump advisers act as agents to a foreign power or saboteurs of national security, or did they adopt false identities to put the nation at risk? These questions go beyond establishing probable cause in a counterintelligence investigation; they go to the heart of the US democratic process. To investigate, electronically surveil, or spy on an opposing political campaign requires unadulterated evidence of egregious wrongdoing. Using the power of law enforcement and the national security apparatus of the US government to gather information on a political opponent in the midst of a highly contentious campaign must meet the highest bar of probable cause. We don't believe the facts of this case come close to that bar.

According to FBI guidelines, the definition of counterintelligence is "information gathered and activities conducted to protect against espionage or other intelligence activities, sabotage, or assassinations conducted by, for or on behalf of foreign powers, organizations or persons, or international terrorist activities, but not including personnel, physical, document or communications security programs."[1] Some intelligence experts have told us collusion of a political campaign with foreign individuals to win an election doesn't rise to a national security threat worthy of a counterintelligence investigation; it calls for a criminal probe of possible corruption, but not an intelligence operation. Others, however, maintain such collusion meets the necessary requirements in a counterintelligence case, especially if a "foreign government" and espionage are involved.

We don't believe the facts and information at the FBI's disposal before opening a counterintelligence operation met that bar regarding collusion between Russia and the Trump campaign. We believe facts were overlooked that showed a different story—an effort to create a narrative that would sabotage the Trump campaign's efforts to win the White House. We aren't questioning the credibility of FBI agents in the field, but we are casting doubts about the actions and motives of higher powers in the Obama administration. From the information known to us, it seems they wanted the collusion narrative to stick, and they were going to make sure that objective was accomplished.

The pieces were already in play. Joseph Mifsud seemed to be pushing evidence into the Trump campaign with the promise of damaging emails on Clinton from the Russians. Donald Trump Jr. had been lured into a meeting with a Russian lawyer. A spy with CIA connections had been dispatched to gather information on Carter Page—if there was any to be found. But most of all, Christopher Steele had delivered parts of his magical dossier to inform or corroborate any allegation against Trump or the campaign.

As all the information came together from the different players—including intelligence from the British—the FBI opened a full investigation on July 31, 2016, into Russian interference and collusion by the Trump campaign. While the first prong of the investigation—interference—has its own twists and turns, we know Russians meddled in our election, at least to the point of waging an information war. The investigation, and the subsequent special counsel probe, has borne fruit on that account and indicted several Russian operatives for interference. This national security threat was real, as it has been in many elections leading up to this one. The methods the Russians used might have been different in the past, but the aim was the same as it has been for decades—disrupt democracy to delegitimize and weaken it.

The second prong of the investigation, however, that the Trump campaign conspired with the Russians, is a different matter. This focus is the point of contention between Trump and law-enforcement officials. This is the point that has driven a wedge among varied factions of American voters. This is the point that has disrupted our political system and ripped apart our social fabric since the election. For these reasons, we will focus our attention on the apparent illegitimacy of this prong of the investigation, not Russian interference in general. It is also the most "sensitive" prong of the investigation and deserves special consideration.

A full counterintelligence investigation into a political candidate's campaign isn't just any inquiry; it's designated by FBI guidelines as "sensitive," and it is not to be initiated lightly. Special considerations are to be made when deciding to pursue the matter, such as

- *seriousness/severity of the violation/threat;*
- *significance of the information sought to the violation/ threat;*
- *probability that the proposed course of action will be successful;*
- *risk of public exposure, and if there is such a risk, the adverse impact or the perception of the adverse impact on civil liberties and public confidence; and*
- *risk to the national security of the public welfare if the proposed course of action is not approved (i.e., risk of doing nothing).*[2]

When dealing with a sensitive investigative matter such as this, the Obama administration was trusted to take particular care, as the FBI's own guide puts it, "when considering whether the planned course of action is the least intrusive method if reasonable based upon the circumstances of the investigation."[3] Instead of using caution, the Obama administration bulldozed ahead, giving approval for a "sensitive matter investigation" with very little information, and running it, not out of the field office, but from FBI headquarters.

This decision isn't without precedent—it happened in the 1996 Atlanta Olympic bombing case. That investigation, of course, was a disaster, as the honchos at FBI headquarters accused the wrong man of the crime while the real perp hid away in the hills. In most instances, it's best to rely on the agents in the field, but the investigation of Trump's collusion with Russia was top heavy—and from the very top, as indicated by a text between counterintelligence agent Peter Strzok and his lover, FBI lawyer Lisa Page, claiming, "The White House is running this."[4]

As a sensitive counterintelligence operation and national security concern, it wouldn't be surprising if Obama knew about the investigation, but he should not have been "running" it. According to counterintelligence experts, it is likely that Deputy Director Andrew McCabe personally oversaw the day-to-day operation of this sensitive matter, giving approval along the way, but how much information went directly to Obama on a regular basis isn't known. A great deal, if he was indeed running the investigation.

Whether it involves sensitive matters or not, a counterintelligence investigation isn't to be opened on a whim or be based on outlandish allegations or flimsy information that would never hold up in court. This is why any investigation, not just one as sensitive as this, is supposed to begin carefully with due diligence. At every stage, caution and the least intrusive methods must be used—from an assessment of the threat, to a preliminary investigation, and then to a full investigation. These three stages are integral to most counterintelligence operations, and directives for each must be followed exactly to protect privacy rights, the safety of the nation, and the course of justice. Those directives are outlined in various guidelines but, most significantly, the four-hundred-page FBI *Domestic Investigations and Operations Guide* (DIOG).

Stages of the Investigation

An assessment begins when information of a threat or crime that puts the nation at risk comes to the attention of law enforcement. "The FBI cannot be content to wait for leads to come in through the actions of others," FBI guidelines state. "Rather, we must be vigilant in detecting criminal or national security threats to the full extent permitted by law, with an eye towards early intervention and prevention of criminal or national security incidents before they occur."[5] Every assessment—especially one involving political opponents—"must have an authorized purpose and clearly defined objectives."[6]

To find out if there's any credence to the complaints, observations, or information reported, law enforcement uses nonintrusive means to gather information—public records, voluntary interviews in which the true intentions of law enforcement are explained to the person being interviewed, information from other departments, and so on. If they find no information or reasonable allegation to support suspicions of a national security threat, the assessment ends. If, however, they find information that could be articulated in a court of law and information that legitimizes suspicions, law enforcement will open a preliminary investigation. This could happen quickly or after several weeks. During a preliminary stage, law enforcement can use intrusive methods to gather materials, including information-sharing with foreign governments and undercover operations.

If the preliminary investigation discovers an "articulable factual basis"[7]—not merely concerns or allegations—of a national threat or a criminal-law violation that endangers the country, then a full investigation is opened. The predication to open such an investigation must be clearly documented for approval. The first paragraph of that report must have stated facts to justify the time and expense of opening a full investigation, especially one that has cost taxpayers millions of dollars, as did the Russia investigation and continuing Mueller probe.

It seems the FBI was looking high and low for something legitimate to put in that first paragraph and propel the investigation forward to the stage when they could use all methods available to them to gather information, including highly intrusive means. One can understand why this would be the case since counterintelligence operations typically deal with very serious matters such as terrorism and espionage. One of those intrusive methods is seeking Foreign Intelligence Surveillance Act (FISA) warrants to electronically spy on subjects of the investigation. So that first paragraph must be based on facts and worthy of digging into the private lives of American citizens.

Counterintelligence investigations come in different varieties. This type was likely a *positive foreign intelligence* investigation, which seeks intelligence to help protect the United States—in this case from the Russians and evidently from the Trump campaign as well. It was not an "enterprise investigation" as has been stated in some media reports. An enterprise investigation allows for more intrusive methods earlier in the operation and examines "groups of persons associated together"[8] who are committing a crime or threatening national security. Guidelines authorize an enterprise investigation only "on the most serious criminal or national security threats,"[9] such as racketeering and terrorism.

The information before the FBI in the summer of 2016 hardly rose to this level, and many counterintelligence experts we consulted agree that an enterprise investigation would have been inappropriate. Additionally, an enterprise investigation cannot use FISA warrants because its focus is organized crime. The FBI sought several FISA warrants during the course of the investigation, thereby proving that this was a regular foreign intelligence operation that required agents to follow guidelines for all three stages.

The assessment stage of the counterintelligence investigation likely began around March 2016 when Paul Manafort and Carter Page joined the team. Also during this time, Glenn Simpson was continuing to gather opposition research on Trump and homing in on his Russian business contacts as a possible treasure trove of compromising material. Information that came to light in the spring of 2018 casts a sliver of doubt on this possibility. Texts between Strzok and Page indicate that the operation might have begun even sooner. A text from December 2015 asked if "all our oconus lures" have been approved. "Oconus lures" is jargon for spies outside the continental United States.[10] The target of the spies was not named, nor was a campaign referenced, but this communication opens the door to the possibility that the Obama administration was spying on the Trump campaign before Manafort, Page, or Papadopoulos were on the scene. Who was the source of the FBI's information and why were they sending spies overseas? Was Simpson sharing his theories about Trump and Russian organized crime with someone at the Justice Department even at this early date? Or did it have to do with the investigation into the Clinton emails and not Russian interference?

When the assessment stage started, and when it progressed into a preliminary investigation, is one of the great mysteries of this operation. Given the lack of information available on collusion, it's hard to believe the baseless accusation deserved anything more than an assessment in 2015. Only later, after the DNC reported a breach of its servers, did a justifiable cause to open a preliminary investigation into the Trump campaign become tenuously manifest. All it takes to open a preliminary investigation is a reasonable allegation—and considering the fact that the FBI never examined the servers, this is all they had—but even then, there was no information on *collusion*.

As Comey testified, the *full investigation* opened on July 31 after the FBI supposedly received information from the Australians about campaign adviser George Papadopoulos— information, as we have already explained, that contained no articulable *facts* indicating collusion. Regardless, the full powers of the Justice Department were unleashed to investigate the Trump campaign in the middle of the summer. The presidential campaign of an opposing political party became a target in a counterintelligence investigation, with all the governmental authority that entails. Why? Based on what information or reasonable allegations? What information justified pushing the investigation forward in its examination of the campaign, and was its use of intrusive measures to spy on Trump advisers compliant with the DIOG?

No Warnings, No Prevention

Former CIA director John Brennan told Congress, "I encountered and am aware of information and intelligence that revealed contacts and interactions between Russian officials and US persons involved in the Trump campaign that I was concerned about because of known Russian efforts to suborn such individuals, and it raised questions in my mind...whether or not the Russians were able to gain the cooperation of those individuals." However, "I don't know whether or not such collusion existed."[11]

No one can "know" for certain if something has occurred without an investigation, but the basis of moving an inquiry from a mere assessment to a preliminary and full investigation has to be more than a highly politicized CIA director's personal "concerns." A counterintelligence investigation is particularly complicated because it's an investigation into whether individuals are agents of a foreign power. It's not a criminal investigation, though certainly crimes can be discovered during the inquiry. Because of this focus, our government must be guarded in its use of such powers, especially during an election, which should remain free of meddling not only by foreign governments but also by our own.

The progression of the Trump-Russia collusion investigation and methods used during each stage call into question the motives behind those driving the inquiry. First, only the Trump team was under suspicion despite Clinton's long history of compromising interactions with Russians. Second, the Trump campaign was not warned in the spring of 2016 of a possible security threat in its midst, despite clear directives from federal guidelines to give such a defensive warning. The decision for law enforcement to intervene and prevent damage to US national security was rejected by the Obama Justice Department at an early stage, and the Trump campaign wasn't warned until late in the summer—and, even then, it was merely a general caution.

When the House Intelligence Committee questioned former attorney general Loretta Lynch about the investigation and why the Trump team had not been warned earlier that members of their campaign could possibly be Russian agents or that they were being contacted by Russians, Lynch told the committee that during her first meeting in early spring with Andrew McCabe and FBI Director Comey about Page, "one of the possibilities the three of us discussed was whether or not to provide what is called a defensive briefing to the campaign, wherein there would be a meeting with a senior person with the Trump campaign to alert them to the fact that...there may be efforts to compromise someone with their campaign." Lynch added, "It is not an uncommon thing...in intelligence matters."[12]

The FBI issued no warning about Page or anyone else at that time, even though, according to the House report, the topic "was again discussed by the administration's most senior policymakers after Director Comey briefed the National Security Council Principals about the Page information in 'late spring' 2016. The Trump campaign did not receive a general counterintelligence briefing until August 2016, and even then, it was never specifically notified about Papadopoulos, Page, Manafort, or General Flynn's Russia ties."[13] No names were provided, only a general threat posed by Russia and China. This, and more, however, should have been communicated to the Trump campaign before the investigation progressed into later stages. It appears as if the Obama administration wanted the opposing campaign in a presidential election to step into a trap instead of warning them of the danger. This alone is a scandal "by omission."

Another questionable move by investigators involved electronic surveillance. One of the most intrusive methods to gather information—a FISA warrant—was sought before the

full investigation was opened on July 31, 2016, in violation
of DIOG guidelines, which state that FISA warrants can only
be sought during the *full* investigation. The court denied the
request, robbing the FBI of an effective means to gather information. After this, a human source was sent to make contact
with a Trump adviser in England. The use of a human source to
gather information overseas is an extremely intrusive and risky
technique that should not be used unless absolutely necessary.
Yet, this method was used while the FBI refused to insist on
examining the scene of the crime—the DNC servers that were
supposedly hacked by the Russians. If intrusive methods were
to be used to sniff around Trump campaign members, why not
use aggressive means to get to the bottom of the only crime that
had been committed and the basis of the investigation—the
purported cyberattack on the DNC by the Russians?

Finally, the FBI failed to notify Congress about the investigation, informing only the White House. When pressed during
hearings about why the FBI broke protocol by not informing the
House Oversight Committee, FBI director James Comey halt-
ingly said it was because the investigation was "too sensitive."[14]
Yet, Congress's oversight committee must be informed precisely
because of the sensitive nature of these matters. The DIOG states
in no uncertain terms, "Congress, acting primarily through the
Judiciary and Intelligence Committees, exercises regular, vigor-
ous oversight into all aspects of the FBI's operations."[15] The
guidelines continue,

> *To this end, the National Security Act of 1947 requires the FBI*
> *to keep the intelligence committees (for the Senate and House*
> *of Representatives) fully and currently informed of substantial*
> *intelligence activities. This oversight has significantly increased*
> *in breadth and intensity since the 1970s, and it provides*

important additional assurance that the FBI conducts its investigations according to the law and the Constitution.[16]

Instead of complying with standard procedure and giving the American people this assurance, the Obama Justice Department launched a full investigation of the Republican presidential campaign under a shadow of secrecy.

The grave responsibility of the FBI to pursue early intervention and take actions to prevent a national security threat appeared to yield to political interests. Director of National Intelligence James Clapper said he had the same "information" as Brennan, and his "dashboard warning lights were on because of that." However, like Brennan, he "didn't have any evidence—I don't care how you want to caveat it—of collusion."[17] Yet the Obama administration pushed the investigation into a full-blown inquiry without facts instead of alerting the campaign of possible danger and stopping any further damage to the electoral process.

Lynch, McCabe, and Comey's refusal to brief the campaign violated standard protocol but also the DIOG, which states that investigators are tasked with "detecting and interrupting criminal activities at their early stages, and preventing crimes from occurring in the first place" instead of "allowing criminal plots to come to fruition."[18] Investigators can't passively observe a national security threat if it can be prevented. Law enforcement must be proactive, yet the Obama administration made no such effort. This begs the question—if the national security threat were real, why not intervene? Was this about protecting the nation or something else? The job of law enforcement is not simply to catch criminals and foreign agents when they're putting US security at risk but to stop them.

No Facts on "Collusion"

Instead, on flimsy and contrived information, the investigation of the Trump campaign and collusion with Russia moved forward. Assessing any possible threat is one thing, but pressing into a full investigation without facts of a crime or a national security threat violates standard procedure. Clapper told MSNBC's Andrea Mitchell that "no evidence" of collusion between Trump campaign aides and Russians "rose to that level, at that time, that found its way into the intelligence community assessment, which we had pretty high confidence in."[19] According to Clapper, the preliminary investigation revealed no probable cause of any collusion, yet the investigation kept following this dead-end trail.

The FBI claims the full investigation in July was kickstarted by Australian intelligence about Papadopoulos, thereby implicating the Trump campaign, but when the FBI finally disclosed an "electronic communication" to House Intelligence Committee chairman Devin Nunes after he threatened them with contempt, he found contrary information. Nunes told Maria Bartiromo on *Sunday Morning Futures* "there was no official intelligence that was used to start this investigation."[20] Nunes referenced the Five Eyes agreement on intelligence-sharing between the English-speaking nations: United States, Canada, Britain, Australia, and New Zealand. "We are not supposed to spy on each other's citizens, and it's worked well," he told Bartiromo. "And it continues to work well. And we know it's working well because there was no intelligence that passed through the Five Eyes channels to our government. And that's why we had to see that original communication."[21]

Nunes said he was looking into the State Department to find out how information about Papadopoulos was obtained by the FBI. "We know a little bit about that because of what some of the State Department officials themselves have said about that," he said. "We have to make sure that our agencies talk and they work out problems. We have to make sure that they don't spy on either American citizens or that we're not spying on British citizens."[22]

Nunes speculated that the source of the information could be a couple of close Clinton associates, including Cody Shearer and Sidney Blumenthal, who had been feeding the State Department information that "was somehow making its way to the FBI."[23] According to the *Sydney Morning Herald*, Downer's information was also being "steered" toward the FBI by Australia's ambassador to the United States, Joe Hockey, in late July 2016.[24] Only days after the official investigation was opened, Peter Strzok, who was the FBI's deputy chief of counterintelligence, made a mysterious trip to an "embassy" in England. As reported by Chuck Ross at the *Daily Caller*,

> [Redacted name] talked about the Embassy. It's the longest continuously staffed establishment in London, Strzok wrote to Page in an Aug. 2, 2016, text message. The Australian embassy in London matches Strzok's description.
>
> Papadopoulos was not interviewed by FBI agents until Jan. 27, 2017, nearly six months after the start of the investigation. That six month delay is puzzling to both congressional investigators and to Papadopoulos. He has wondered to associates why, if he was actually suspected of conspiring with the Russian government, the bureau would have waited so long to contact him.[25]

According to the *Sydney Morning Herald*, "It remains uncertain precisely the degree to which Australia's reporting of the Downer-Papadopoulos conversation sparked the original investigation given US authorities were getting information also from other friendly governments and from within the US."[26] The other "friendly governments" likely includes Britain, and it is becoming clearer as more information is coming out that the FBI was using information from the CIA.

CIA Contributions

Brennan confirmed this when he told the House Select Committee on Intelligence in May 2017 that he "was aware of intelligence and information about contacts between Russian officials and US persons." This information, he said, "served as the basis for the FBI investigation to determine whether such collusion—cooperation occurred."[27] Brennan continues,

> *I wanted to make sure that every information and bit of intelligence that we had was shared with the bureau [FBI] so that they could take it. It was well beyond my mandate as director of CIA to follow on any of those leads that involved US persons. But I made sure that anything that was involving US persons, including anything involving the individuals involved in the Trump campaign, was shared with the bureau.*[28]

How did Brennan receive this information and from whom? What intelligence did he give the FBI that they didn't already have? The only individuals the FBI wouldn't have known about who made "contacts" with Russians were Papadopoulos, and Trump Jr. in early June at the Trump Tower meeting. How did Brennan know about these meetings, and what compelled him to pester the FBI to open an investigation? Was British intelligence spying on the Trump team or obtaining that information incidentally in other operations and passing it to the CIA who, in turn, gave it to the FBI?

If so, this could be problematic because guidelines on national security investigations, as outlined in the DIOG, do not allow information sharing with foreign agencies when it is just an "intelligence matter" before any preliminary or full investigation has opened. Reportedly, British intelligence had been passing information to US intelligence officials since late 2015, early 2016. Though the British intel community has denied this—as has Tony Blair, who supposedly hinted to Trump that the Brits had been spying on his campaign—a member of the intelligence community has shared with *The American Spectator* significant information on the interaction between former CIA director John Brennan and British intelligence:

> A member of the intelligence community tells TAS that he was approached by FBI investigators inquiring about Brennan's improprieties at the CIA. He was startled to hear them venting aloud about Brennan's practice of using British intelligence officials to spy on the Trump campaign, including American contractors hired by the British who were working from the 12th floor of a building in Crystal City, Virginia, and an NSA building in San Antonio, Texas. Brennan, they fumed, was using British intelligence agents so that he could deny, if asked, that he had spied on the Trump campaign.
>
> Just as Hillary outsourced her spying on Trump to the ex-British spy Christopher Steele, Brennan turned to his counterparts in British intelligence for dirt on Trump, and the British through various planted stories have taken credit for this idiotic dirt-digging (which consisted of treating disinformation as real or over-interpreting inconclusive material), the most obvious one appearing in the Guardian: "British Spies Were First to Spot Trump Team's Links With Russia."[29]

Information from Edward Snowden's NSA leaks in 2013 sheds some light on the relationship between US and UK intelligence agencies in the past. According to *The Guardian*, from 2010 to 2013, the NSA paid out at least 100 million pounds (about 150 million dollars, according to the conversion rate at that time) in top-secret payments to the UK spy agency Government Communications Headquarters (GCHQ). Before releasing the documents describing the payments, "Snowden warned about the relationship between the NSA and GCHQ, saying the organisations have been jointly responsible for developing techniques that allow the mass harvesting and analysis of internet traffic. 'It's not just a US problem,' he said. 'They are worse than the US.'"[30]

Revelations about the relationship between the two agencies led to accusations by privacy activists that GCHQ was essentially doing work for the NSA that the NSA couldn't do on its own, given the restrictions of American law.[31] One document from 2010 read that the NSA had "raised a number of issues with regards to meeting NSA's minimum expectations." As a result, GCHQ "still remains short of the full NSA ask."[32] As for the NSA's motivation in contracting with GCHQ, the documents reveal that Britain's relatively lax surveillance laws were a "selling point." For instance, and this is a critical point, the law prohibits the NSA from spying on Americans living in the United States. Having the GCHQ do that for them is a circumvention of the spirit of American law, yet we know of at least one instance of this occurring from a GCHQ anti-terrorism success story. They spoke of their contributions when it came to the NSA's investigation of a Muslim American citizen responsible for attempting to detonate a car bomb in New York City in 2010. It's a great story, but it's also confirmation of the existence of an information-sharing relationship.

In another leaked GCHQ classified document from 2013, they said the agency should have "exploited to the full our unique selling points of geography, partnerships [and] the UK's legal regime."[33] We know, according to public reporting, that British intelligence began "accidentally" intercepting information on the Trump team. According to *The Guardian*, "Britain's spy agencies played a crucial role in alerting their counterparts in Washington to contacts between members of Donald Trump's campaign team and Russian intelligence operatives."[34] The article notes, "Both US and UK intelligence sources acknowledge that GCHQ played an early, prominent role in kickstarting the FBI's Trump-Russia investigation, which began in late July 2016." So, according to these reports, it was British intel, not the Aussies, that started the investigation.

The GCHQ maintains they never used targeted surveillance to gather information but picked it up by chance as part of routine spying on Russian intelligence. Meanwhile, the head of GCHQ Robert Hannigan, who passed information to CIA director John Brennan in 2016, stepped down just four days after Trump was inaugurated. So abrupt was the resignation that he told staffers only hours before making his decision public. Hannigan's exit naturally prompted speculation about why he stepped down, so he responded, saying he was doing so for "personal" reasons, mainly family. Typically, under such circumstances, someone would put in two weeks' notice, especially if they're responsible for the operation of one of the world's most powerful intelligence-gathering agencies.

As for the information Hannigan passed to the CIA, *The American Spectator* reports,

> *Brennan then took that material to Harry Reid who promptly leaked it to the New York Times: "Brennan used GCHQ*

information and intelligence from other partners to launch
a major inter-agency investigation. In late August and
September Brennan gave a series of classified briefings to the
Gang of Eight, the top-ranking Democratic and Republican
leaders in the House and Senate."

In Brennan's counterintelligence briefing to Reid, according to a report by Sara Carter, he "alluded to the unverified allegation that members of the Trump campaign may be colluding with the Russians."[35] This information "expanded the number of people who were aware of the unverified allegations and played a significant role in the increase of leaks to the media, according to the information obtained by the committee."[36]

Yet, as Brennan said himself, he still found no evidence of collusion. Regardless of this fact, the FBI decided to open a full investigation not only into Russian interference in the election, which affected both campaigns, but, in Comey's words, to investigate "the nature of any links between individuals associated with the Trump campaign and the Russian government and whether there was any coordination between *the campaign and Russia's efforts* [emphasis added]."[37] The investigation was not only of Russia or individuals working with Russia as foreign agents, but of the Trump campaign itself.

Stefan Halper

As first reported by Chuck Ross of the Daily Caller, two months before the 2016 election, George Papadopoulos received a random meeting request from foreign policy expert Stefan Halper, a University of Cambridge professor and member of the Cambridge Intelligence Seminar founded by officers in British intelligence. Halper asked Papadopoulos to fly to London to discuss international relations and the possibility of

Papadopoulos writing a policy paper on a gas field in the Mediterranean for three thousand dollars. Halper paid for his flight to England, and during their conversations, Halper suddenly turned to the subject of Russia, asking Papadopoulos, "You know about hacking the emails from Russia, right?"[38] Where did that question come from? Papadopoulos smelled a fishing expedition and offered him no information.

The subject wasn't broached again. During Papadopoulos's visit to London, they had dinner and visited a club popular among diplomats. "They were accompanied by Halper's assistant, a Turkish woman named Azra Turk," Ross reported. "Sources familiar with Papadopoulos's claims about his trip say Turk flirted with him during their encounters and later on in email exchanges."[39] Papadopoulos's contact with Halper didn't extend much past that trip. According to Ross, Papadopoulos accepted Halper's proposal to write the paper and submitted it the next month, but "there are no public records of Halper releasing reports" on the topic of Papadopoulos's research. After this, Halper's contact broke off.

Papadopoulos says Halper wasn't the only suspicious person to approach him. There were two others. Papadopoulos's wife, Simona Mangiante, told the Daily Caller that one of the contacts offered to pay him thirty thousand dollars a month during his time with the Trump team.[40] According to Mangiante, "It looks to be one among a series of attempts to entrap George. The question today to me [is whether] these people are simply shady businessmen or are they part of a greater attempt to entrap George in illegal activity."[41]

Mangiante said the person who contacted Papadopoulos with the money offer was Sergei Millian, the businessman who is thought to be the source of the golden shower story in the

Steele dossier. According to Ross, "Papadopoulos and Millian met for the first time at around the same time the FBI opened its counterintelligence investigation, code-named "Crossfire Hurricane."[42]

The other suspicious contact was "with an Israeli national on the Greek island of Mykonos," Mangiante told Ross. The man offered Papadopoulos money to discuss business in Cyprus and Israel, but Papadopoulos turned down the offer because he suspected it was a trap.[43]

Entrapment seemed to be part of the plan, whether it was foreign operatives or domestic informants, such as Halper. A low-level Trump adviser was at the center of it, but Papadopoulos wasn't the only campaign member Halper approached in 2016. He also contacted Sam Clovis, Trump campaign co-chair, and Carter Page, an energy consultant and foreign policy adviser to the campaign.

Halper and Clovis met only once, and they mostly talked about China. Later, Halper asked the campaign co-chair if he could get a position on the Trump team, but nothing ever came of the request. Clovis told Tucker Carlson of Fox News that he and Halper discussed information related to foreign policy and nothing else, though looking back, the meeting seemed odd. Several weeks later, Clovis received emails with attachments from Halper, but he didn't open them. "I have no idea what was in them but they were mostly titled, 'papers that dealt with China,'" Clovis told Carlson.[44]

Halper met Page on July 11 at a University of Cambridge symposium on "2016's Race to Change the World." The event was attended by individuals associated with British intelligence, including Sir Richard Dearlove, former head of MI6. According to reports, a graduate assistant of Halper's invited Page sometime in late May or early June to attend the symposium. Dearlove and Halper were both members of the Cambridge Intelligence Seminar, established by the official historian of MI5 and deeply connected to British intelligence.

Dearlove, like many in the British government, would have had reason to oppose a Trump presidency and likely was supportive of Halper's efforts. The former British spy is infamously known for downplaying the threat of Muslim terrorists, claiming in 2014, "this new conflict is essentially Muslim on Muslim." At a speech to the Royal United Services Institute, he said,

> Counter-terrorism activity will remain an important requirement but it should no longer dominate our national security thinking and planning, rather a problem we have learned to live with and that should seldom be given, either by the Government or the media, the oxygen of publicity.
>
> I feel deeply uncomfortable to see our national media making national security monsters out of rather misguided young men from our Muslim communities who frankly, I think, cut rather pathetic figures.[45]

Dearlove's views placed him in direct opposition to Trump, who suggested harsh policies to deal with ISIS and Muslim terrorists—an issue that upset the Brits so much they threatened to ban him from the country. At the symposium Page attended, Dearlove closed out the event by speaking on the global effects of the 2016 US presidential campaign.

Page had never been a part of the symposium before that summer and was essentially invited out of the blue. Unlike Halper and Dearlove, he didn't speak at the event. The symposium was merely an opportunity for Halper to connect with Page in a friendly manner—contact he maintained through the next year, including meeting at Halper's farm in Virginia. Page has since described his interactions with Halper as benign, just one academic talking with another. An email from July 28, 2017, reflects the tone of their relationship:

> *Dear Carter,*
>
> *I thought I'd write as the summer wears on to ask how you are and what your plans are at this point. It seems attention has shifted a bit from the "collusion" investigation to the "contretemps" within the White House and, how—or if—Mr. Scaramucci will be accommodated there. I must assume this gives you some relief—*
>
> *We are here in Virginia enjoying a warm but quiet summer. Be in touch when you have time. Would be great to catch up.*
>
> *Stef*[46]

Who is Stefan Halper, and why did he contact not one but three Trump campaign advisers in the summer of 2016? Glenn Simpson of Fusion GPS first hinted at the answer when he testified to Congress that the information in Christopher Steele's dossier mirrored that of *an FBI informant in the Trump campaign.* This information came from Steele's FBI contact in Rome, agent Michael Gaeta, whom he had worked with on another case. Simpson told Congress the FBI believed "Chris's information might be credible because they had other intelligence that indicated the same thing and one of those pieces of intelligence was a human."[47]

Senator Chuck Grassley jumped on the comment, writing a letter to Simpson's attorney and asking him to clarify the "inside source" comment for the record. Grassley never received the requested response, only a note from Simpson's lawyer saying, "Mr. Simpson stands by his testimony."[48] In the spring of 2018, Simpson's comment captured the attention of the public, leading to widespread speculation about who this person could be, why he was spying on the Trump campaign, when did he begin his secret activities, and why hadn't the FBI promptly informed Congress.

News media scrambled to discover the name of the source. *The New York Times* filled in some of the details on his identity in an article published in May:

> *The informant, an American academic who teaches in Britain, made contact late that summer with one campaign adviser, George Papadopoulos, according to people familiar with the matter. He also met repeatedly in the ensuing months with the other aide, Carter Page, who was also under FBI scrutiny for his ties to Russia.... The informant is well known in Washington circles, having served in previous Republican administrations and as a source of information for the C.I.A. in past years, according to one person familiar with the source's work.*[49]

The description was so obvious to many who knew of Halper that media outlets soon began reporting him as the alleged spy in the camp. "Not to keep you in suspense any longer," *Mother Jones* wrote, "by several accounts the informant was Stefan Halper, a guy who worked in the Nixon, Ford, and Reagan administrations and is now Director of American Studies at Cambridge University."[50]

Carter Page

We don't know when Halper first began working for the FBI (or CIA) to gather information on individuals within the Trump campaign. From all indications, he started with contacting Page, who had already been under surveillance in the past after Russian spies tried to recruit him in 2013. Page had given unclassified information on the future of the energy industry to an undercover Russian spy, though according to a complaint filed against the Russians, Page did not know their true intentions and thought they were helping him develop business contacts. The FBI informed Page in June of that year that he was being recruited, but Page found it difficult to believe because he didn't have anything to provide them of significance. Instead of acting as a Russian agent, Page cooperated with the FBI's investigation of the Russians who tried to recruit him.[51]

The FBI, however, kept an eye on Page and even interviewed him in March 2016 about his Russian connections, the same month he joined the Trump campaign as a low-level adviser. This interview, according to Page, had nothing to do with Russian collusion or the election, but unrelated events that happened in 2013. In early July, Page, independent of the campaign, traveled to Moscow to give a speech at the New Economic School, where he criticized US policy. Because of this, and Page's business connections in Russia, the FBI believed he could be the main conduit between the Trump team and Russian government officials—a point highlighted in Steele's unverified memos. The assumption appears to be based on no viable information.

Page has refuted this allegation, stating under oath that he was not working with the Russian government to help the Trump campaign. As late as early November 1, 2016, *The New York Times* reported that intelligence officials admitted "no evidence has emerged that would link him or anyone else in his business or political circle directly to Russia's election operations."[52] In its exhaustive report on the Russia investigation, the House Intelligence Committee agreed, concluding from its own inquiry that there was no evidence of conspiracy regarding Page or other members of the team. Yet, a FISA warrant was issued to spy on Page in October 2016, and according to the FISA application that was released in July 2018, the FBI used Steele's unverified dossier as justification for the surveillance. Most of the application was redacted, so this is all the public knows of the source material presented to the judge, but the FBI informant who made contact with Page could very well be hidden within the blacked-out lines.

When asked about his interactions with Halper, Page said they didn't discuss anything that would implicate himself or the Trump campaign as a national security threat, so any information Halper possibly relayed to the FBI would have been inconsequential. That's unless Halper gave them false accounts to get FISA warrants. This is conceivable since communications between the two suddenly ended after the last FISA warrant was issued to spy on Page in 2017.[53]

"Least Intrusive Methods"

The date of Halper's entrance as an informant for the FBI is significant because the DIOG's guidelines on how a national security investigation should be conducted are specific about which techniques can be used at certain points during the inquiry. The first step in a counterintelligence investigation is to obtain a threat assessment. During this period, the FBI can investigate possible threats to national security by using public records, non-pretextual interviews, and contacts with other departments. It cannot information-share with other governments, and it cannot use undercover agents, spies, or confidential informants. Only when a threat assessment stage moves to the preliminary investigation stage can a spy be used.

Even at this stage and into a full investigation, the least intrusive methods are to be used. This is repeated ad nauseam in the DIOG, e.g., "If the threat is remote, and individual's involvement is speculative, and the probability of obtaining probative information is low, intrusive methods may not be justified, i.e., they may do more harm than good."[54] Using a human source or an undercover agent, while technically allowed in a preliminary investigation, was inappropriate given the lack of information on the Trump team colluding with the Russians.

When the public first became aware of Halper's role as a spy in the Trump camp, much ado was made over the designation given and the seriousness of his actions. Some insisted he wasn't a "spy" and therefore "nonintrusive." This distinction, however, is nonsensical. Halper was covertly trying to gather information from the Trump team. This is "spying" and, according to the DIOG, it is an intrusive method—one that should be used infrequently. What's odd is the insistence that he be called an informant because informants are typically part of an organization, and they feed law enforcement information from their own sphere. Halper was not part of the Trump campaign; he was on the outside looking in, not an informant dishing out— in other words, a spy.

Yet, Halper wasn't a trained undercover agent either. Who then was he working for? Who hired him? Someone at the CIA, or was it, as Glenn Simpson indicated in his testimony and as former director of national intelligence James Clapper speculated, the FBI? Clapper admitted that the FBI might have had someone trying to find out "what the Russians were doing to try to substantiate themselves in the campaign or influence or leverage it."[55] His reference to "the campaign" instead of "campaigns" further confirms that law enforcement was spying not on individuals associated with Russian interference in the election but the Trump campaign.

Whether the FBI was using a confidential human source (CHS) or an undercover agent doesn't matter when it comes to the undeniable fact that the operation was undercover. A CHS is untrained and can be anyone from an individual with a criminal record to the concerned neighbor around the corner. An undercover agent is a highly trained law-enforcement operative whose testimony in court is more credible than a CHS because of their intense training. When gathering information overseas, as they did in the 2016 investigation, the FBI typically uses an undercover agent, not a CHS, because they don't want someone who is untrained in the field creating an international incident when providing information on a foreign nation or individual.

The FBI did not send a professional to England to talk to Page or Papadopoulos. Instead, they sent Halper, an experienced source with a long history of CIA connections, but untrained. To get approval for this atypical decision, the FBI would have needed to get the green light from many different levels of authority, particularly from the CIA director, who at that time was John Brennan—an outspoken adversary of Trump and someone who was already gathering information on the Trump campaign from foreign sources. Whether it was through the FBI or on his own, was Brennan the man poking around to get information on the Trump campaign? If so, what were his motivations?

Despite these irregularities, if Halper was working for the FBI during a preliminary investigation on Russian interference and links to the Trump campaign, this use of a human source would be permitted. However, if Halper was spying on the Trump campaign in a mere threat assessment period before there was articulable information that members of the campaign were foreign agents or that a foreign power was using the campaign, then the FBI would have violated the DIOG guidelines on national security investigations. For the investigation to enter the preliminary stage when a spy can be activated, there must be information or allegations indicating that

- *an individual is or may be an international terrorist or an agent of a foreign power;*
- *a group or organization is or may be a foreign power or an agent of a foreign power;*
- *an individual, group, or organization is or may be engaging, or has or may have engaged, in activities constituting a threat to the national security (or related preparatory or support activities) for or on behalf of a foreign power;*
- *a crime involved in or related to a threat to the national security has or may have occurred, is or may be occurring, or will or may occur;*
- *an individual, group, or organization is, or may be, the target of a recruitment or infiltration effort by an international terrorist, foreign power, or agent of a foreign power under circumstances related to a threat to the national security; or*
- *an individual, group, organization, entity, information, property, or activity is, or may be, a target of international terrorism, espionage, foreign computer intrusion, or other threat to the national security.*[56]

An agent of a foreign power as it relates to US citizens is any person who

- *knowingly engages in clandestine intelligence-gathering activities for or on behalf of a foreign power, which activities involve or may involve a violation of the criminal statutes of the United States;*
- *pursuant to the direction of an intelligence service or network of a foreign power, knowingly engages in any*

other clandestine intelligence activities for or on behalf of such foreign power, which activities involve or are about to involve a violation of the criminal statutes of the United States;

- *knowingly engages in sabotage or international terrorism, or activities that are in preparation therefore, for or on behalf of a foreign power;*
- *knowingly enters the United States under a false or fraudulent identity for or on behalf of a foreign power or, while in the United States, knowingly assumes a false or fraudulent identity for or on behalf of a foreign power; or*
- *knowingly aids or abets any person in the conduct of activities described in subparagraph [the first three bullet points] or knowingly conspires with any person to engage in such activities.*[57]

When an investigation moves from one stage to another, investigators must have quality information that could potentially stand up in court. The FBI, however, didn't seem to be looking toward an eventual court case, but political interests. The investigation was reportedly being run from the top down, with the field office playing second fiddle to less-experienced agents up the chain of command. The further an investigation moves from the objectivity of the investigators on the ground, the more political it becomes. The FBI appeared to be bulldozing through stages of the investigation and rushing to use intrusive methods, including one of the most intrusive—FISA warrants that allow for electronic surveillance.

Where was the cause for these intrusive measures when it came to collusion by the Trump team? The House Intelligence Committee found no evidence that anyone in the campaign was a threat to national security, committed a crime that threatened national security, identified as a terrorist, used fake identities, or colluded with Russia to sabotage the United States, and there was no articulable information on any of these allegations in the spring and summer of 2016. Why, then, was Halper hired to spy on Trump campaign advisers? The only crime that supposedly occurred, which could be seen as a national security threat, was the hacking of the DNC servers in late spring. But there was no information showing that anyone on the Trump campaign had anything to do with the cyberattack, and no intelligence agency has ever examined the servers. The FBI had looked into connections between Trump Tower servers and banks in Russia, but, as *The New York Times*, reported, "The FBI ultimately concluded that there could be an innocuous explanation, like a marketing email or spam, for the computer contacts."[58] The criminal investigation involving the Trump Tower servers was dropped because there was no evidence of a crime.

Paul Manafort was hired under a cloud of suspicion, but that involved his business in Ukraine, not Russian interference in the US election. "The focus in that case was on Mr. Manafort's ties with a kleptocratic government in Ukraine—and whether he had declared the income in the United States—and not necessarily on any influence over Mr. Trump's campaign," an official told *The New York Times*.[59]

In April 2016, Mifsud offered Papadopoulos information on Clinton, but it was never delivered, and no indication of collusion was evident. Following his meeting with Mifsud, Papadopoulos told Alexander Downer about the offer of damaging material, but the FBI wasn't supposedly aware of this until late July after the Australians informed the FBI about the conversation with Papadopoulos. Halper had already been activated to check out Page before they received this information.

In early June, a Russian lawyer with connections to the firm that hired Steele to gather opposition research on Trump contacted Trump Jr. for a meeting, but nothing came of it. No information was exchanged. No one appeared to knowingly engage in clandestine behavior that put the nation at risk, and this could have been easily discovered at the time by investigators.

That leaves only Page as a possible link to the Russians. His speech in Moscow alerted the FBI to possible "trouble," but there was no information that he was helping the Russians interfere in the election on Trump's behalf, and there was no information that he had anything to do with the purported DNC breach. His speech and business connections with Russians didn't provide reasons to use such an intrusive method to gather information. There was no indication that he was acting as a foreign agent, a terrorist, or a saboteur.

It seems there would need to be much more than one speech to push the investigation further using intrusive methods. Even though the Steele dossier later accused Page of meeting with Russian officials during his trip to Russia, the FBI wouldn't have known this because they said they didn't receive the Steele dossier until the fall of 2016. So, why use such methods on the international stage to spy on Page? Maybe because previous efforts to spy on the Trump team had failed.

In June, before the counterintelligence investigation had become a full investigation, the FBI submitted a FISA request to electronically surveil members of the Trump team. FISA rejected that request, something that is rarely done as the FISA court is typically accommodating to such requests.[60] Given the lack of probable cause to spy on members of the Trump campaign, it's no wonder the FISA court said no.

The FBI, however, should never have sought the warrant in the first place. First, they wrongly sought a FISA warrant as an extension of a criminal investigation, or to put it more precisely a re-contextualized criminal investigation posing as a counterintelligence probe. The criminal investigation of the computers in Trump Tower and financial connections to Russian banks discovered no wrongdoing, so the investigation ended. The FBI, however, used this pretext to seek a FISA warrant in the counterintelligence investigation to spy on members of the Trump team and possibly Trump himself. If the FBI were trying to discover whether a crime had occurred, it should have sought a regular wiretap, not a warrant for foreign intelligence surveillance. Investigators didn't have that option, so they sought a FISA warrant instead.

To get this warrant in a foreign intelligence investigation, investigators would have needed proof that someone in the Trump camp was an agent of a foreign power who was engaging in or planning an attack on the United States, sabotage or international terrorism, or clandestine intelligence activities by an intelligence service of a foreign power. Or, they would have needed factual bases that someone was committing espionage or acting as a double agent. That's a seriously high bar. Additionally, not all foreign activities are a threat to national security—such as an international fraud scheme—so investigators needed solid information that the campaign was itself a serious danger to the country. There is no indication that they had even the most tenuous proofs of such activities.

This apparent attempt to abuse the FISA court, however, isn't the only irregularity with this request. It blatantly violated federal regulations of investigations. The FBI sought a FISA warrant in a counterintelligence investigation during a preliminary stage when

FISA warrants are strictly forbidden. According to the DIOG, the FBI can use all methods of investigation during a preliminary investigation "except mail opening, physical search requiring a Federal rules of criminal procedure Rule 41 search warrant or a FISA order, electronic surveillance requiring a judicial order or warrant."[61] The FBI violated federal guidelines by seeking a FISA warrant before it had opened a full investigation into Russian interference and the Trump campaign.

The effort failed because the FISA court didn't give them what they wanted—and what they wanted was to find evidence that the Trump team was colluding with the Russians. They wanted not just rumor, information, or allegations; they needed evidence to move the inquiry into a full investigation. Brennan had been pressing them to open an investigation. Steele had given them information he had gathered, but they needed articulable facts. They didn't have them in June, so they took another step to gather proof—send a spy into the camp.

It is more than possible that Halper was activated by the CIA and/or FBI to find compromising information on the Trump campaign to fuel the narrative that it was colluding with Russia. Halper would have been the perfect man for the job. He has connections to the CIA and MI6 and boasts a long history of gathering information for law enforcement, government entities, and established Republicans. From 2012 to 2016, he was paid more than one million dollars by the Department of Defense's Washington Headquarters Services for his services in "research and development in the social sciences and humanities."[62]

Halper's History

Halper's talent for digging up dirt on opposing political candidates is nothing new. In 1979 to 1980, he worked on the campaign of George Bush, who was competing with Ronald Reagan for the Republican nomination. The Bush campaign was considered quite unusual because of the number of former CIA operatives who were part of it (nearly twenty-five at one point). "Simply put, no presidential campaign in recent memory—perhaps ever—has attracted as much support from the intelligence community as the campaign of former CIA director Bush," the *Washington Post* reported in 1980.[63] Bush's top foreign policy and defense adviser was Ray Cline, former deputy director of the CIA and also the father-in-law of Stefan Halper.

The Bush campaign with its host of CIA operatives swept into the Reagan campaign when Bush lost the nomination, and Reagan named him his vice president. Halper went with them and became instrumental in gathering research, work that was not always on the straight and narrow. In 1983, when he was director of policy coordination and handled communications for Bush, he and others were accused of obtaining debate briefing materials on Reagan's opponent, Jimmy Carter, and circulating them among campaign operatives during the campaign. The scandal was aptly called Debategate. William Casey, then director of the CIA, was accused of passing the materials to James Baker, the campaign's debate manager, though he denied it. A report released by a House subcommittee named Halper as one of the people who "either received or circulated nonpublic information from inside the Carter camp," *The New York Times* reported.[64]

The Reagan campaign reportedly "conducted a data-gathering operation to collect inside information on Carter foreign policy and used a number of former CIA officials in the effort." Halper "was in charge of the operation," though he denied any involvement.[65] In interviews conducted by the FBI at the time,

Carter aides insisted there were many people involved in the campaign infiltration and passing on of information.

This history sheds light not only on Halper's capability to gather information for political purposes but also his extensive connections with the CIA and the Bushes, who have been stalwart anti-Trumpers. Despite being a Republican, Halper was no fan of Trump and preferred Clinton. He told a Kremlin-controlled news outlet during the campaign exactly why—itself an odd choice since he was so concerned about Russian infiltration at Cambridge Intelligence Seminar (CIS), of which he was a member. When asked about US-British relations and the impact of the 2016 election, Halper told Sputnik,

> *The victory of Hillary Clinton, who is more experienced and predictable than her Republican rival Donald Trump, in the US presidential elections will be more beneficial for the US-UK relations.*
>
> *I believe [Hillary] Clinton would be best for US-UK relations and for relations with the European Union. Clinton is well-known, deeply experienced and predictable. US-UK relations will remain steady regardless of the winner although Clinton will be less disruptive over time.*[66]

Halper's bias toward Clinton, his background in political intrigue, and his close associations with the CIA, FBI, and establishment politicians make him an obvious choice to spy on the Trump campaign for the Obama administration. The ease with which Halper's identity was uncovered discredits claims by those in the DOJ that he was a "top-secret intelligence source" and that revealing his name "could risk lives by potentially exposing the source, a US citizen who has provided intelligence to the CIA and FBI." Democratic senator Mark Warner went so far as to warn his colleagues that they would be committing a crime if they disclosed the name of the spy and thereby undermined "the ongoing investigation into Russian interference in our election."[67] Halper, however, is hardly some deeply hidden covert agent for the Obama administration. As *The New York Times* reported, "The informant is well known in Washington circles, having served in previous Republican administrations and as a source of information for the C.I.A. in past years, according to one person familiar with the source's work."[68]

Halper's connection to British intelligence is also well known. He is a close associate of former MI6 chief Richard Dearlove, whose career in British intelligence spanned four decades. During this period, Dearlove worked with Christopher Steele, who consulted him on the Trump dossier in the fall of 2016. Dearlove was also present at the symposium Page attended at the organizers' request. This triad of connections begs the question, was there information sharing among the three? Did material in Steele's dossier about Page come from Halper or the other way around? Would Halper make up information about Russian collusion? It's not inconceivable since Halper has made false claims about Russian influence and infiltration in the past. As reported by Chuck Ross,

> *A historian and Russian intelligence researcher at Cambridge, Svetlana Lokhova, told [the Daily Caller] that Halper is behind allegations made about her and Flynn during the retired general's visit to Cambridge in 2014, when he served as director of the Defense Intelligence Agency.*
>
> *"Stef Halper, who is currently under [Department of Justice] investigation for his activities, has been revealed by [The New York Times] as the source of the false allegations about me and General Flynn," said Lokhova, who was born in Russia and has British citizenship.*[69]

Lokhova was accused of being a Russian agent assigned to recruit Flynn. Their brief interactions over dinner, in which Lokhova showed Flynn a postcard sent to Joseph Stalin in 1912, caused Halper to be "concerned" and report it to the authorities. No evidence of wrongdoing has been discovered, and no other academics at the conference expressed the same concerns as Halper.

Lokhova told the BBC that the idea that she would try to recruit Flynn in the presence of so many former British spies was "ludicrous." Her life has been "completely changed" because of the accusation. "In Britain, I am now being accused of being a Russian spy," she said. "In Russia, some think I am a British spy. And I am neither. I am just a historian who writes about an area that has become incredibly politicised."[70]

In December 2016 after Trump's surprising win, Halper made international headlines when he and two other colleagues, including Dearlove, announced they were leaving the Cambridge Intelligence Seminar (CIS) because of "unacceptable Russian influence on the group."[71] They claimed the source of the "Russian infiltration" was a digital publishing house called Veruscript, which donated money to CIS, and one of its journals was a front for Russian intelligence. Veruscript lashed out in a statement, saying the allegation was "wholly unfounded": "All claims and allegations are false and without substance, and the company has retained legal advice to assess the reputational damage caused to the company as a result of such sensational reporting."[72]

The donation—a mere two thousand pounds—was made through the *Journal of Intelligence and Terrorism Studies*, which Veruscript shuttered following the accusations. The decision, they said, was made "for the benefit of its other titles and on-going academic publishing activity," "that closing the services of this unique product was the most appropriate action at this time."[73] According to *The Telegraph*, no "concrete evidence yet [has been] found to suggest the claims [of Russian infiltration] are true."[74]

Was Halper's spying for the FBI more of the same? Digging up dirt on an opposing candidate, passing information along to cohorts in the CIA, and inventing Russian infiltration narratives? If so, Halper's experience would have been a valuable resource in a scheme to entrap the Trump campaign.

Crossfire Hurricane

In August, after the FBI counterintelligence investigation dubbed Crossfire Hurricane officially opened, former CIA director John Brennan hurried to Capitol Hill to brief members of Congress on possible election interference. According to *The New York Times*,

> In an Aug. 25 briefing for Harry Reid, then the top Democrat in the Senate, Mr. Brennan indicated that Russia's hackings appeared aimed at helping Mr. Trump win the November election, according to two former officials with knowledge of the briefing.
>
> In the August briefing for Mr. Reid, the two former officials said, Mr. Brennan indicated that the C.I.A. focused on foreign intelligence.[75]

The briefing had Brennan's desired effect—pushing for more intrusive methods to spy on the Trump campaign and Page in particular. On August 27, Reid wrote to James Comey telling him he had "recently become concerned" that Russia's meddling in the election was "more extensive than widely known." Interestingly, the only member of the Trump campaign mentioned in the letter was Carter Page. He had become the focus of the investigation and the only possibility to get a FISA warrant for spying—first on him and, by extension, those he communicated with, past and present. According to journalist Sara Carter, one congressional investigator told her he believed actors in the FBI had a hand in Brennan's briefing to Reid to legitimize the surveillance of Carter Page:[76]

> *Documents obtained by congressional investigators suggest possible coordination by Obama White House officials, the CIA and the FBI into the investigation into President Donald Trump's campaign. Those senior Obama officials used unsubstantiated evidence to launch allegations in the media that the Trump campaign was colluding with Russia during the run-up to the 2016 presidential election.*
>
> *The documents, which include text messages from embattled FBI Special Agent Peter Strzok and his paramour Lisa Page, also reveal that former Obama White House Chief of Staff Denis McDonough was involved in the initial investigation into Trump's campaign. Comey, Brennan, and McDonough were the "highest-ranking officials at the FBI, CIA and White House" and were working in concert to ensure an investigation was initiated, congressional members told this reporter.[77]*

As congressional investigators told Fox News, the CIA and FBI should remain "independent agencies," and "coordination between political actors at the White House and investigators would be inappropriate."[78]

It's likely Brennan shared information from Steele's memos with Reid, a point supported by BuzzFeed when they published the full dossier, commenting, "Harry Reid spokesman Adam Jentleson tweeted Tuesday that the former Senate Democratic leader had seen the documents before writing a public letter to FBI Director James Comey about Trump's ties to Russia."[79] Brennan's briefing, and Reid's subsequent letter to Comey, came just weeks after a particularly cryptic text was sent from Strzok to Page:

> I want to believe the path you threw out for consideration in Andy's [McCabe] office—that there's no way he gets elected— but I'm afraid we can't take that risk. It's like an insurance policy in the unlikely event you die before you're 40.[80]

What "insurance policy" was Strzok referencing if not the FBI's Russia investigation? In early August, Page texted Strzok, "Maybe you're meant to stay where you are [in the investigation] because you're meant to protect the country from that menace." Strzok thanked her, adding, "It's absolutely true that we're both very fortunate. And of course I'll try and approach it that way. I just know it will be tough at times. I can protect our country at many levels, not sure if that helps."[81]

Strzok's political bias is more than evident from his texts, causing the inspector general to have no "confidence" that Strzok's involvement in the Russia investigation was "free from bias," particularly when Strzok decided to prioritize the Russia probe over Clinton's email investigation immediately before the election.[82] Strzok appeared to insert his political interests into decisions about the investigations, pushing forward the Russia probe to secure Trump's defeat.

Former US attorney and independent counsel of the United States Joseph diGenova said, "No amount of sugar coating or *post hoc* explanation of this and other texts can conceal the couple's animus against Trump and support for Clinton. Strzok's messages illustrate his commitment to Clinton's victory and Trump's defeat or, if Trump won, to an 'insurance policy.'"[83] He continues,

The term "insurance policy" obviously refers to the Trump-Russia collusion investigation, which to this day remains a probe with no underlying crime. This is not the talk of professional investigators, but of corrupt agents who have created two standards of justice based on their political leanings. It looks like a reprise of the schemes undertaken during an earlier era, under FBI Director J. Edgar Hoover, that led to the creation of the Church Committee—a committee on which I served, and which tried to reform the FBI to prevent it from meddling in domestic politics.[84]

The Steele dossier was "at the heart of the Russia collusion scheme," diGenova said. The FBI used the opposition research document to drive the investigation forward even though it had never been verified by the FBI. "Comey and then-CIA Director John Brennan laundered the Steele Dossier through the US intelligence community to give it an aura of credibility and get it to the press," he added.[85]

Reid's letter to Comey about the investigation was made public in a *Times* article on August 29, 2016. Following its publication, Strzok texted Page a link to the story, with the message "here we go." According to congressional investigators, the two "knew it would create public calls for an investigation into Russian interference,"[86] even though the FBI had already begun an investigation in secret without alerting the congressional oversight committee.

The narrative that Trump had colluded with the Russians was circulating in the public sphere thanks to DNC media operatives, but not everyone believed it or took it seriously. Reporters remained skeptical, and voters were more titillated by the latest sexual harassment accusations swirling around Trump than collusion with Russia. But, if the story that had been drifting in the public domain were backed by reports of an FBI investigation, it would be legitimized. And that's exactly what happened. The leak pushed the narrative into the realm of plausibility just as the election was reaching its final stretch.

Page, however, was still worried Trump would be elected despite the odds. Almost frantic, she wrote to Strzok: "[Trump's] not ever going to become president, right? Right?!" He responded with a text that they would later withhold from congressional investigations until it surfaced in the inspector general's report. "No. No he won't. We'll stop it," Strzok ominously tweeted. The IG report stated this text "is not only indicative of a biased state of mind but, even more seriously, implies a willingness to take official action to impact the presidential candidate's electoral prospects. This is antithetical to the core values of the FBI and the Department of Justice."[87]

Despite his promises, Stzrok didn't stop Trump. In an election that shocked the nation and the world, Trump became the forty-fifth president of the United States. The investigation that had been promised as an "insurance policy" failed, but this didn't stop the effort to take down the president-elect. The investigation continued, turning its eye on Trump's national security advisor Mike Flynn.

Michael Flynn

On December 29, 2016, while Flynn was on vacation in the Dominican Republic just weeks before Trump's inauguration, he received a phone call from Russian ambassador Sergey Kislyak.[88] Earlier that day, President Barack Obama forced the closure of Russian-owned compounds in New York and Maryland as punishment for interfering with the election. This lame-duck move by the Obama administration gave Kislyak a reason to call Trump's incoming national security advisor. Kislyak was, of course, being monitored by the US government, and any contacts he made would have been recorded. One could conclude this was a roundabout way to spy on Flynn in search of a crime. The Russia investigation was still necessary to take out Trump, only now it would be used for impeachment. They just needed proof of collusion, and surveillance of Page wasn't finding it. It was possible Flynn would deliver the missing evidence.

Flynn took Kislyak's call, though he had to have known it would be intercepted and monitored. It was a risk to talk to the ambassador, particularly with accusations of collusion swirling around the Trump campaign. Obviously, Flynn didn't think he could be the target of a setup, but that's what happened. On January 24, 2017, Flynn was questioned by special agents Strzok and Joe Pientka about the phone conversation.[89] The FBI had intercepted and listened to Flynn's entire conversation in which sanctions on Russia were discussed. They knew what was said. Instead of gathering information in a counterintelligence investigation, the investigators questioned Flynn on the contents of his own conversation, looking for any deviations from the script laid out in front of the FBI.

According to a senior FBI agent interviewed by journalist Sara Carter in June 2018 after the IG report had been released, the interview with Flynn was problematic in several ways. The agents never told him it was a formal interview or that they suspected him of lying, never giving him a chance to explain. The senior agent familiar with the case was particularly disturbed by revelations of Strzok's extreme anti-Trump bias and his intimate involvement in both the Clinton and Russia investigation. You don't want people "tainted" to perform that kind of interview, he said. "You want to get what's called a clean team to do the interviews…people who haven't had access to any of this highly sensitive information to perform the interview and you give them sort [of] rough guidelines [of] what you want them to talk about and then hopefully they'll get the person to admit to it."[90]

The agent told Carter that Flynn was "very forthcoming about 99 percent of the things that happened, if he misremembered, or if he was exhausted because the guy probably had about four hours of sleep a night during that time, it didn't matter in the end. They wanted to get him. All he had to do was misremember one time that he talked to the guy. Then they could automatically [bring] him up on that one charge."[91]

The two-page complaint against Flynn cites false statements to the FBI regarding his discussion with Kislyak on December 29 and a separate conversation on December 22. The relevant statements were the following:

> (i) On or about December 29, 2016, FLYNN did not ask the Government of Russia's Ambassador to the United States ("Russian Ambassador") to refrain from escalating the situation in response to sanctions that the United States had imposed against Russia that same day; and did not recall the Russian Ambassador subsequently telling him that Russia had chosen to moderate its response to those sanctions as a result of his request.

And,

> (ii) On or about December 22, 2016, FLYNN did not ask the Russian Ambassador to delay the vote on or defeat a pending United Nations Security Council resolution.[92]

When James Comey briefed a number of Capitol Hill lawmakers about the bureau's counterintelligence operation, two sources familiar with the meetings said Comey told lawmakers the FBI agents who interviewed Flynn didn't believe he lied or intentionally provided any misleading answers.[93] Comey would later deny those claims in 2018 on his book tour, but a House Intelligence Committee report confirmed that "General Flynn pleaded guilty to making a false statement to the Federal Bureau of Investigation regarding his December 2016 conversations with Ambassador Kislyak, even though the agents did not detect any deception during Flynn's interview."[94] The report added that then-FBI deputy director Andrew McCabe also testified that the FBI agents who interviewed Flynn "didn't think he was lying."[95]

The dispute over Flynn's truthfulness allowed Deputy Attorney General Sally Yates to express "concern" that Flynn could be blackmailed by Russia simply because he deviated from the transcript of the recorded call with Kislyak. She claimed to be concerned about potential violations of the Logan Act, a rarely enforced law that had been on the books since 1799 prohibiting Americans from corresponding with foreign governments "relating to controversies or disputes which do or shall exist"[96] between the two countries.

The Logan Act is vague, potentially unconstitutional, and would have legal ramifications for several individuals if it were enforced, e.g., Jimmy Carter's peace efforts as a private citizen, Dennis Rodman traveling to North Korea, or Jane Fonda parading around with the Viet Cong. Even the act's namesake, George Logan, wasn't deterred by it and traveled to Britain in 1810 to try to de-escalate tensions that eventually led to the War of 1812.[97]

Only two people have been indicted under the Logan Act, in 1803 and 1852. That's an average of less than one person per century. No one has been convicted under the act. It's hardly an ideal legal avenue to prosecute someone during a critical presidential transition involving dealings with a foreign power. Yet, this is the law that propelled the Russia collusion narrative into the Trump presidency.

The story about Flynn's conversations with Kislyak was quickly leaked to the media. *Washington Post* columnist David Ignatius first reported it, using information only those intimate with the case and determined to find proof of collusion could provide. In the article "Why Did Obama Dawdle on Russia's Hacking?" Ignatius reports,

> *According to a senior US government official, Flynn phoned Russian Ambassador Sergey Kislyak several times on Dec. 29, the day the Obama administration announced the expulsion of 35 Russian officials as well as other measures in retaliation for the hacking. What did Flynn say, and did it undercut the US sanctions?*[98]

This report was published in early January, but the FBI wouldn't interview Flynn until after Trump took office. How then would Ignatius know that anyone would be concerned about his discussion of sanctions?

Ignatius also mentioned the law that would surface in the case. "The Logan Act (though never enforced) bars US citizens from correspondence intending to influence a foreign government about 'disputes' with the United States," Ignatius wrote. "Was its spirit violated? The Trump campaign didn't immediately respond to a request for comment."[99] Of all possible laws to propose regarding an inquiry into Flynn, what are the odds that the *Washington Post* reporter would choose one that had never yet been enforced, but it would be the exact one leveled against Flynn?

NSA Surveillance Expands

While all eyes were focused on the incoming administration, Obama authorized the NSA to share surveillance data with the sixteen other US intelligence agencies, as Director of National Intelligence James Clapper and Attorney General Loretta Lynch initially approved the changes in procedures. In effect, the agency's trove of raw data became wide open to the entire intel community. According to *The New York Times*,

> *Previously, the N.S.A. filtered information before sharing intercepted communications with another agency, like the C.IA. or the intelligence branches of the F.B.I. and the Drug Enforcement Administration. The N.S.A.'s analysts passed on only information they deemed pertinent, screening out the identities of innocent people and irrelevant personal information.*
>
> *Now, other intelligence agencies will be able to search directly through raw repositories of communications intercepted by the N.S.A. and then apply such rules for "minimizing" privacy intrusions.*[100]

With the change, those names are no longer shielded. The government can, in essence, spy on someone by proxy. Patrick Toomey of the American Civil Liberties Union told *The New York Times* that the expansion eroded privacy rights. "Rather than dramatically expanding government access to so much personal data, we need much stronger rules to protect the privacy of Americans," Toomey said. "Seventeen different government agencies shouldn't be rooting through Americans' emails with family members, friends and colleagues, all without ever obtaining a warrant."[101]

A statement by the ACLU called for Congress to intervene to stop this breach of trust between Americans and the government:

The procedures released today allow more agencies to directly access information collected by the NSA without a warrant under procedures that are grossly inadequate. This raises serious concerns that agencies that have responsibilities such as prosecuting domestic crimes, regulating our financial policy, and enforcing our immigration laws will now have access to a wealth of personal information that could be misused. Congress needs to take action to regulate and provide oversight over these activities.[102]

The decision to expand access to personal information didn't happen accidentally. It's possible that this kind of intelligence sharing was already occurring between the NSA and some intelligence agencies during the election to build the Russia collusion narrative. Obama merely needed to give it an official status of legality after the fact. The timing of the new procedures supports this theory since they occurred just days before Trump would take control of the White House. Perhaps Obama needed to make the change because the NSA was already under scrutiny for abuses. With the new procedures, those abuses would go away.

A year before, on January 7, 2016, the inspector general's office of the NSA internally released the "Report on the Special Study of NSA Controls to Comply with the FISA Amendments Act Targeting and Minimization Procedures."[103] The report found that the NSA's protocols regarding surveillance were not being followed. When it came to upstream data collection (data intercepted by phone calls or through the internet), the report found that the NSA was only following proper protocol 5 percent of the time. As a result, the communications of Americans inside the United States were being intercepted, stored, and even analyzed.

Suspecting widespread noncompliance with long-standing procedures, Mike Rogers, the NSA's director in the Obama administration, ordered the agency's compliance officer to run a full audit on 702 compliances in mid-2016. FISA section 702 "allows the government to obtain the communications of foreigners outside the United States, including foreign terrorist threats,"[104] without a warrant. Section 702, however, "cannot be used to intentionally target a US citizen, or to intentionally target any person known to be in the US... [and] cannot be used to target a person outside the US if the purpose is to acquire information."[105] This rule is supposed to prevent Americans from being surveilled without a warrant, but sometimes it happens unintentionally. When this occurs during foreign surveillance, Americans are protected by having their names masked.

In October, just before the election, Rogers was briefed by the NSA's compliance officer on the results of the audit. Rogers then reported to the DOJ and the FISA court on October 24—and returned to the FISA court two days later with additional information. The court would later issue a memorandum revealing the results of his audit:

> *The October 26, 2016 Notice [containing the information Rogers learned from the audit] disclosed that an NSA Inspector General (IG) review...indicated that, with greater frequency than previously disclosed to the Court, NSA analysts had used US-person identifiers to query the result of Internet "upstream" collection, even though NSA's section 702 minimization procedures prohibited such queries...this disclosure gave the Court substantial concern.*
>
> *At the October 26, 2016 hearing, the Court ascribed the government's failure to disclose those IG and OCO reviews at the October 24, 2016 hearing to an institutional "lack of*

candor" on NSA's part and emphasized that "this is a very serious Fourth Amendment issue."[106]

Rogers' role in this situation was significant due to his impromptu visit to Trump Tower nine days after Trump won the election. On November 17, Rogers met with the newly minted president-elect without giving President Obama advance notification. The next day, Trump suddenly moved his presidential transition operation from Trump Tower in Manhattan to one of his properties in Bedminster, New Jersey. Reaction from the sitting president was swift. Obama immediately called for the termination of Rogers at the NSA, stating that Rogers wasn't doing enough to combat the influence of the (former) Islamic State online. This reason is ironic, considering Obama had blocked three-quarters of all anti-ISIS air strikes requested by US military pilots. The timing was also odd. Obama was a lame-duck president. Why did he care about Rogers' record on combating terrorism?

Did he care because Rogers had informed Trump that the Obama administration had been spying on his team at Trump Tower? Is this why Rogers didn't tell Obama what he was doing? A surveillance operation would be consistent with Trump's team immediately moving to Bedminster, and it correlates with his tweets months later that the Obama administration "wiretapped" him.

In March of 2017, Devin Nunes revealed that the communications of President Donald Trump and associates were likely picked up after the election by intelligence agencies conducting surveillance on foreign targets. Nunes cited intelligence reports "that clearly show that the president-elect and his team were…at least monitored."[107] "It looks to me like it was all legally collected, but it was essentially a lot of information on the president-elect and his transition team and what they were doing," Nunes continued, noting that the information had "little or no apparent intelligence value."[108]

Obama's national security advisor Susan Rice appeared surprised by the claims and denied them in a PBS interview. Host Judy Woodruff asked, "We've been following a disclosure by the chairman of the House Intelligence Committee, Devin Nunes, that in essence, during the final days of the Obama administration, during the transition, after President Trump had been elected, that he and the people around him may have been caught up in surveillance of foreign individuals in that their identities may have been disclosed. Do you know anything about this?" To this, Rice replied, "I know nothing about this. I was surprised to see reports from Chairman Nunes on that count today."[109]

By September, thanks to questioning before the House Intelligence Committee, it was revealed that Rice couldn't have possibly been surprised by Nunes' allegations, because she was one of those doing the unmasking. CNN broke the story, headlined "Exclusive: Rice Told House Investigators Why She Unmasked Senior Trump Officials."[110]

In mid-December, Rice unmasked the identity of various Trump-team members from surveillance of the crown prince of the United Arab Emirates, Sheikh Mohammed bin Zayed al-Nahyan, when he was in New York attending a meeting with Michael Flynn, Jared Kushner, and Steve Bannon. Rice claimed to be bothered by the timing of the meeting and by the UAE not notifying the US government of al-Nahyan's planned travel to the United States. Apparently, that faux pas justified surveilling al-Nahyan and then unmasking the identities of the American citizens he met.

CNN tried to provide cover for Rice in the article, quoting Republican Florida representative Tom Rooney, who said he "didn't believe Susan Rice did anything illegal"[111]—even though Nunes himself said the information "looks to me like it was all legally collected."[112] Legality, however, was never the question; it was whether an incumbent president was gathering intelligence on the Trump team.

Rice's unmasking was part of a broader theme—a surge in unmasking requests during Obama's final year in office, as the presidential race was heating up. In July 2017, *The Washington Free Beacon* reported that former Obama UN ambassador Samantha Power "appears to be central to efforts by top Obama administration officials to identify individuals named in classified intelligence community reports related to Trump and his presidential transition team, according to multiple sources."[113] Power revealed the names of at least 260 people during her last year as UN ambassador and increased her pace to one per day in the final months of Obama's presidency.

Power's role in unmasking was odd because it's not something a UN ambassador typically does, and unmasking requests are quite rare. When she testified behind closed doors to the House Intelligence Committee on October 13, 2017, Power said, "they [the unmasking requests] may be under my name, but I did not make those requests."[114] Representative Trey Gowdy told Fox News this might be Power's claim, but the intelligence community assigned the requests to her; so, she was either acting on her own or covering for someone else.

One thing is clear, however—the unmasking had nothing to do with concerns of Russian interference. Rice failed to tell the truth about her knowledge of it, and Power probably did too. If the unmaskings had no malicious intent, why skirt the truth? It's hardly coincidental that during the final year of Obama's presidency, when Trump became the GOP nominee, these unmasking requests surged.

On inauguration day, Rice apparently tried to find cover by giving the Obama administration an alibi for a strange meeting held two weeks before about law-enforcement activities related to Russian hacking. Just minutes after Trump was sworn in as president, Rice sent a bizarre email to herself regarding the contents of the meeting on January 5, 2017:

> *On January 5, following a briefing by IC leadership on Russian hacking during the 2016 Presidential election, President Obama had a brief follow-on conversation with FBI Director Jim Comey and Deputy Attorney General Sally Yates in the Oval Office. Vice President Biden and I were also present... President Obama began the conversation by stressing his continued commitment to ensuring that every aspect of this issue is handled by the Intelligence and law enforcement communities "by the book." The President stressed that he is not asking about, initiating or instructing anything from a law enforcement perspective. He reiterated that our law enforcement team needs to proceed as it normally would by the book. From a national security perspective, however, President Obama said he wants to be sure that, as we engage with the incoming team, we are mindful to ascertain if there is any reason that we cannot share information fully as it relates to Russia.... The President asked Comey to inform him if anything changes in the next few weeks that should affect how we share classified information with the incoming team. Comey said he would.*[115]

What possible purpose could this email serve except to create an alibi for a suspicious meeting? If the witch hunt into

Trump's Russian ties were indeed "by the book," Rice would have no need to remind herself.

SPECIAL COUNSEL PROBE

On May 9, 2017, Trump wrote the following letter to FBI director James Comey:

> *Dear Director Comey,*
>
> *I have received the attached letters from the Attorney General and Deputy Attorney General of the United States recommending your dismissal as the Director of the Federal Bureau of Investigation. I have accepted their recommendation and you are hereby terminated and removed from office, effective immediately.*
>
> *Donald J. Trump*

Attorney General Jeff Sessions recommended removing the director based on Deputy Attorney General Rod Rosenstein's evaluation of Comey's work on the Clinton email investigation. Rosenstein wrote in his memorandum to Sessions:

> *I cannot defend the Director's handling of the conclusion of the investigation of Secretary Clinton's emails, and I do not understand his refusal to accept serious mistakes; it is one of the few issues that unites people of diverse perspectives.*
>
> *The Director was wrong to usurp the Attorney General's authority on July 5, 2016, and announce his conclusion that the case should be closed without prosecution. It is not the function of the Director to make such an announcement. At most, the Director should have said the FBI had completed its investigation and presented its findings to federal prosecutors. The Director now defends his decision by asserting that he believed Attorney General Loretta Lynch had a conflict. But*

the FBI Director is never empowered to supplant federal prosecutors and assume command of the Justice Department.

Compounding the error, the Director ignored another longstanding principle; we do not hold press conferences to release derogatory information about the subject of a declined criminal investigation.... The Director laid out his version of the facts for the news media as if it were a closing argument, but without a trial. It is a textbook example of what federal prosecutors and agents are taught not to do.

Although the President has the power to remove an FBI director, the decision should not be taken lightly.... The way the Director handled the conclusion of the email investigation was wrong. As a result, the FBI is unlikely to regain public and congressional trust until it has a Director who understands the gravity of the mistakes and pledges never to repeat them. Having refused to admit his errors, the Director cannot be expected to implement the necessary corrective actions.

Sessions' recommendation was soon lost on the public, as the media placed the entire responsibility for the firing on Trump, refusing to acknowledge that he was acting on the recommendation of the Justice Department. *The New York Times* called Comey's firing a "stunning development" that "raised the specter of political interference by a sitting president into an existing investigation by the nation's leading law enforcement agency. It immediately ignited Democratic calls for a special counsel to lead the Russia inquiry."[116]

These calls intensified after Comey leaked to the press notes of private meetings with Trump that the director claimed to have written down as "insurance" in case Trump lied about their conversations. Comey later called Trump "morally unfit" to serve in office and told ABC News that "a person who sees moral equivalence in Charlottesville, who talks about and treats women like they're pieces of meat, who lies constantly about matters big and small and insists the American people believe it, that person's not fit to be president of the United States, on moral grounds."[117]

Given this judgment of Trump, Comey said he was morally compelled "to write it down [the content of the meetings] and write it down in a very detailed way." At least two of the memos reportedly contained classified information, which prompted a review by the Justice Department inspector general. In response, Comey showed astonishing gall by claiming the memos he wrote were personal and that he leaked them to the media as "a private citizen." Comey told Congress,

> I asked—the president tweeted on Friday after I got fired that I better hope there's not tapes. I woke up in the middle of the night on Monday night because it didn't dawn on me originally, that there might be corroboration for our conversation. There might [be] a tape. My judgment was, I need to get that out into the public square. I asked a friend of mine to share the content of the memo with a reporter. Didn't do it myself for a variety of reasons. I asked him to because I thought that might prompt the appointment of a special counsel. I asked a close friend to do it.[118]

This disregard for confidentiality and adherence to rules by the FBI director caught the attention of the inspector general, who found that Comey had been insubordinate and suffered "serious error in judgment" during the Clinton email investigation. He acted outside of his responsibilities as an investigator to direct the course of the investigation and even used a private email to conduct FBI business.[119]

One of Comey's most disruptive memos came from February 14 in which he recorded Trump saying, "I hope you can see your way clear to letting this go, to letting [Michael] Flynn go. He is a good guy. I hope you can let this go." The comment made it appear as if Trump was issuing an order to end the Russian interference investigation, even though this wasn't the case—a point Comey later conceded. In testimony before Congress, he was asked if the president ever asked him to stop the FBI investigation, to which Comey replied, "Not to my understanding." He added that he believed the president was offering him "direction," not an order. Comey then clarified that the Russia and Flynn investigations were separate and that closing the Flynn investigation would not have stopped the Russia probe. The two were "touching each other, but separate," he explained.

Comey's leaked memo had the effect he intended, as it fueled demands for a special counsel to replace the failing counterintelligence probe. Michael Schmidt of *The New York Times* wrote, "The documentation of Mr. Trump's request is the clearest evidence that the president has tried to directly influence the Justice Department and FBI investigation into links between Mr. Trump's associates and Russia."[120] Believing this to be the case, Deputy Attorney General Rod Rosenstein, now in charge of the Russia case due to Attorney General Jeff Sessions' recusal, appointed Robert Mueller on May 17, 2017, to head the investigation into Russian interference.

Where's the Crime?

Despite being lauded by many as highly appropriate, the special counsel brought no legitimacy to an already illegitimate investigation, one that began with "evidence" supplied by opposition research in a political campaign and setups of Trump campaign advisers. Appointing a special counsel was simply another miscarriage of justice because the grounds on which the deputy attorney general made his decision violated federal regulations. Rosenstein bluntly stated his decision was not grounded on criminal law: "My decision was not based on finding that crimes have been committed or that any prosecution is warranted. I have made no such determination." A criminal-law violation, however, is the *required* grounds for appointing a special counsel. According to federal regulation 28 CFR 600.1, the acting attorney general "will appoint a Special Counsel when he or she determines that criminal investigation of a person or matter is warranted."[121] But Rosenstein made no such decision. Instead, he determined "that based *upon the unique circumstances* [emphasis added], the public interest requires me to place this investigation under the authority of a person who exercises a degree of independence from the normal chain of command."[122] Rosenstein added,

> *Each year, the career professionals of the US Department of Justice conduct tens of thousands of criminal investigations and handle countless other matters without regard to partisan political considerations. I have great confidence in the independence and integrity of our people and our processes. Considering the unique circumstances of this matter, however, I determined that a Special Counsel is necessary in order for the American people to have full confidence in the outcome. Our nation is grounded on the rule of law, and the public must be assured that government officials administer the law fairly. Special Counsel Mueller will have all appropriate resources to conduct a thorough and complete investigation, and I am confident that he will follow the facts, apply the law and reach a just result.*[123]

"Without regard to partisan political considerations"—yet, this was the very basis of the appointment since there was no criminal-law cause. Some have cited obstruction of justice as "the crime," but there could have been no such obstruction by Trump in a counterintelligence investigation headed by the FBI director, who can be fired by his boss, the president. The only reported crime committed during the election was the unconfirmed hacking of the DNC computers by foreign entities, but there was no evidence that Trump or anyone associated with him in his campaign was complicit in that crime. In fact, Comey admitted that Trump was not under investigation, despite having surveilled team members and reportedly infiltrated his campaign with an FBI informant.

Not only was there no crime committed by the Trump team regarding Russia collusion, the investigation that had been ongoing since July 2016 was a *counterintelligence* investigation. Comey made this point clear in March 2017 when he testified that he had been "authorized by the Department of Justice to confirm that the FBI, as part of our *counterintelligence mission* [emphasis added]," was to investigate "the Russian government's efforts to interfere in the 2016 presidential election." As part of this investigation, the FBI looked into possible links between the Trump campaign and the Russian government. "As with any counterintelligence investigation," Comey added, "this will also include an assessment of whether any crimes were committed."[124]

Finding criminal activity during a counterintelligence investigation, however, is not the same as conducting a criminal investigation. The focus of counterintelligence is not a crime committed by an American citizen but the activity of a foreign country—in this instance Russia. Information needs to be gathered in these circumstances, not to pursue justice in a court of law, but to employ government powers to stop the hostile actions of a foreign nation. This falls under the purview of the executive branch, which means Trump had the authority to handle it according to his judgment.

As time passed with no finding of Trump-Russia collusion, the focus of the investigation changed to obstruction of justice—the last hope of a dying effort to oust Trump. This allegation against Trump has become a constant refrain used by his opponents to threaten him with impeachment if he even hints at firing Mueller or Rosenstein. This threat, however, has no foundation in reality. Trump, as the president and thereby the boss of Mueller and Rosenstein, has every right to remove the special counsel. Additionally, there can be no obstruction of justice because there is no criminal investigation to obstruct.

This distinction is a point lost on the media and many in America who think Trump has been under a criminal investigation. It is also lost on some lawmakers and the investigators themselves. The special counsel probe is an extension of a counterintelligence investigation. If it were, indeed, criminal in nature, those crimes should have been named in the beginning. They were not named. Instead, Mueller was given sweeping authority to investigate individuals to find violations of criminal law. In a constitutional republic, this isn't the way it works. In the United States, law enforcement is tasked with investigating crimes in search of the people who did it. They do not examine people in search of crimes. If people were the focus and not the crimes, then nearly every person in the country would be found guilty of violating some law.

The special counsel investigation has been a farce from the beginning, starting with the failure to name crimes, then packing the legal team with Democrats and Democratic donors. As reported by Matt Zapotosky at the *Washington Post,*

- *13 of the 17 members of Mueller's team have previously registered as Democrats, while four had no affiliation or their affiliation could not be found.*
- *Nine of the 17 made political donations to Democrats, their contributions totaling more than $57,000.*
- *Six donated to Hillary Clinton, Trump's opponent in the 2016 race.*[125]

"Lawyers at the Justice Department," the *Post* stated, "— from which Mueller drew the bulk of his team—are generally thought to be left-leaning."[126] The seventeen attorneys include Zainab Ahmad, Greg Andres, Lawrence Rush Atkinson, Ryan Dickey, Michael Dreeben, Kyle Freeny, Andrew Goldstein, Adam Jed, Scott Meisler, Elizabeth Prelogar, James Quarles, Jeannie Rhee, Brian Richardson, Brandon Van Grack, Andrew Weissmann, Aaron Zebley, and Aaron Zelinsky.

Dreeben, whose voter registration is unknown, is an appellate attorney for the Office of the Solicitor General. He donated one thousand dollars to Clinton in 2006 and a combined one thousand dollars to Obama in 2007 and 2008. Quarles, whose voter registration is unknown, is a former partner at WilmerHale. He donated over 7,000 dollars to Obama in the last decade and 2,700 dollars to Clinton's 2016 presidential campaign.

Rhee, a registered Democrat and former partner at WilmerHale, also donated a total of 5,400 dollars to Clinton. Rhee donated a combined 4,800 dollars to Obama in 2008 and 2011, along with smaller contributions to the DNC and Democrats running for Congress. Even more significant, Rhee represented the Clinton Foundation, heading off Freedom of Information Act requests that had to do with Clinton's private email server.[127] She was also the personal attorney of Ben Rhodes, Obama's deputy national security advisor, who was instrumental in the effort to convince the public and Congress to support the Iran nuclear deal.[128]

Weissmann, a registered Democrat who served as general counsel at the FBI and was an assistant US attorney for the Eastern District of New York, donated a combined 2,300 dollars to Obama's campaign in 2008. In 2006, he contributed at least 2,000 dollars to the DNC. Andres, a registered Democrat and a former partner at Davis Polk and former assistant US attorney for the Eastern District of New York, donated at least 2,700 dollars to Senator Kirsten Gillibrand in 2017, along with smaller donations to other Democratic candidates. His impartiality came into question when Tucker Carlson of Fox News reported that he sent an email to outgoing attorney general Sally Yates that lauded her for refusing to enforce Trump's travel ban. "I am so proud and in awe," he wrote. "Thank you so much. All my deepest respect."[129]

Attorneys are supposed to leave their political biases at the door, but in an environment that has been highly politicized, the absence of Republican lawyers on the team calls into question the team's objectivity. Even Mueller's objectivity has been called into question because of ties that could create possible biases. Since leaving the FBI in 2013, Mueller has worked at the law firm WilmerHale, most of whose lawyers lean to the left. Nearly 85 percent of the firm's lawyers donated to Obama.[130]

Mueller has also been scrutinized for his use of George Nader in his investigation of the Trump campaign. Nader, a Lebanese-American, is a businessman-turned-diplomat who has tried to peddle Middle Eastern influence in Washington for decades, from the Clinton administration, to Obama's, and finally to Trump's. During the Trump era, Nader became an adviser of sorts to the ruler of the United Arab Emirates, and he frequented the White House during Trump's first year. Because of this, Mueller queried Nader about his role in framing Trump's policies and any flow of money from several countries into the Trump White House.

Of particular interest to Mueller is two meetings that occurred while Nader was working with the UAE: one in Trump Tower in which the UAE crown prince Sheikh Mohammed bin Zayed al-Nahyan met with Jared Kushner, Michael Flynn, and Steve Bannon, and another a month later in the Seychelles, islands in the Indian Ocean, attended by a Russian businessman close to Putin and Erik Prince, founder of the private military firm Blackwater (now Academi) and brother of Trump's secretary of education, Betsy DeVos. The meeting, brokered by the UAE, was reportedly to set up back-channel communications between President-elect Trump and Moscow.

During this time, National Security Advisor Susan Rice learned about the meeting in New York between al-Nahyan and the three (at the time) unidentified Americans from intelligence intercepts from foreign sources. After receiving the information, Rice requested the identities of the US persons, also known as unmasking. Typically, US citizens whose communications are inadvertently picked up when intelligence sources are surveilling foreign individuals are kept hidden to protect their privacy. Trump questioned the legality of Rice's decision to unmask Kushner, Flynn, and Bannon.

Mueller focused on Nader in his effort to discover if he helped the UAE buy political influence, making him a key figure in the special counsel's investigation of Trump. Nader agreed to cooperate with Mueller, exchanging immunity for providing him with any information on meetings between the UAE and Trump team members. This isn't particularly noteworthy on its own, but Nader's connections lead to some significant entanglements for Mueller.

Nader's legal representation is Kathryn Ruemmler, attorney for the Clinton Foundation. Significantly, Ruemmler is also Susan Rice's lawyer. She served as long-term White House counsel and played a role in making the Obama administration less than transparent. According to *The New York Times*, "Examples of Ms. Ruemmler's influence are wide-ranging.... Ms. Ruemmler took a hard line in internal debates about keeping executive branch documents secret, like memos from the Justice Department's Office of Legal Counsel sought by congressional overseers, or in Freedom of Information Act lawsuits. Her arguments—that disclosing them would chill candid advice to presidents—have contributed to Mr. Obama's transition from promising greater transparency to being criticized even by his own allies for excessive secrecy."[131]

When President Obama's national security team, including Deputy National Security Advisor Ben Rhodes, pushed to release a comprehensive timeline of events documenting the Benghazi attack that would also synthesize the views of the various government agencies into one report right ahead of the 2012 election, it was Ruemmler who shot that idea down and advised them to keep quiet.[132]

Ruemmler is also directly connected to Mueller. She served as a prosecutor on the DOJ's Enron task force under Andrew Weissmann, one of Mueller's top attorneys on the special counsel probe. The task force was handpicked by Mueller. While on the task force, Ruemmler was implicated in numerous forms of prosecutorial misconduct. As Sidney Powell, who authored a book on the case called *Licensed to Lie*, wrote, "Ms. Ruemmler signed a letter to defense counsel in the Merrill Lynch/Enron case that was false and deceptive, and she hid evidence that showed they were innocent. The Fifth Circuit reversed 12 out of 14 counts of conviction."[133] Nothing happened to her. "Thanks to the protection of Robert Mueller and President Obama," Powell wrote, she never suffered any real consequences for her misconduct in the Enron case.[134]

In addition to being troubled by these questionable connections, Republicans in Congress have demanded that Mueller resign because he was FBI director when the Obama administration made a surreptitious uranium deal with Russia. As reported in *Newsweek*, "At the time the Obama administration was considering the deal, the FBI had evidence of Russian bribery and required a confidential informant to sign a non-disclosure agreement, [Congressman Matt] Gaetz noted based on government documents. The Department of Justice waited until 2014 to file charges."[135] Also overseeing the investigation and possible cover-up in the Uranium One deal was Rod Rosenstein and Andrew McCabe.

Rosenstein has received further criticism for his involvement in the continuation of FISA warrants based on fake opposition research. According to a Republican congressional memo, Rosenstein approved an application to extend surveillance on Carter Page. Republican lawmakers have said Rosenstein and others have not sufficiently explained why they allowed the spying to continue and why they failed to properly vet the application for a warrant.[136]

These apparent conflicts of interest have made Rosenstein and Mueller a target of Trump's criticism. As reported in *The New York Times*,

> *A White House spokesman, Hogan Gidley, said in a statement: "The president has been clear publicly and privately that he*

wants absolute transparency throughout this process. Based on numerous news reports, top officials at the FBI have engaged in conduct that shows bias against President Trump and bias for Hillary Clinton. While President Trump has the utmost respect and support for the rank-and-file members of the FBI, the anti-Trump bias at the top levels that appear to have existed is troubling."[137]

A Flood of Leaks

By the time the special counsel was appointed, partisan politics had already run amuck in the Justice Department, so skepticism about possible bias during the investigation is more than warranted. The inspector general's report supports this assumption, citing instances of bias. None were in favor of Trump, only of Clinton, with one agent even referring to the Trump campaign with the clarion call, "Viva le resistance."[138]

At every turn, from the intelligence community to the FBI, an effort to embarrass or expose Trump has been ever-present in Washington, D.C. The number of leaks plaguing Trump's administration since his inauguration is proof alone of the highly politicized nature of the Trump-Russia inquiry—a practice within the FBI that had been prevalent since the Clinton email investigation, a point made by the inspector general:

We identified numerous FBI employees, at all levels of the organization and with no official reason to be in contact with the media, who were nevertheless in frequent contact with reporters.... We have profound concerns about the volume and extent of unauthorized media contacts by FBI personnel that we have uncovered during our review.

In addition, we identified instances where FBI employees improperly received benefits from reporters, including tickets to sporting events, golfing outings, drinks and meals, and admittance to nonpublic social events. We will separately report on those investigations as they are concluded, consistent with the Inspector General Act, other applicable federal statutes, and OIG policy.[139]

The IG concluded that this pervasive leaking "appears to be a cultural attitude among many in the organization."[140]

This culture didn't disappear when Trump became president. According to a Senate committee report, "State Secrets: How an Avalanche of Media Leaks Is Harming National Security," the number of leaks during the first 126 days of Trump's presidency was unprecedented:

Under President Trump's predecessors, leaks of national security information were relatively rare, even with America's vibrant free press. Under President Trump, leaks are flowing at the rate of one a day, an examination of open-source material by the majority staff of the Committee on Homeland Security and Governmental Affairs shows. Articles published by a range of national news organizations between January 20 and May 25, 2017, included at least 125 stories with leaked information potentially damaging to national security. Even a narrow search revealed leaks of comparable information during the Trump administration that were about seven times higher than the same period during the two previous administrations.

From the morning of President Trump's inauguration, when major newspapers published information about highly sensitive intelligence intercepts, news organizations have reported on an avalanche of leaks from officials across the US government. Many disclosures have concerned the investigations of alleged Russian interference in the 2016 election, with the world learning details of whose communications US intelligence agencies are monitoring, what channels are being monitored, and the results of those intercepts. All such revelations are potential violations of federal law, punishable by jail time. [141]

A list of the leaks as reported by the Committee on Homeland Security and Governmental Affairs can be found in Appendix II.

During this period, leaks occurred at a rate of nearly one a day, with most having to do with the Russia investigation. Many of those leaks revealed "closely-held information such as intelligence community intercepts, FBI interviews and intelligence, grand jury subpoenas, and even the workings of a secret surveillance court."[142] The sources are cited as "current and former US officials, some clearly from the intelligence community. One story cited more than two dozen anonymous sources."[143] Unlike with the Obama or Bush administrations, almost all of the leaks during the Trump presidency were about the president himself or his administration. According to the report,

Many stories presented President Trump in a negative and often harsh light, with some seemingly designed to embarrass the administration. For example, a Mother Jones article detailed a memo telling intelligence analysts to keep President Trump's daily briefings short and to avoid nuance; a Reuters piece reported on how the National Security Council frequently puts his name in briefings so he will keep reading; and The Washington Post wrote a story on how the President "badgered, bragged and abruptly ended" a phone call with the Australian Prime Minister. This Post story was one of several that quoted directly from President Trump's private calls with foreign leaders, a rare occurrence under previous presidents. [144]

Leaks regarding Russia-related intelligence were dangerous because of the national security information that was revealed.

In the effort to "out" Trump, the leakers disclosed to the world that "US intelligence agencies are routinely monitoring Russian officials, including within the Kremlin." They also revealed "the communications channels being monitored; whose conversations have been picked up on telephone wiretaps; the contents of some of these communications; and, in at least one case, which agency is doing the monitoring."[145]

According to the report, the most publicized leaks during that period related to Comey's memos and his firing, with the director admitting his role in leaking the information to the media "in hopes of getting a special counsel appointed."[146] On May 16, the day before Rosenstein appointed the special counsel, several leaks made the headlines: "Comey Memo Says Trump Asked Him to End Flynn Investigation," "Notes Made by FBI Director Comey Say Trump Pressured Him to End Flynn Probe," "Trump Officials on Comey Memo: 'Don't See How Trump Isn't Completely F*cked,'" and "Sources: Trump Shared Classified Info with Russians." The very next day, nine news stories contained leaked information.

As leaks dripped nearly daily, Freedom Watch, a conservative activist organization, filed a lawsuit in November 2017 demanding that the court order the DOJ to investigate leaks during the special counsel investigation. "Considering their nature, it is clear that the majority of these leaks are coming from Special Counsel Robert Mueller and his staff, most of whom are suffering from serious conflicts of interest," the complaint stated. Larry Klayman, founder of Freedom Watch and a former federal prosecutor, accused Mueller of "representing his establishment benefactors in both political parties to see the presidency of Donald Trump destroyed."[147]

The complaint listed several examples of leaks Freedom Watch argued had to come from Mueller's staff. An NBC article reported,

> *Federal investigators working for Special Counsel Robert Mueller are keenly focused on President Donald Trump's role in crafting a response to a published article about a meeting between Russians and his son Donald Jr., three sources familiar with the matter told NBC News. The sources told NBC News that prosecutors want to know what Trump knew about the meeting and whether he sought to conceal its purpose.*[148]

Another from *The Wall Street Journal*:

> *Special counsel Robert Mueller is examining what role, if any, former national security adviser Mike Flynn may have played in a private effort to obtain Hillary Clinton's emails from Russian hackers, according to people familiar with the matter. The effort to seek out hackers who were believed to have stolen Mrs. Clinton's emails, first reported by The Wall Street Journal, was led by a longtime Republican activist, Peter W. Smith.*[149]

The complaint accused Mueller and his staff of leaking to CNN:

> *Russian officials bragged in conversations during the presidential campaign that they had cultivated a strong relationship with former Trump adviser retired Gen. Michael Flynn and believed they could use him to influence Donald Trump and his team, sources told CNN.*[150]

Freedom Watch cited these and other examples as reasons for a court-ordered investigation of the leaks. Conflicts of interest were also cited, including an attorney who represented the Clinton Foundation. "Attorney Jeannie S. Rhee…was ethically required to decline a position that places her in a conflict of interest as a staff attorney for Mr. Mueller," the complaint said. "Mr. Mueller's hiring of Ms. Rhee—and others—is in itself an ethical violation of the USDOJ standards and professional rules." Freedom Watch maintained that Mueller's "refusal to correct this unethical conduct speaks volumes and loudly proclaims the true nature of Mr. Mueller's intentions and undertaking."

A federal court judge refused to order the FBI to investigate the leaks based on Freedom Watch's failure to prove injury. US District Judge Amy Berman Jackson wrote in December 2017,

> *The problem in this case is that even if the allegations in the complaint concerning bias or wrongdoing on the part of the Special Counsel are accepted as true on their face, and even if plaintiff is correct that these allegations "clearly warrant thorough ethics investigation and discipline," plaintiff has not—neither in its complaint nor in response to the order to show cause—set forth any facts that would establish that it or any of its members...has suffered an invasion of a legally protected interest that is concrete and particularized, and actual or imminent.*[151]

Earlier in the summer, Rosenstein was compelled to make a public statement about leaks after the *Washington Post* published a report that Mueller and his team were looking into the business dealings of Trump's son-in-law, Jared Kushner. "Americans should exercise caution before accepting as true any stories attributed to anonymous 'officials,'" Rosenstein said, "particularly when they do not identify the country—let alone the branch or agency of government—with which the alleged sources supposedly are affiliated."[152] Following the leaks, the Trump administration called the investigation a witch hunt, and allies of the president have continued to question the actions and motives of Mueller's team, though the exact source of the leaks has never been proven.

Leaking has not only created a political storm throughout the investigation, but it has also damaged reputations. The constant leaks compelled Paul Manafort to file a motion to investigate several anonymous sources that accused him of colluding with the Russians during the campaign. This allegation has never been proven, though Manafort has been indicted on other charges related to his work in Ukraine and financial dealings, including tax evasion, bank fraud, and failure to file as a foreign agent. As reported by Josh Gerstein at *Politico*, Manafort's lawyers argued "that government officials had engaged in repeated leaks of classified information, grand jury secrets and sensitive investigative details that have jeopardized his right to a fair trial."[153] According to the motion,

> *In the fall of 2016, the former chairman to Donald J. Trump's presidential campaign, Paul J. Manafort, Jr., became the target of an apparent "leaks" campaign conducted by numerous unidentified government officials. Over the following sixteen months, current and former government officials—including law enforcement agents—disclosed confidential and ostensibly classified information to multiple media sources in an effort to substantially prejudice and adversely impact Mr. Manafort.*
>
> *From October 2016 through February 2018, countless press articles were published and disseminated regarding the government's investigation and prosecution of Mr. Manafort. Numerous reports contained information from government sources that was clearly subject to grand jury secrecy, was potentially classified intelligence information, or was simply false.*[154]

The leaks regarding Manafort's "collusion with the Russians" began long before he was indicted on other charges. "The government-source leaks concerning surveillance of Mr. Manafort with foreign individuals is particularly troubling," his lawyers wrote. They continue,

> Despite multiple discovery and Brady requests in this regard, the Special Counsel has not produced any materials to the defense—no tapes, notes, transcripts, or any other material evidencing surveillance or intercepts of communications between Mr. Manafort and Russian intelligence officials, Russian government officials (or any other foreign officials). The Office of Special Counsel has advised that there are no materials responsive to Mr. Manafort's requests.[155]

The natural conclusion one would draw from this is, as Manafort's lawyers stated, "these government leaks were intentionally designed to create a false narrative in order to garner support for the appointment of a Special Counsel to investigate Manafort for purportedly coordinating with Russian intelligence/government officials despite the lack of any such evidence."[156] Mueller's team has denied this allegation, of course, but they have not supported an effort to uncover the source of the leaks, something one would think law enforcement would be committed to discovering. Instead, Mueller opposed Manafort's motion for a hearing, arguing that he has failed to prove the leaked information was "specific to the grand jury investigation." In other words, Mueller maintains the leaks could have come from many different sources outside the grand jury. While this could be true, the fact remains that there has been an unprecedented number of leaks surrounding investigations that should have been airtight.

Essential to due process is the confidentiality of information during an investigation so that innocents who are being examined in the course of an inquiry aren't exposed and thus condemned as guilty in the court of public opinion. Yet, this is what has happened with the Trump-Russia collusion investigation. Leaks have framed facts out of context and have fueled a narrative that has never been supported by evidence.

These leaks are also illegal—an ironic twist as investigators have sought a crime while all around them crimes have been committed. As stated in the House Intelligence Committee report on Russian interference, "Leaks of classified information are criminal acts, and have the potential to damage US national security interests, at home and abroad." Leaks related to the "Russian active measures" to sow discord in the election reached back into 2015 and 2016. According to the House report,

> At the time of these leaks, the information contained within them was still classified. These leaks of classified information endangered US national security by revealing key information about US intelligence capabilities to its adversaries, including assessments on adversary intentions. The Committee finds the timing of these leaks particularly concerning. These leaks happened during the early stages of the IC's ongoing assessment of Russian active measures, thus permitting adversaries to not only potentially discover US intelligence capabilities, but also provided adversaries, including the Russians, the opportunity to thwart or manipulate the IC's ongoing assessment.[157]

Most of the leaks pushed the narrative that the Russians wanted to or had helped Trump get elected. On December 9, the *Washington Post* reported that the CIA had determined that Russia interfered in the election to help Trump.[158] In an article titled, "Russian Hackers Acted to Aid Trump in Election,

US Says," *The New York Times* echoed the words of a classified Intelligence Community (IC) report: "We now have high confidence that they [the Russians] hacked the DNC and the RNC, and conspicuously released no documents from the Republican organization, one senior administration official said."[159] In mid-December, both NBC News[160] and CNN[161] reported that Putin was involved in the hack, echoing a classified IC report.

One of the most egregious leaks came in January 2017 when information about Steele's dossier was leaked to CNN. As stated in the House report,

> It is important to note that Evan Perez, Jim Sciutto, Jake Tapper, and Carl Bernstein of CNN reported on January 12, 2017, that President-elect Trump was briefed on classified information indicating that the Russians have compromising personal or financial information that the Russians could use against President-elect Trump. The Committee's investigation revealed that President-elect Trump was indeed briefed on the contents of the Steele dossier and when questioned by the Committee, former Director of National Intelligence James Clapper admitted that he confirmed the existence of the dossier to the media.
>
> When initially asked about leaks related to the ICA in July 2017, former DNI Clapper flatly denied "discuss[ing] the dossier [compiled by Steele] or any other intelligence related to Russia hacking of the 2016 election with journalists." Clapper subsequently acknowledged discussing the "dossier with CNN journalist Jake Tapper," and admitted that he might have spoken with other journalists about the same topic. Clapper's discussion with Tapper took place in early January 2017, around the time IC leaders briefed President Obama and President-elect Trump, on "the Christopher Steele

information," a two-page summary of which was "enclosed in"
the highly classified version of the ICA.[162]

This leak, which wrongly legitimized an unverified dossier that had been published by BuzzFeed, sought to further damage Trump before he even stepped into office. That effort has continued throughout his presidency and has infested the special counsel probe.

What Hath the Investigation Wrought?

After more than a year of investigation and ongoing disruption to the presidency and the US political system, the special counsel investigation has failed on several fronts. George Papadopoulos did not turn out to be the traitorous operative many hoped he would be. Instead, he was charged for lying to the FBI with no evidence of collusion. The same is true of Mike Flynn, whose phone conversation with the Russian ambassador ended with a "no there, there." Instead of a grand conspiracy charge, he was indicted for lying to investigators—a lie they said was unintentional. "According to two sources familiar with the meetings," Byron York reported in the *Washington Examiner*, "Comey told lawmakers that the FBI agents who interviewed Flynn did not believe that Flynn had lied to them, or that any inaccuracies in his answers were intentional." Nine months later, however, Flynn admitted to lying. "What happened?" York asked. "[S]ome lawmakers are trying to figure out what occurred between the time Comey told Congress the FBI did not believe Flynn lied and the time, several months later, when Flynn pleaded guilty to just that." This turn of events led many congressional lawmakers to "find the Flynn case troubling, from start to finish."[163] Whatever happened, one thing we know—there was no evidence of collusion.

The same is true with others targeted by investigators—
Carter Page, Donald Trump Jr., and Jared Kushner, all of whom
were painted by the media as villains with deep ties to the
Kremlin. None has faced a single charge. Page, who remained
under surveillance into the summer of 2017 with yet another
FISA warrant, had been interviewed extensively. As reported
in the *Washington Post* based on more leaks from anonymous
sources, FBI agents grilled him for hours:

> *Over a series of five meetings in March, totaling about 10
> hours of questioning, Page repeatedly denied wrongdoing
> when asked about allegations that he may have acted as a kind
> of go-between for Russia and the Trump campaign, according
> to a person familiar with Page's account.*
>
> *The interviews with the FBI are the most extensive known
> questioning of a potential suspect in the probe of possible
> Russian connections to associates of President Trump. The
> questioning of Page came more than a month before the
> Russian investigation was put under the direction of Special
> Counsel Robert S. Mueller III.*[164]

Despite the "frank and open conversations," as Page
described them, the investigation moved no closer to providing
evidence of criminal wrongdoing.

Kushner came under FBI examination because of his
meeting with the Russian ambassador to discuss setting up
back-channel communications between the Trump transition
team and Putin. Kushner's actions, many believed, would surely
be proof-positive that the Trump campaign had been colluding with the Russians. Never mind that setting up these forms
of communication is common. As Trump's national security
advisor H. R. McMaster said in response to the Kushner inquiry,
"We have back-channel communications with a number of

countries. So, generally speaking, about back-channel communications, what that allows you to do is communicate in a
discreet manner."[165] Not only this, but setting up secure channels after supposedly colluding with the Russians throughout
the campaign is nonsensical. If the communications were
already established, Kushner would not need to make such
arrangements after Trump was elected.

As the investigation progressed into the summer of 2017, a
ranking member of the House Intelligence Committee, Democrat Adam Schiff, admitted that the nearly year-old investigation
into collusion hadn't produced "proof you could take to a jury."
But that doesn't mean they should stop investigating, Schiff told
ABC News's Martha Raddatz. "Indeed, it would be negligent
for us not to investigate. If a foreign government…has something that they can hang over the head of our president or our
administration that can influence US policy, it is very much in
our national security interest to know it."[166] Never mind that
there was no evidence that a foreign government had any such
thing. But these were "unique circumstances," so the noncrim-
inal investigation continued, as Mueller added one Democrat
after another to his ever-expanding team of investigators.[167]

On June 14, 2017, Mueller decided to widen the Russia
investigation even further, including an examination of whether
Trump had tried to obstruct justice. If the collusion allegation
didn't work out, this was the fallback. As the *Washington Post*
reported, Mueller's decision to broaden the scope marked "a
major turning point in the nearly year-old FBI investigation,
which until recently focused on Russian meddling during the
presidential campaign and on whether there was any coordination between the Trump campaign and the Kremlin."[168] The
report was, once again, based on leaks:

Five people briefed on the interview requests, speaking on the condition of anonymity because they were not authorized to discuss the matter publicly, said that Daniel Coats, the current director of national intelligence, Mike Rogers, head of the National Security Agency, and Rogers's recently departed deputy, Richard Ledgett, agreed to be interviewed by Mueller's investigators as early as this week. The investigation has been cloaked in secrecy, and it is unclear how many others have been questioned by the FBI.[169]

Obviously, the cloak of secrecy had a lot of holes in it. Trump took to Twitter to deliver his response:

They made up a phony collusion with the Russians story, found zero proof, so now they go for obstruction of justice on the phony story. Nice[170]

Mueller began investigating the possibility of Trump's obstruction of justice based on Comey's firing, but Comey himself admitted Trump didn't order him to stop the investigation, and no other officials could be found to show Trump's purported intention of squelching investigators from "finding the truth." In June, Senator Marco Rubio asked National Intelligence Director Dan Coats if Trump had requested that Coats "influence an ongoing investigation." Coats ominously refused to comment, saying he didn't think it was appropriate to talk about private conversations with the president in an open hearing. "I am willing to come before the committee and tell you what I know and don't know," Coats said. "What I'm not willing to do is to share what I think is confidential information that ought to be protected in an open hearing, and so I'm not prepared to answer your question." However, in a statement issued by the DNI spokesman, Coats said he "has never felt

pressured by the President or anyone else in the Administration
to influence any intelligence matters or ongoing investigations."

NSA director Mike Rogers also declined to answer the
question, but he added, "In the three plus years that I have been
the director of the National Security Agency, to the best of my
recollection I have never been directed to do anything I believe
to be illegal, immoral, unethical or inappropriate." In September, the new FBI director, Christopher Wray, joined others in
confirming that Trump wasn't obstructing justice. "I can say
very confidently that I have not detected any whiff of interference with that investigation."[171]

Yet the media continued to beat this drum, and Mueller
believed he had reason to move forward. He impaneled a grand
jury late in the summer, which normally indicates that criminal charges will be coming down the pike. What are those
crimes? Why hasn't the American public been told that the
counterintelligence investigation is now a criminal inquiry?
Why hasn't Trump been informed of their suspicions regarding an actual crime? No answers have been forthcoming, but
the investigation, based only on "unique circumstances" and no
criminal-law violations, has continued.

From September 2017 until the spring of 2018, Mueller's
team gathered hundreds of thousands of documents; interviewed hundreds of people; spent millions of dollars; and
worked with attorneys in the Southern District of New York
to arrange for the raid of the law offices of Michael Cohen,
Trump's personal attorney, in an unprecedented case of potentially violating client-attorney privilege, yet there is still no
evidence of collusion. An extensive report by the House Permanent Select Committee on Intelligence undercut the special
counsel with its finding that no collusion occurred between the
Trump campaign and Russia. It did, however, find

- *a pattern of Russian attacks on America's European allies;*
- *Russian cyberattacks on US political institutions in 2015–2016 and their use of social media to sow discord;*
- *a lackluster pre-election response to Russian active measures;*
- *concurrence with the intelligence community assessment's judgments, except with respect to Putin's supposed preference for candidate Trump;*
- *how anti-Trump research made its way from Russian sources to the Clinton campaign; and*
- *problematic contacts between senior intelligence community officials and the media.*[172]

The majority investigation came to the following conclusion:

In the course of witness interviews, reviews of document productions, and investigative efforts extending well over a year, the Committee did not find any evidence of collusion, conspiracy, or coordination between the Trump campaign and the Russians. While the Committee found several of the contacts between Trump associates and Russians—or their proxies, including WikiLeaks—were ill-advised, the Committee did not determine that Trump or anyone associated with him assisted Russia's active measures campaign.[173]

The Democrats, however, refused to let go of the narrative, stating in their own report that they "remain committed to continuing the investigation." They accused the committee's majority of having "shattered its commitment by rushing to end its investigation prematurely." The Democrats went on to attack the majority report, casting it as an irresponsible piece of political hackery:[174]

They have engaged in a systematic effort to muddy the waters, and to deflect attention away from the President, most recklessly in their assault on the central pillars of the rule of law. Their report, as with their overall conduct of the investigation, is unworthy of this Committee, the House of Representatives, and most importantly, the American people, who are now left to try to discern what is true and what is not.

The Majority's report reflects a lack of seriousness and interest in pursuing the truth. By refusing to call in key witnesses, by refusing to request pertinent documents, and by refusing to compel and enforce witness cooperation and answers to key questions, the Majority hobbled the Committee's ability to conduct a credible investigation that could inspire public confidence.[175]

The minority report is filled with unjustifiable whining about the Republicans "promoting baseless allegations of wrongdoing by the Obama Administration and our law enforcement agencies." The Democrats maintained, without viable proof and without investigating many of the points we have raised in this book, that "important evidence has been found on the issues of collusion and obstruction." Therefore, they insist, "much work remains on these and other vital lines of inquiry and key unanswered questions."[176]

As the Mueller probe has progressed, these vital lines of inquiry have led to several indictments, including Russian nationals accused of interfering in the election and Russian military officers indicted on charges of hacking the DNC computers. None of these indictments, however, involve collusion. The "unanswered questions" appear to have been answered: Russia meddled in the US presidential election, as they've done in the past, but no evidence can be found of a Russian conspiracy involving the forty-fifth president of the United States.

PART 3

THE REAL STORY

FROM THE CRITICAL STAGES of the 2016 election until now, we have been inundated with the narrative that Russia injected itself into the US electoral process for the sole purpose of electing its "preferred candidate" Donald Trump—a businessman who never had political power to make deals with the Kremlin, a successful capitalist committed to spreading economic freedom throughout the world, and a lifelong champion of American patriotism. Trump's history and experience contradict the Marxist-laced ideology of Russian nationalism espoused by Vladimir Putin, and considering Russia's ideological hatred for everything Trump represents, he doesn't quite have the makings of a Putin puppet.

Hillary Clinton, on the other hand, is a more likely candidate. Her leftist ideology mirrors her mentor's, Saul Alinsky, the radical Marxist organizer who believed, just as Putin does, that "conflict is the route to power." Clinton's "reset" of US-Russia relations worked in the Kremlin's favor, as it weakened the United States and empowered Russia on the world stage. Both the Clintons and Russia fared well financially during and after the Uranium One deal. Shortly after the Russians announced they were acquiring a majority stake in Uranium One, former president Bill Clinton gave a speech in Moscow for five hundred thousand dollars. Before this, as the Russians gained greater control of Uranium One, the company and investors donated millions to the Clinton Foundation.

With cash flowing in her direction from Russia, Clinton approved, along with other Obama administration department heads, the transfer of 20 percent of US uranium to Russian-controlled companies—an agreement that strengthened Russia's quest to become a power player in global energy. According to *The Hill*, between 2010 and 2012, Russia's nuclear energy company, Rosatom, "made more than $10 billion in new uranium sales agreements with US firms during Clinton and Obama's 'reset.'"[1]

Before Clinton gave the Uranium One deal her stamp of approval, the FBI was investigating a Russian plot involving corrupt business dealings in the United States to advance Putin's goal of dominating the global nuclear energy market. An undercover agent in the racketeering investigation testified to Congress that "he [the informant] was told by Russian nuclear executives that Moscow had hired the American lobbying firm APCO Worldwide to influence the Clintons and US policy and that they expected the firm to provide in-kind support for the Clintons' Global Initiative." The informant didn't know the outcome of this supposed arrangement, and APCO has vehemently denied any connection between its work with the Russian business Tenex (Techsnabexsport, a nuclear technology company) and the Clinton Global Initiative (CGI),[2] but the Clinton Foundation hasn't been forthcoming about the amount of support APCO has given to CGI. As reported by John Solomon in the fall of 2017,

> *The [Foundation's disclosure] site, created to detect conflicts of interest for Secretary of State Hillary Clinton because of her family's various charitable efforts, shows APCO gave between $25,000 and $50,000 over the last decade.*
>
> *But according to interviews and internal documents reviewed by The Hill, APCO was much more generous and*

provided hundreds of thousands of dollars in pro-bono services and in-kind contributions to the Clinton Global Initiative (CGI) between 2008 and 2016.[3]

According to an APCO report submitted to the United Nations Global Compact, the company "significantly increased its pro-bono support for CGI" in 2011. This increase happened to come "as APCO was paid $3 million in 2010 and 2011 to work for Rosatom, Russia's state-owned nuclear company," Solomon reports. "Rosatom paid APCO to lobby the State Department and other federal agencies on behalf of its Tenex subsidiary, which sought to increase its commercial uranium sales in the United States."[4] The executive chairwoman of APCO told *The Hill*, "All activities on these two unconnected activities were appropriate, publicly documented from the outset and consistent with regulations and the law. Any assertion otherwise is false, unfounded and a lie."[5]

With a reliable FBI informant reporting that the Russians claimed otherwise, this has only added to the Uranium One controversy—a scandal that has continued to dog the Clintons for years. Of all the deals that might have transpired behind the scenes, we know for a fact that millions of dollars were poured into Clinton coffers from Russia as the United States handed over control of a significant portion of its uranium to Putin. As you can see from Clinton's record, she had the experience, ideology, and political power to benefit the Kremlin, not Trump.

RUSSIAN INTERFERENCE

Russia, however, had only one thing in mind when it interfered in the US presidential election, and it wasn't necessarily to help any one candidate win. Through disruption and chaos, trolls, bots, and agitators, it sought to weaken the United States by casting doubt on the very principles that undergird the American democratic system. As Deputy Attorney General Rod Rosenstein said after months of investigating Russia's meddling, Russian nationals "allegedly conducted what they called information warfare against the United States, with the stated goal of spreading distrust towards the candidates and the political system in general."[6]

In the end, this interference affected both the Trump and Clinton campaigns, creating no clear advantage for either candidate. The actions of foreign nationals were designed to sow discord in the US democratic process by exploiting racial tensions, organizing and infiltrating rallies, and using social media to manipulate perception and spread fake news.

Contrary to statements by many in the media, Russian interference in US elections isn't new. Consider the 1984 election, when the Soviets launched a disinformation campaign casting President Ronald Reagan as the primary threat to world stability. According to a Heritage Foundation report, "The Kremlin rulers have seized every opportunity to worsen US-Soviet relations and increase international tension.... Americans must understand that Moscow is trying to cast their votes for them."[7]

In 2016, Russia was reaching into its old bag of tricks while using new methods and platforms, though this time both candidates were targeted. Even if you believe, as some do, that Russia wanted to damage Clinton in particular, the motivation wasn't to defeat her but to ensure that if she achieved her expected victory, her presidency would be weakened. This would force her to be more apt to bow to Russian interests as she had done in the past.

Despite Russia's history of election meddling and reports from investigators confirming that its purpose was to create chaos and not to elect one favored candidate, the narrative that Trump conspired with the Russians has been maintained both in the media and in an ongoing investigation by Special Counsel Robert Mueller. The probe, just like the counterintelligence investigation before the election, has failed to prove collusion. By continuing to move forward without substantial evidence of a crime, the special counsel investigation has revealed what it has always been: an investigation, not of a crime, but of a person—or as Trump put it in a tweet, "The single greatest witch-hunt in history."[8]

The goal is Trump's removal, whether he committed a crime or not. When the special counsel investigation was initiated, the Justice Department didn't even bother to name any crimes it suspected the Trump team had committed. Special-counsel regulations require that specific crimes are identified in an investigation, but this didn't happen. With this investigation, the Department of Justice is, as Andrew McCarthy bluntly puts it, "not following the normal rules, in which a prosecutor is assigned only after evidence of an actual crime has emerged."[9] The goal is not justice but Trump's removal, either through impeachment or delegitimizing the Trump presidency with an ongoing investigation.

This effort raises the question of why these actors are so determined to remove Trump when there's no legal basis for it. One reason is pure politics. Democrats don't want Barack Obama's policies reversed, and they don't wish Trump's victory to be a repudiation of his presidency. They want Obama's legacy preserved unblemished. As for the Never-Trump Republicans who have been just as resolved to oust Trump as the Democrats, they want the power he took by becoming the unlikely president "of the people" returned to the safekeeping of the establishment class.

There's no question the motivating force in framing Trump was politics, but we believe the timeline of events and criss-crossing web of actors reveal that the effort to sabotage the Trump campaign, and then to cover it up with more investi-gations, was not just sleazy electoral warfare but much more. It was an elaborate scheme driven by four key players: the Clinton campaign; Obama and his administration, with the support of Republicans rooted in the administrative state; the intelligence agencies of both the United States and the United Kingdom; and, to a lesser degree, Ukrainian officials, working alone or with the DNC. These four groups form a complicated web of cross-purposes—different motives, same goal. As an Obama aide said regarding the varied objectives of Russia when inter-fering in the US election, "All these potential motives aren't mutually exclusive."[10]

HILLARY CLINTON AND BARACK OBAMA

Victory, a right owed to a "faithful Democrat" after so many years in public service, is the most obvious motive to topple an opposing candidate's campaign with scandal. But for Hillary Clinton there was much more to it. Scandals of her own eclipsed her years as secretary of state. She was in the midst of an FBI investigation that could have put her behind bars. She needed to win to keep incriminating details related to her suspicious and possibly illegal activities while at the State Department buried. The list is long—her involvement with the transfer of US uranium to Russia; connections to Russian lobby organi-zations through the Democratic lobbying firm, the Podesta Group; millions of dollars transferred to the Clinton Founda-tion from Russian businessmen; and, of course, her use of a nongovernment email server to communicate from Russia. It was imperative that she escape Trump's campaign promise to lock her up. What better way than to transfer her own Russian entanglements to Trump? Any trails that snaked her way would be diverted to the Republican nominee. After all, he had Russian connections of his own. It wouldn't be hard to do.

Clinton's Private Server

The email issue is particularly significant because of the involvement of the former president. Any legal proceedings to hold Clinton accountable, which Trump promised on the campaign trail, would effectively reveal the content of Barack Obama's interactions with the secretary of state on that private email server. This could be potentially problematic for Obama, if not in legal terms, then certainly as a blow to his legacy.

Because of the need for transparency in government, and to protect classified information, all government officials are required to use secured state-issued email servers when working on official business. These servers are protected from hacking by hostile agents so that national security is preserved. Officials are also kept accountable through the use of state email systems, as their communications are accessible to inquiries and investigations when necessary. In 2012, Clinton defied this regulation of government communications by setting up an unsecured private email server, which she used to pass on classified information.

Clinton's private server was unearthed during an investigation into the September 2012 attack on the US diplomatic mission in Benghazi, Libya, which led to the deaths of four Americans. In August 2014, the congressional Benghazi committee requested the State Department turn over thousands of documents about those events. After receiving the reports, they saw that former Secretary of State Clinton had used a private server to handle government business. This discovery later launched an FBI investigation into her mishandling classified materials, which uncovered evidence that Clinton had used this personal email domain to communicate with Obama from Russia on July 1, 2012. According to an FBI report,

> *Secretary Clinton's use of a personal email domain was both known by a large number of people and readily apparent. She also used her personal email extensively while outside the United States, including from the territory of sophisticated adversaries. That use included an email exchange with the President* [emphasis added] *while Secretary Clinton was on the territory of such an adversary. Given that combination of factors, we assess it is possible that hostile actors gained access to Secretary Clinton's personal email account.*[11]

That Obama interacted with Clinton on her private email was confirmed in the inspector general's report in June 2018 on the Clinton email investigation, in which the OIG stated that FBI analysts and a prosecutor told the OIG that "former President Barack Obama was one of the 13 individuals with whom Clinton had direct contact using her clintonemail.com account."[12]

On March 2, 2015, *The New York Times* broke the story on Clinton's email server in an article titled, "Hillary Clinton Used Personal Email Account at State Department, Possibly Breaking Rules." The Obama administration went into "downplay and deny" mode, as Attorney General Loretta Lynch privately told FBI director James Comey to refer to the Clinton probe as a "matter" rather than an investigation. Also at this time, Clinton's campaign manager and former Obama adviser John

Podesta emailed Clinton aide Cheryl Mills, asking if they could withhold information sent between Obama and Clinton because "that's the heart of executive privilege."[13] Later that same month, Clinton wiped her server clean with BleachBit so that, in the words of Representative Trey Gowdy, "even God couldn't read them."[14]

Former White House press secretary Josh Earnest, however, failed to keep information about Obama's use of Clinton's private email out of the public realm. During a press briefing, he let it slip that "the president, as I think many people expected, did over the course of his first several years in office trade emails with his secretary of state."[15] This comment conflicted with Obama's statements that he learned of Clinton's private server "the same time everybody else learned it, through news reports."[16] Not coincidentally, Clinton campaign secretary Josh Schwerin emailed former White House communications director Jennifer Palmieri after Obama made the contradictory comment: "Jen you probably have more on this but it looks like POTUS just said he found out HRC was using her private email when he saw it on the news." The email was forwarded to Cheryl Mills, who forwarded it to Podesta, adding, "We need to clean this up."[17]

More was revealed about Obama's involvement with Clinton's emails in September 2016 when *Politico* reported that Obama had used an alias to communicate (presumably without detection) with Clinton and others, a point also later confirmed in the inspector general's report. The FBI uncovered the email address months before when interviewing Clinton's deputy chief of staff, Huma Abedin, in April. She was shown an email exchange between Clinton and Obama but didn't recognize the address Obama had used. "Once informed that the sender's name is believed to be a pseudonym used by the president," *Politico* reported, "Abedin exclaimed: 'How is this not classified?' Abedin then expressed her amazement at the president's use of a pseudonym and asked if she could have a copy of the email."[18]

Additionally, a draft of Comey's exoneration letter dated June 30, 2016 (five days before publicly absolving Clinton), included a passage referencing the email exchange between Clinton and Obama on July 1, 2012, when she was in Russia. The line "That use included an email exchange with *the President* [emphasis added] while Secretary Clinton was on the territory of such an adversary" was inexplicably removed from Comey's final letter.[19] The content of those emails will never be known by the public because Obama took Podesta's advice in October to use the "confidentiality tradition" to keep the emails secret.

Obama's communication with Clinton over her private nonsecure server (and denying his knowledge of it), however, just scratches the surface of potential wrongdoing. If Clinton were charged in a trial promised by then-candidate Trump, the contents of Obama's emails would take center stage. And with Clinton charged, Obama's executive privilege would have to yield to the demands for evidence in a criminal prosecution.

It doesn't take much imagination to know that the president wanted this scandal to go away. On October 11, 2015, CBS aired an interview with Obama in which he said Clinton's use of a private server was a "mistake," it didn't "pose a national security problem," and it was "not a situation in which America's national security was endangered."[20] Obama set the course of the investigation right there. As John Giacalone, the former executive assistant director of the FBI's National Security Branch, told the Office of

Inspector General in its investigation of the FBI's handling of the Clinton email investigation, "We open up criminal investigations. And you have the President of the United States saying this is just a mistake.... That's a problem, right?" Yes, that's exactly right. Randy Coleman, former assistant director of the FBI's Counterintelligence Division, echoed that sentiment, telling the OIG, "[The FBI had] a group of guys in here, professionals, that are conducting an investigation. And the…President of the United States just came out and said there's no there there." Another official told the OIG, "You're prejudging the results of an investigation before they really even have been started."[21]

In April 2016, in a television interview, Obama continued to insist that Clinton had no intention of threatening national security by mishandling classified emails on her private server:

She would never intentionally put America in any kind of jeopardy. What I also know is that there's classified and then there's classified. There's stuff that is really top secret, and then there's stuff that is being presented to the president, the secretary of state, you may not want going out over the wire.

I continue to believe she has not jeopardized America's national security. There's a carelessness in terms of managing emails that she has owned and she recognizes. But I also think it is important to keep this in perspective.[22]

In June after that statement, Attorney General Lynch had a bizarre meeting with Bill Clinton on a tarmac in Arizona, which led many to suspect that they discussed the FBI's investigation into Clinton's emails. Later, the public learned that FBI investigator Peter Strzok and his mistress, FBI lawyer Lisa Page, exchanged texts at that time in which Strzok said the meeting "looks like hell," to which Page replied, "It's a real profile in courage since she knows no charges will be brought."[23]

And that's just what happened. On July 5, 2016, Comey echoed Obama, stating that Clinton didn't intend any harm, and he exonerated her:

> *Although there is evidence of potential violations of the statutes regarding the handling of classified information, our judgment is that no reasonable prosecutor would bring such a case. Prosecutors necessarily weigh a number of factors before bringing charges. There are obvious considerations, like the strength of the evidence, especially regarding intent. Responsible decisions also consider the context of a person's actions, and how similar situations have been handled in the past.*
>
> *In looking back at our investigations into mishandling or removal of classified information, we cannot find a case that would support bringing criminal charges on these facts. All the cases prosecuted involved some combination of: clearly intentional and willful mishandling of classified information; or vast quantities of materials exposed in such a way as to support an inference of intentional misconduct; or indications of disloyalty to the United States; or efforts to obstruct justice. We do not see those things here.*[24]

The only blip in this case came when, in October 2016, the FBI found emails from Clinton's private server on Anthony Weiner's laptop. Weiner was married to Abedin, and he was being investigated for allegedly sexting an underage girl. In the course of the investigation, the FBI found the Clinton emails, but they waited weeks before notifying Congress. It wasn't until October 28, 2016, that Comey told lawmakers about the emails and reopened the investigation.

This new wrinkle, however, was quickly ironed away when on November 6, right before the presidential election, Comey informed Congress that the newly found emails didn't change his earlier decision to clear Clinton. She still used a private server and mishandled classified information, but, as Comey said, she didn't intend to do it, though intention should have no bearing on improper use of classified materials. Regardless, Comey let her off the hook—again. The only thing he seemed to feel sorry about was possibly swaying the vote by doing his job and reopening the investigation—something he couldn't avoid because too many people in the agency knew about the emails on Weiner's laptop. In May 2017, Comey testified that any chance that his actions impacted the election made him feel "mildly nauseous."

Hiding the truth about Benghazi, Uranium One, and the contents of those emails from Clinton's private server, especially as they apply to Obama, made defeating Trump vital. The Obama administration couldn't just leave the election to chance—Trump had to be kept out of the White House, and the best way to ensure that outcome was to make the Trump-Russia scandal stick. The only problem was no such scandal existed. It had to be invented and orchestrated. The Russians were already interfering in the election, and the Obama administration certainly didn't do anything to stop it. We know this from Susan Rice's inexplicable directive in the summer of 2016 to "stand down" in response to the White House cyber team wanting to investigate Russian interference further.[25] The meddling had to go on because it was perfect fodder to fuel the Trump-Russia collusion narrative, ensuring that under a cloud of Kremlin influence, Trump would never be elected.

Russia and Iran

Obama likely had other reasons to ensure a Clinton win when it came to keeping his legacy stain-free. Of particular concern would have been the details of his nuclear deal with Iran and

Russia's involvement in building Iran's nuclear program. As reported by John Solomon in *The Hill*, the same FBI informant we mentioned previously from the Uranium One case told Congress what the FBI knew about interactions between Russia and Iran during Obama's presidency:

> *A former undercover informant says he provided evidence to the FBI during President Obama's first term that Russia was assisting Iran's nuclear program even as billions in new US business flowed to Moscow's uranium industry.*
>
> *William Douglas Campbell told The Hill his evidence included that Russia was intercepting nonpublic copies of international inspection reports on Tehran's nuclear program and sending equipment, advice and materials to a nuclear facility inside Iran.*[26]

According to Campbell, Russia was concerned that if its activities were known by the United States, its chances of getting US uranium would be at risk. They were exactly right, but the American people didn't find out because their government kept it hidden. As Solomon reports,

> *"The people [in the Russian nuclear industry] I was working with had been briefed by Moscow to keep a very low profile regarding Moscow's work with Tehran," Campbell said in an interview. "Moscow was supplying equipment, nuclear equipment, nuclear services to Iran. And Moscow, specifically the leadership in Moscow, were concerned that it would offset the strategy they had here in the United States if the United States understood the close relationship between Moscow and Tehran."*[27]

Campbell's notes on FBI debriefings reveal that Russia was using the same money laundering schemes between Moscow and Iran as it did between Russians and Americans. Campbell gathered this information while working as an undercover informant inside the Kremlin-controlled nuclear company, Rosatom.[28] When he gave his reports to the FBI, he said he "got no feedback. They took the reports, and the reports, I assume, went to specific people assigned to analyze the reports and that was the last I heard of it."[29] In 2012, the FBI asked Campbell to find out even more about the Russians assisting Iran, giving him a list of questions, but he didn't gather much. Campbell's inquiries came to a halt after the Russians became suspicious. He was fired from Rosatom before he could continue the work.[30]

Regardless, the FBI had enough information to be quite aware of what was going on between Russia and Iran, yet the Obama administration's favorable treatment of Russia and its generosity concerning US uranium continued unabated. The FBI knew about Russian money laundering in America at the time of the Uranium One deal, and the FBI also knew about Russia's involvement in the development of the Iran nuclear program. But they never told the committee approving the Uranium One deal, and they hushed up knowledge of Russia wheeling and dealing with Iran to build up its nuclear capability.

Why would the Obama administration refuse to release this information? Why allow Iran to build up its nuclear program with Russia's help? The reason was likely political—to shift power in the Middle East away from Israel and toward Iran, a move that would be in keeping with Obama's apparent anti-Israeli ideology. In a sense, the Obama administration played a part in the Iranians building their nuclear program through the Russians, as the United States gave over its uranium to the Kremlin. Considering these events, Obama would have had a vested interest in keeping Trump out of the White House—and he would have had plenty of help: the same officials overseeing the Russian corruption investigation later played key roles in probing the Trump-Russia narrative and Clinton's emails.

The FBI director in charge during the Russia corruption investigation when Campbell submitted his intel on the connections between Russia and Iran was Robert Mueller, now special counsel investigating suspected Trump-Russia collusion. Overseeing the Russian corruption investigation at that time was US Attorney Rod Rosenstein, who currently serves as Trump's deputy attorney general and is responsible for keeping the Mueller investigation going. Finally, the assistant FBI director working with Mueller was Andrew McCabe, who later headed the Clinton email probe and then was fired by Trump for leaking information about the investigation to the press and failing to be forthright about it.

The need to protect Obama's legacy from Trump's intrusions or past revelations would have roused the president to do what he could to guarantee a Clinton win. Obama's motives were mostly political, personal, and not unexpected, given his unique place in American history.

BRITISH INTELLIGENCE

Christopher Steele, a former British spy with extensive connections to the British government and contacts in the upper echelons of the Kremlin, compiled a series of memoranda on Trump in the summer of 2016. He was working for the Democratic National Committee and the Clinton campaign to gather opposition research. The "dirty dossier" became a centerpiece in the Trump-Russia narrative, driving an investigation that assumed Steele's work was genuine, or at least they presented it as such for expediency. In truth, the memos were full of lies and unverified allegations from second- and third-hand sources, some of whom were members of the Russian government.

Leaking false information in the midst of a campaign isn't a foreign concept to British spies. With peculiar similarities, it has happened before. In 1924, just four days before the UK election in October, a letter was published in the *Daily Mail* revealing a Russian plot to mobilize British communist sympathizers in the Labour Party. The purpose was to engage in "agitation-propaganda" and to support a treaty between England and the Soviet Union. The letter was embarrassing to the Labour Party and severely lessened its chances of winning the election. The Conservative Party smelled blood in the water.

The alleged author of the letter was Grigory Zinoviev, a Bolshevik revolutionary and president of Communist International, a global organization that advocated for a worldwide communist society. Zinoviev denied writing the letter, pointing out inconsistencies in content and style:

> *The letter of 15th September, 1924, which has been attributed to me, is from the first to the last word, a forgery. Let us take the heading. The organisation of which I am the president never describes itself officially as the "Executive Committee of the Third Communist International"; the official name is "Executive Committee of the Communist International." Equally incorrect is the signature, "The Chairman of the Presidium." The forger has shown himself to be very stupid in his choice of the date. On the 15th of September, 1924, I was taking a holiday in Kislovodsk, and, therefore, could not have signed any official letter.*[31]

Zinoviev said he wasn't surprised the opposing party would use such methods: "Apparently they seriously thought they would be able, at the last minute before the elections, to create confusion in the ranks of those electors who sincerely sympathise with the Treaty between England and the Soviet Union."[32]

In 1999, British historians confirmed the letter was a fake. MI6, at the time, likely knew it was forged, but they used it anyway because it could help stop a political party with policies the intel community opposed. According to researcher Gill Bennett, British intelligence had developed "uneasiness about their prospects under a re-elected Labour government":

> The security and intelligence community at the time consisted of a "very, very incestuous circle, an elite network" who went to school together. Their allegiances, [Bennett] says in her report, "lay firmly in the Conservative camp."
>
> [T]he forged Zinoviev letter was widely circulated, including to senior army officers, to inflict maximum damage on the Labour government.[33]

According to *The Guardian*, "The exact route of the forged letter to the *Daily Mail* will never be known," though an individual who would later become the head of MI6 "admitted sending a copy to the *Mail*." Bennett put MI6 at the "center of the scandal," as its agents leaked a false document and deceived "the Foreign Office by asserting it [knew] who the source was—a deception it used to insist, wrongly, that the Zinoviev letter was genuine."[34]

As with the framing of Trump, the Zinoviev affair comprised a complex web of actors with different motives working toward the same goal—no individual puppet master constructing a plot from beginning to end. "There was no evidence of a conspiracy in what [Bennett] called an 'institutional sense,'" *The Guardian* reports about the Zinoviev letter.[35] To this day, details of the scandal are not fully known. "The story remains incomplete,"

Bennett said. "The Zinoviev Letter remains, as before, a most extraordinary and mysterious business."[36] The same can be said of the Trump-Russia scandal, and adding to the mystery is the role of British intelligence.

During the campaign of 2016, US and UK intelligence communities, as well as Republican war hawks, were genuinely concerned about national security under a Trump presidency. They were determined to preserve the special relationship of intelligence sharing between the two allies, which they believed was specifically threatened by his campaign promise to reinstate torture as an intel-gathering method. As early as November 2015, they knew Trump was a threat. When asked if he would bring back waterboarding, Trump said at the time, "You bet your ass I would. In a heartbeat. I would approve more than that. It works…and if it doesn't work, they deserve it anyway for what they do to us."[37] The British were worried. If the United States instituted torture in the fashion Trump described on the campaign trail, the information-sharing relationship between US and UK intelligence agencies would be dangerously disrupted, if not severed.

The British were particularly sensitive to Trump's proposed policies during the months leading up to the election because they were embroiled in controversy over past entanglements in America's now-defunct waterboarding program. Torture was a hot-button topic in the United Kingdom. "The absolute prohibition of torture is a cardinal principle of international law," *The Guardian* reported, "and the UK has created specific offences that also cover complicity in torture, even when it happens abroad."[38] UK intelligence agencies were under fire in 2016 for being supposedly complicit in waterboarding. "The UK was undoubtedly lured into crossing this most serious of lines in its rush to cooperate with the US and other security partners in the context of the so-called 'war on terror,'" *The Guardian* report-ed.[39] The British, according to Prime Minister David Cameron, were determined "to get to the bottom of what happened," so Britain's reputation "as a country that believes in freedom, fair-ness and human rights" would be cleared of all stain.[40]

Throughout the campaign Trump continued to promise to reinstate torture if he became president, saying in a New Hampshire debate that he'd "bring back a hell of a lot worse than waterboarding."[41] He kept up the rhetoric even after his nomination, and it became a growing concern to anti-torture war hawks, such as Senator John McCain. CIA director John Brennan was so vehemently opposed to torture that he prom-ised never to obey Trump's order, because he valued the sanctity of the intelligence community: "I will not agree to carry out some of these tactics and techniques I've heard bandied about because this institution needs to endure."[42]

In July of 2016, Trevor Timm, an opinion columnist for *The Guardian*, wrote, "Trump's statements [regarding torture] should be yet another reminder of the terrifying powers of the US president, and we should be doing everything we can to curtail that power, rather than expand it."[43] The comments reflected not only the views of the public but the government as well. Before the election, the UK Intelligence and Security Committee of Parliament visited Washington to meet with various US officials when fears about Trump's policies on torture were at its height. According to its official 2016–2017 annual report,

> *We visited Washington in September 2016, meeting the Central Intelligence Agency, National Security Agency, Office of the Director of National Intelligence, the House Permanent Select*

Committee on Intelligence and the Senate Select Committee on Intelligence. We also spoke to various Washington-based staff from the UK Agencies.

The closeness of the relationship between the UK and US agencies—and the value that both sides place upon—it was apparent throughout our visit.

Our visit took place prior to the election of President Trump. Certain views that the President has expressed—particularly prior to his election—have the potential, if they were to become official policy, to pose difficulties for the UK-USA intelligence relationship. These include, inter alia, the potential for a change in the US relationship with Russia and Iran, and a change in policy on the use of torture and cruel, inhuman or degrading treatment.[44]

The committee interviewed members of the UK intelligence community to get their reaction to Trump's campaign rhetoric. Their response was grave:

Asked about statements made by President Trump during the election campaign, MI5 was quite clear: "Whether this signals a likelihood to return to forms of abuse of detainees, I think we spent enough time in this room talking about that for you to know I would be very highly alert to any sort of changes like that. I have communicated internally already about this in MI5, that, you know, whatever happens, MI5 will operate within the law and by our values. So if any of that changes on the US side, there will be a consequence in the relationship but, you know, we will not collude in any sort of change in that sort of behaviour. Of course we won't. But let's not assume that is going to happen in the US."

Any significant change in US policies relating to detainee treatment would pose very serious questions for the UK-USA intelligence relationship. The US agencies are well aware of the implications for cooperation with the UK and other allies, and the UK agencies are monitoring the situation closely. The UK Government must continue to keep a close eye on any changes in US policy and take swift action if there are signs that these might run counter to British laws and values.[45]

Trump's position on torture softened in the weeks after he was elected, prompting Britain's signals intelligence and security organization, Government Communications Headquarters (GCHQ), to breathe a sigh of relief. Their representative told the intelligence committee they didn't think there would be any change in America's policy on torture, but if "something happened which caused us fundamentally to revisit our presumption of legality [of the US agencies' actions], which we have got now, hard won after many years after all the problems we have discussed [on detainee treatment and rendition], then that would be really difficult."[46]

This easing of concerns among the British happened only after Trump was elected and changed his tune, but during the campaign and just after his win, they believed his presidency would severely damage the goodwill between the two countries. They already found him intolerable because of his proposed ban on Muslims (a statement that led to a petition debated in Parliament to keep him out of the United Kingdom), but the reinstatement of torture could be directly disruptive. As BBC News reported,

The UK and US share a language and much cultural heritage, but, argues Tim Oliver, a fellow in European-North American relations at the London School of Economics, the truly "special" quality in their relationship is the sharing of intelligence, as well as co-operation over nuclear weapons and special forces.

Mr. Oliver says there is a risk this could "sour" because of the "degree of distrust and unease" felt by the government towards Mr. Trump, "an erratic president who appears willing to do anything when it comes to torture, bombing, relations with authoritarian states."[47]

Immediately following Trump's historic win, UK-based information security expert and ex-GCHQ specialist Matt Tait told a British newspaper that Trump's position on torture could mean the end of the relationship between GCHQ and the NSA:

Trump's position on torture is a really big deal. Torture of detainees is directly and unambiguously a violation of the internationally accepted laws of armed conflict—even if used against unlawful enemy belligerents, such as terrorists rather than captured prisoners of war. Trump's comments on torture are important and a unique deviation for US policy. Previous administrations, even when they have engaged in "enhanced interrogation techniques" [EITs] such as under George W. Bush—and even when these EITs escalate to the point that they are widely called "torture"—the US has gone to lengths to assert that the EITs it did use didn't amount to "torture"; declassified legal memos show lawyers within the Bush administration trying to define the line where interrogation becomes torture and push EITs right up to, but not over, that line.[48]

Tait argued that Trump didn't care where the lines were and was more than willing to step over them, that the Republican nominee thought torture was okay, not only as a form of information-gathering, but as a method of punishment. This, Tait said, would make it "impossible for UK intelligence cooperation with the Trump administration across a range of intelligence programs." If there's any risk of the United States engaging in any sort of war crimes, Tait explained, the United Kingdom would have to pull back from sharing its intelligence with their ally across the Atlantic.[49]

Open Rights Group executive director Jim Killock expressed his concerns to *The Register*:

> *If the US openly pursues a policy of torturing those suspected of terrorism, it cannot legally be enabled by the sharing of intelligence from the UK.*
>
> *However, given the close integration of the UK and US intelligence agencies, it will be difficult to separate our data sharing and technologies. This presents a huge challenge for oversight, who need to be aware of the possibility that GCHQ might be urged to help with policies that are indefensible.*[50]

The British were also worried about Trump's access to UK intelligence if he were president. This possibility became a pressing concern after Britain passed its Investigatory Powers Act in October 2016, "which legalises a whole range of tools for snooping and hacking by the security services unmatched by any other country in western Europe or even the US."[51] One of the leading opponents of the act in Britain was afraid that if Trump were elected president, he would abuse access to Britain's extensive intelligence data—a worry increased by the belief that Trump was Russia's willing puppet. Trump would have "access to all the data that the British spooks are gathering," warned Liberal Democrat peer Lord Strasburger, "and we should be worried about that."[52]

Ironically the final stages of the expansive Investigative Powers Act were deliberated as British courts ruled that UK intelligence agencies "operated an illegal regime to collect vast amounts of communications data, tracking individual phone and web use and other confidential personal information, without adequate safeguards or supervision for 17 years."[53] That's a lot of private information the United Kingdom would not want to fall into the hands of a powerful US president in a supposed unholy alliance with one of its greatest enemies, Russia.

UKRAINE AND MANAFORT

In July 2017, Trump tweeted, "Ukrainian efforts to sabotage Trump campaign—'quietly working to boost Clinton.' So where is the investigation A.G."[54] The tweet didn't come out of thin air; the president was referring to Ukrainians who bolstered Clinton's campaign by spreading damaging information on his campaign manager, Paul Manafort.

During the months leading up to the election, Ukrainian government officials met with members of the US media and government, their trips managed and funded through a think tank accused of lobbying on behalf of foreign governments. The lobbying efforts were orchestrated by a Ukrainian oligarch, Victor Pinchuk, who was working with a longtime pal of Bill Clinton. Additionally, a Ukrainian-American DNC consultant played matchmaker with US journalists and Ukrainian officials to get the word out on Manafort. Alexandra Chalupa was obsessed with Manafort and his work with the former pro-Russian president, Viktor Yanukovych. She, like many in Ukraine, was worried that Manafort was a Russian agent embedded in the Trump team to exert Putin's control. The minute Manafort was hired, Chalupa went on a crusade to expose him as the Russian troll she believed him to be.

Adrian Karatnycky, a senior fellow at the Atlantic Council and codirector of the Ukraine in Europe Initiative, wrote an impassioned response to Trump's tweet on how Ukrainian involvement in the US election wasn't as bad as the Russians and therefore deserves a pass. "Unlike Russian interference, the Ukrainian government did not hack any e-mail accounts of Trump campaign officials or advisers nor did it promote Hillary Clinton through media it owns or controls," he writes. "All Ukraine stands charged with is discussing the role played by Trump's then campaign chairman Paul Manafort in its own domestic politics."[55]

The argument that "our bad isn't as bad as theirs" doesn't erase the guilt of doing something bad. The fact is, as Karatnycky admits, Ukrainians did inject themselves into the US election, not only by funneling open-source material to the press in a relentless crusade against Manafort, but also by releasing confidential information that helped Clinton. Ukrainian parliamentarian Serhiy Leshchenko leaked documentation that Yanukovych's pro-Russian party earmarked 12 million dollars for Manafort for unknown services. The information might not have come from the Ukrainian president himself—though this is possible—but it was delivered to the American media through a Ukrainian lawmaker. Leshchenko might be at odds with President Petro Poroshenko in Ukraine, as Karatnycky explains in his post, but this doesn't change the fact that a member of the Ukrainian government, among others, sought to disrupt the US election.

Leshchenko told the *Financial Times*: "A Trump presidency would change the pro-Ukrainian agenda in American foreign policy. For me it was important to show not only the corruption aspect, but that he is [a] pro-Russian candidate who can break the geopolitical balance in the world." According to Leshchenko, most of Ukraine's politicians are "on Hillary Clinton's side."[56]

Karatnycky maintains that Russia's actions were worse by comparison because they involved hacking and Putin's controlling hand, orchestrating electoral interference from the top. Ukraine, on the other hand, is divided into factions with no one person controlling all operations—and they're friendly with the United States, unlike Russia. But just because government operatives aren't working in sync and their nation is an ally to the West doesn't make interfering in US elections permissible, no matter how trivial in comparison.

Meddling might not be illegal, but it is unethical, as an outside entity is trying to play a part in a democratic process reserved for American citizens. The Russians were sowing discord and creating chaos in general, but the Ukrainians who interfered in the election favored one candidate over another. This effort by Ukrainians might have been merely a blip in election history if it had been the only interference happening at the time, but it stood alongside other efforts with the same goal, making it significantly more consequential.

The DNC and the Ukrainian government have insisted there was no plot to boost Clinton by going after Trump's campaign manager, but a *Politico* investigation found that Ukrainian officials were involved.[57] The crusade against Manafort and his eventual ousting from the campaign was proof of this.

A defender of Ukraine's interests, Karatnycky's response to *Politico*'s investigation would no doubt be the same as it was to Trump's tweet about Ukrainian interference:

> *The information Leshchenko made public about alleged illegal cash payments to Manafort came from two sources. One was the National Anti-Corruption Bureau of Ukraine (NABU), an office created with US and EU technical assistance, and established as an independent body.*

Moreover, even the original source of information about Manafort did not come from the president's or government's loyalists but was provided by a disaffected former deputy head of Ukraine's Security Service (the SBU). The information this official supplied was deliberately withheld from Poroshenko and the SBU and eventually shared only with NABU, investigative Ukrainian media, and Leshchenko.[58]

But, as an insider in the Ukrainian government told *Politico*, Poroshenko likely knew about it.[59]

Regardless, one thing we do know is a lawmaker from Ukraine strategically inserted information about Manafort into an election. Additionally, DNC operative Alexandra Chalupa met with individuals in the Ukrainian government to gather information that would be damaging to Manafort and by extension Trump. Journalists published that information, fueling the false narrative that the Trump team colluded with the Russians.

A FAILED SCHEME KEEPS GOING

Whether the motivation was CYA mixed with good old-fashioned ambition, safeguarding the political legacy of a historic president, national security and the preservation of a powerful relationship between allies, or a passionate desire to maintain a US foreign policy agenda favorable to a particular country, each of these actors wanted the same thing: they wanted Trump defeated, and they acted to make that happen.

Their efforts failed, but the scheme kept going. The FBI's counterintelligence investigation into Russian interference and Trump collusion eventually morphed into Robert Mueller's special counsel probe whose *raison d'être* appears to be to cover up the real scandal—a scandal hinted at by Trump through more controversial tweets on March 4, 2017:

Terrible! Just found out that Obama had my "wires tapped" in Trump Tower just before the victory. Nothing found. This is McCarthyism![60]

Is it legal for a sitting President to be "wiretapping" a race for president prior to the election?[61]

The very next year, on March 5, 2018, Trump tweeted something similar, no doubt in response to the continued investigation by Mueller into still unproven collusion between Trump and Russia:

Why did the Obama Administration start an investigation into the Trump Campaign (with zero proof of wrongdoing) long before the Election in November? Wanted to discredit so Crooked H would win. Unprecedented. Bigger than Watergate! Plus, Obama did NOTHING about Russian meddling.[62]

Representative Devin Nunes, chairman of the House Intelligence Committee, who released a memo alleging illegality on the part of the FBI during the campaign, echoed this sentiment: "The truth is, the [Democrats] are covering up that Hillary Clinton colluded with the Russians to get dirt on Trump to feed it to the FBI to open up an investigation into the other campaign."[63] According to James Robbins of *USA Today,*

The memo's central indictment is that top Obama administration officials knowingly and willfully used unverified information paid for by the Hillary Clinton campaign, some of which came from Russian intelligence, in a secret court document to justify a counterintelligence investigation of the Trump campaign during the 2016 presidential election. This corrupt process was later the basis for a campaign to sabotage the incoming Trump administration and to fuel a witch hunt against the president.[64]

Very few people in the media believed Trump's "conspiracy theory." In reaction to the "Trump Tower wiretap" tweet, CNN's Don Lemon scoffed, "Everyone in this room is dumber for having listened to that." In a feeble attempt at humor, author Stephen King quipped, "Not only did Obama tap Trump's phones, he stole the strawberry ice cream out of the mess locker." California congressman Ted Lieu spoke directly to Trump: "If there was a wiretap at Trump Tower, that means a fed judge found probable cause of crime, which means you are in deep shit."

Trump had accused the former president's administration of violating our most sacred laws, putting in jeopardy our democratic process, and threatening the privacy rights of American citizens—all for political gain. So momentous was the mere suggestion of criminality that the tweets were either lies created by a delusional mind or the truth. If a lie, our current president is a madman or master manipulator. If the truth, our former president was involved in a scandal that threatens the very foundation of our free republic, and the Department of Justice under his command has diminished its credibility through abuse of power, abandoning the rule of law for the arbitrary rule of political will.

The media and political class chose to believe Donald Trump was a madman. Instead of examining how various players intersected with one another to tell a different story, they stuck with the narrative that a pragmatic businessman from New York colluded with Vladimir Putin and Russian operatives to become president. Reality was much different, involving an intersection of players with different motives and the same goal of sabotaging the Trump campaign and presidency with false accusations, illegal spying, and entrapment. This is the real story, and it's the greatest scandal in American political history.

APPENDIX I

TIMELINE

2012

July 1 – Hillary Clinton improperly uses her unsecured private email server to email President Barack Obama from Russia.

2013

Early November – Donald Trump is in Russia for the 2013 Miss Universe pageant. Trump meets with both Emin and Aras Agalarov, who purchased the licensing rights off Trump for the pageant. It's in a hotel on this trip that the alleged "golden shower" incident described in Christopher Steele's dossier is said to have occurred.

2015

March 4 – John Podesta emails Cheryl Mills and urges Obama to claim executive privilege for his email exchanges with Clinton.

March 7 – Obama claims on television that he learned about the Clinton email scandal from news reports.

Mid-March – Loretta Lynch, in private, directs FBI director James Comey to call the FBI's probe into Clinton's email server a "matter" instead of an "investigation."

Late March – Clinton's emails are wiped with BleachBit so that, in the words of Trey Gowdy, "even God cannot read them."

Late 2015 – DNC contractor Alexandra Chalupa begins investigating Trump's alleged Russia ties.

British intelligence agency GCHQ becomes aware of "suspicious interactions" between figures connected to Trump and suspected Russian agents. They continue passing on information to US intelligence authorities until summer of 2016.

2016

Mid-January – Alexandra Chalupa warns the DNC about Paul Manafort and Russia.

Early March – Fusion GPS approaches Perkins Coie.

March 14 – George Papadopoulos meets Joseph Mifsud (the professor) in Italy.

Mid-March – The NSA's Mike Rogers orders an audit of 702 "About" queries.

The FBI interviews Carter Page about his contacts with Russian intelligence.

March 19 – Alexandra Chalupa begins consulting with the DNC on Trump's alleged ties to Russia.

March 21 – Trump identifies George Papadopoulos as one of his foreign policy advisers.

March 24 – Papadopoulos meets Mifsud in London, accompanied by a woman falsely presented as Vladimir Putin's niece.

March 25 – Democratic operative Alexandra Chalupa meets with top Ukrainian officials in Washington, D.C., with the aim of exposing ties between Trump, his top campaign aide Paul Manafort, and Russia.

March 28 – Trump names Manafort as his campaign convention manager. Manafort leads the effort in getting commitments from convention delegates.

Late March – Chalupa briefs DNC staffers on Russia's alleged ties to Manafort and Trump. According to *Politico*, Ukrainian embassy officials and Chalupa then coordinate "an investigation with the Hillary Team" into Manafort.

Early April – Chalupa begins working with Michael Isikoff, a reporter who would publish information from Christopher Steele's dossier at Yahoo News in September, which he obtained directly from Steele.

April 12 – Marc Elias, a lawyer from Perkins Coie representing the Clinton campaign and DNC, retains Fusion GPS to conduct opposition research on Donald Trump. The FBI later pays Steele for his research. The Clinton campaign and DNC continue to fund Fusion GPS through the end of October.

April 19 – The DNC pays a six-figure expense to Perkins Coie.

April 25 – Obama for America begins paying Perkins Coie. The payment is for "legal services."

April 26 – Papadopoulos meets Mifsud in London again and is promised information on Clinton. Isikoff publishes a story detailing Manafort's business dealings with a Russian oligarch.

Late April – Abnormalities in the DNC's email system are detected.

Early May – Papadopoulos tells Australian diplomat Alexander Downer that the Russians have "dirt" on Hillary Clinton.

Perkins Coie begins payments to Fusion.

June 3 – Donald Trump Jr. receives an email from Rob Goldstone, a publicist for Emin Agalarov. Goldstone wrote in the email that "The Crown prosecutor of Russia met with his [Emin's] father Aras this morning and in their meeting offered to provide the Trump campaign with some official documents and information that would incriminate Clinton and her dealings with Russia and would be very useful to your father. This is obviously very high level and sensitive information but is part of Russia and its government's support for Mr. Trump."

June 7 – Goldstone writes another email to Trump Jr.: "Emin asked that I schedule a meeting with you and the Russian government attorney who is flying over from Moscow for this Thursday."

June 9 – Russian lawyer Veselnitskaya meets with Glenn Simpson early in the day in a Manhattan courtroom. Later, Donald Trump Jr., Paul Manafort, and Jared Kushner meet Veselnitskaya at Trump Tower. Goldstone is also present at the meeting. Veselnitskaya provides none of the information regarding Clinton she claimed she had. This wasn't made public until a year later, when *The New York Times* reported on the meeting on July 8, 2017.

June 10 – Veselnitskaya and Simpson are both present at the same dinner. Simpson denies that the two discussed the Trump Tower meeting, and he would later claim he first learned about it from the media like everyone else.

According to *The Hill*, a number of edits to Comey's letter exonerating Clinton were made "on or around June 10." Among them was a recommendation from FBI agent Peter Strzok, changing language referring to Clinton's behavior as "grossly negligent" in handling classified information. Another significant edit was the changing of "reasonably likely" with regard to the hacking of her emails by hostile actors to "possibly." Comey's earliest draft of the letter dates back to May 2.

June 14 – The *Washington Post* breaks a story that hackers gained access to the DNC's servers.

Mid-June – Fusion GPS hires former MI6 spy Christopher Steele to conduct opposition research into Donald Trump, in what would later become the infamous "dossier."

The US Foreign Intelligence Surveillance Court (FISC) denies a FISA warrant to spy on Trump campaign members because it names Trump specifically.

June 17 – The *Washington Post*'s front-page story links Trump to Russia. The headline reads "Inside Trump's Financial Ties to Russia and His Unusual Flattery of Vladimir Putin."

June 20 – Manafort becomes Trump's campaign manager, following the firing of Corey Lewandowski.

Steele proposes bringing his research with Fusion to the FBI.

June 27 – Bill Clinton and Loretta Lynch have a mysterious "tarmac meeting," which leads many to suspect that it was to discuss the FBI's investigation into Clinton's emails. Strzok later observes in a text dated July 1 that the timing of the meeting "looks like hell," to which his coworker FBI lawyer Lisa Page replied, agreeing that "it's a real profile in courage since she knows no charges will be brought."

June 30 – An internal draft of James Comey's remarks concluding the FBI's Clinton email investigation circulates. Among the comments that didn't make it to the final draft was one referencing a July 1, 2012, email that President Obama had sent to Clinton. "The President" was changed to "another senior government official" before being removed entirely.

Late June/Early July – Peter Strzok meets with Christopher Steele.

July 5 – Comey holds a press conference and reads a statement effectively exonerating Clinton, claiming she didn't "intend" to break the law, although intent is not a component of the relevant crimes.

Early July – Steele meets with FBI. This occurred after a July 4 meeting in which he shared what became the first chapter of the dossier with a "friend" in London.

July 22 – WikiLeaks releases nearly 20,000 of the over 44,000 hacked DNC emails they would end up releasing in total. WikiLeaks founder Julian Assange denies that the origin of the emails is Russian.

July 25 – The FBI confirms their investigation into the DNC hack.

July 29 – The DNC publicly claims that their computer network has also been hacked. Guccifer releases more emails.

The Foreign Intelligence Surveillance Court rejects an FBI request to wiretap Carter Page.

July 31 – The FBI launches a formal counterintelligence investigation regarding Russian interference in the US election.

Late July – The FBI counterintelligence operation begins looking into the Trump campaign.

Alexandra Chalupa leaves the DNC to work full-time on her "research" into Manafort, Trump, and Russia.

August 14 – *The New York Times* reports on cash payments that pro-Russian interest groups in Ukraine made to Paul Manafort a decade prior.

August 15 – Peter Strzok sends a text to Lisa Page about "an insurance policy in the unlikely event you die before you're 40…" referring to an insurance policy in the unlikely event of a Trump presidency. This text, among others, aren't made public until December 2017.

CNN reports that the FBI is conducting an inquiry into Manafort's payments from the aforementioned pro-Russian interests in Ukraine.

August 19 – Manafort resigns as Trump campaign chairman.

Late August – The FBI initiates a new wiretap against now-former Trump campaign manager Paul Manafort. This wiretap extends through early 2017.

September 2 – Lisa Page texts Strzok that "[President Obama] wants to know everything we're doing."

Early September – Christopher Steele becomes an FBI source, with the DOJ's Bruce Ohr as his point of contact. Steele told Ohr, whose wife was also working for Fusion GPS when Steele was, that he was "desperate that Donald Trump not get elected."

Mid-September – Steele meets with his State Department friend Jonathan Winer to discuss the dossier.

Steele flies to Rome to meet with and brief the FBI on his "research."

September 23 – Michael Isikoff publishes a Yahoo News article about Carter Page's trip to Moscow in July 2016, citing Steele's dossier.

September 26 – The Obama administration asks the Foreign Intelligence Surveillance Court (FISC) to allow the National Counterterrorism Center to "access sensitive, unmasked intel" on Americans from the FBI and NSA. The court approves the request.

Late September – Jonathan Winer meets with Clinton ally Sidney Blumenthal to exchange negative information on Trump.

Christopher Steele and Glenn Simpson meet with reporters from *The New York Times*, *The Washington Post*, Yahoo News, *The New Yorker*, CNN, and ABC.

October 3 – The FBI seizes computers belonging to Anthony Weiner, the husband of Clinton aide Huma Abedin.

October 7 – Director of National Intelligence James Clapper issues a statement with the Department of Homeland Security stating that the Russian government is responsible for hacking the DNC's emails as part of their efforts to disrupt the 2016 election.

October 19 – Steele writes his final report for the dossier, and the FBI authorizes payment to him.

October 21 – A FISA request is granted to spy on Carter Page after the Justice Department and FBI applied a second time, thanks to new "evidence" from Steele's dossier and what appeared to be corroborating evidence from a Michael Isikoff article.

October 28 – Comey briefly reopens the Clinton email investigation due to the emails discovered on Anthony Weiner's computer weeks prior. Simpson and Steele begin shopping the dossier to the media afterward.

Late October – Steele breaks with the FBI, citing dissatisfaction with their work. The FBI later says it was they who broke ties with Steele for leaking to the media.

Despite having broken ties with the FBI, Steele reportedly maintains contact with Bruce Ohr.

October 31 – *Mother Jones*'s David Corn is the first to write about the dossier in an article, citing an "unidentified former spy."

November 6 – Comey, for the second time, closes the FBI's investigation into Clinton's private email server.

November 8 – Donald Trump is elected the forty-fifth president of the United States.

November 17 – NSA director Mike Rogers meets Trump in Trump Tower and is criticized for not telling Obama about the meeting first. Trump abruptly announces that his presidential team meetings will no longer be held in Trump Tower and will now be held in Bedminster, New Jersey.

November 18 – Trump leaves Trump Tower to conduct interviews in Bedminster. Against Obama's recommendation, Trump hires Lt. General Michael Flynn as his national security advisor.

November 18–20 – Senator John McCain and his adviser David Kramer attend a security conference in Halifax, Nova Scotia, where they learn about Steele's dossier from former UK ambassador to Russia, Sir Andrew Wood.

December 15 – Obama intelligence officials unmask members of the Trump team and surveil the crown prince of the United Arab Emirates (Sheikh Mohammed bin Zayed al-Nahyan) when he visits Trump Tower. Susan Rice later defended the decision and stated that Steve Bannon, Jared Kushner, and Michael Flynn were "unmasked" during the surveillance.

On the same day, DNI Clapper relaxes the NSA's rules regarding the sharing of raw intelligence data.

December 22 – Flynn asks Russian ambassador Sergey Kislyak if Russia would vote against, or delay voting on, an upcoming UN Security Council resolution vote condemning Israel. Russia ended up voting in favor of the resolution despite Flynn's request.

December 29 – Obama expels thirty-five Russian diplomats from the United States in retaliation for alleged Russian interference in the 2016 election.

On the same day, Kislyak calls Flynn while he's in the Dominican Republic and discusses sanctions in retaliation for Obama's actions. The call is intercepted and recorded by US intelligence officials.

In the phone call with Kislyak, Flynn asks that Russia refrain from retaliating to the US sanctions. Kislyak agrees that Russia would "moderate its response to those sanctions" as a result of his request, according to charges later filed against Flynn by the US special counsel's office. (Flynn's conversation with the Russian ambassador would not become public until next year.)

2017

Early January – The wiretap continues against Trump campaign chair Paul Manafort, which captures his conversations, including the times he spoke with Trump.

Loretta Lynch signs off on the intelligence-sharing rules that DNI Clapper proposed on December 15, easing the difficulty in sharing raw surveillance data within the government.

January 6 – The Office of the Director of National Intelligence releases a declassified intelligence report claiming: "Russian President Vladimir Putin ordered an influence campaign in 2016 aimed at the US presidential election." The report says Russian intelligence services gained access to the Democratic National Committee computer network for nearly a year, from July 2015 to June 2016, and released hacked material to WikiLeaks and other outlets "to help President-elect Trump's election chances."

Comey meets alone with Trump to brief him on the allegations contained in Steele's dossier. Comey later said in a testimony that the purpose of the meeting was "to alert the incoming President to the existence of this material, even though it was salacious and unverified..."

January 10 – The "failing pile of garbage" (Trump's words) BuzzFeed publishes Fusion's dossier. Trump tweets, "FAKE NEWS – A TOTAL POLITICAL WITCH HUNT!"

January 12 – The *Washington Post* breaks the story that Flynn and Kislyak spoke on December 29, the day that the United States announced new sanctions on Russia in response to the cyberattacks during the 2016 presidential election. *Post* columnist David Ignatius correctly identifies the arcane Logan Act as the legal ammunition that was about to be fired at Flynn, and reveals that the two had discussed sanctions (before it was officially confirmed that they had). His source for the story is a "senior US government official."

Obama finalizes Clapper's new data-sharing rules.

The Justice Department's inspector general announces a probe into Comey regarding alleged misconduct during the Clinton email investigation.

The FBI's Carter Page FISA warrant gets its first ninety-day renewal and is signed by Comey and Deputy Attorney General Sally Yates.

January 15 – Mike Pence says, regarding Flynn's call with Russian ambassador Kislyak, that the two did not discuss US sanctions on Russia.

January 20 – Trump is inaugurated. Less than thirty minutes after he's sworn in, Susan Rice sends an email to herself regarding the Obama administration's inquiry into Russian interference in the US election. She writes, "President Obama began the conversation by stressing his continued commitment to ensuring that every aspect of this issue is handled by the Intelligence and law enforcement communities 'by the book.' The president stressed that he is not asking about, initiating or instructing anything from a law enforcement perspective. He reiterated that our law enforcement team needs to proceed as it normally would by the book."

Senator Lindsey Graham flagged the email as "odd and disturbing."

January 22 – Flynn is sworn in as National Security Advisor, and *The Wall Street Journal* reports that US counterintelligence agents have been investigating Flynn's communications with Russian officials.

January 23 – GCHQ head Robert Hannigan, who took over in 2014, abruptly resigns, citing "personal" reasons. CNN would later report on April 14 that British intelligence had "passed Trump associates' communications with Russians on to US counterparts."

January 24 – Sally Yates becomes acting attorney general and sends Peter Strzok and another FBI agent to the White House to question Flynn. Comey would reportedly tell members of Congress in private that those agents didn't believe Flynn lied during questioning.

January 27 – The FBI interviews George Papadopoulos.

Late January – Perkins Coie denies paying for the dossier. The nonpartisan Campaign Legal Center later announces in October 2017 that Hillary for America (her presidential campaign) and the DNC had failed to disclose legally required information about the funding of the dossier.

February 8 – Jeff Sessions becomes the attorney general.

February 9 – The *Washington Post* publicly reports that Flynn and Kislyak "privately discussed US sanctions against Russia with that country's ambassador to the United States during the month before President Trump took office, contrary to public assertions by Trump officials."

February 13 – The *Washington Post* reports that the DOJ opened an investigation into Flynn about a potential Logan Act violation.

February 14 – Mike Flynn resigns.

February 16 – Trump is asked "Did you direct Mike Flynn to discuss the sanctions with the Russian ambassador?" at a press conference. Trump denies the allegation.

Papadopoulos is interviewed a second time by the FBI.

March 4 – Trump fires off several tweets accusing Obama of wiretapping Trump Tower and "tapping my phones in October" during the "very sacred election process."

March 20 – Comey confirms the existence of an FBI counterintelligence investigation at a hearing of the House Intelligence Committee. He specifies that the FBI is investigating "the Russian government's efforts to interfere in the 2016 presidential election and that includes investigating the nature of any links between individuals associated with the Trump campaign and the Russian government and whether there was any coordination between the campaign and Russia's efforts."

March 22 – Representative Devin Nunes, chairman of the House Intelligence Committee, holds a press conference to announce that he had reviewed intelligence reports that show "incidental collection" on some unnamed Trump transition team members had occurred after the election. Nunes says that he believes this information raises further red flags about the intelligence community improperly unmasking US citizens.

Susan Rice later says in a PBS interview regarding Nunes claims, "I know nothing about this…I really don't know to what Chairman Nunes was referring."

March 24 – Fusion declines Senator Chuck Grassley's document requests and refuses to answer his questions about potential ties to Russia. Grassley sends Simpson a letter challenging him for not turning over the documents requested.

March 31 – Grassley requests documents from Fusion GPS again and alleges that they've acted as an agent for Russia without properly registering as a foreign agent.

Early April – A second wiretap on Carter Page is approved.

April 3 – Various news agencies report that Susan Rice has requested and reviewed "unmasked intelligence" on Trump associates.

May 3 – Comey says at a Senate Judiciary Committee hearing that the FBI had opened investigations on more than one "US persons" in connection with their investigation into whether the Trump campaign colluded with Russia in the 2016 election. He declines to answer if Trump is under investigation, adding, "I'm not going to comment on anyone in particular, because that puts me down a slope of—because if I say no to that, then I have to answer succeeding questions. So what we've done is brief the chair and ranking on who the US persons are that we've opened investigations on. And that's—that's as far as we're going to go, at this point."

May 5 – Fox News reports that Comey considered the anti-Trump dossier so important that it be included in January's final intelligence report on Russian influence in the 2016 election. Comey previously called parts of the dossier "salacious and unverified."

May 8 – Deputy Attorney General Rod Rosenstein learns that Trump intends to fire Comey. Rosenstein later would tell Congress, "On May 8, I learned that President Trump intended to remove Director Comey and sought my advice and input. Notwithstanding my personal affection for Director Comey, I thought it was appropriate to seek a new leader." Rosenstein then set out to write a memo outlining his concerns about Comey's leadership.

May 9 – Trump fires Comey. A White House statement says that Trump acted "based on the clear recommendations" of Attorney General Jeff Sessions and Deputy Attorney General Rod Rosenstein. In a memo, Rosenstein cites Comey's handling of the FBI's investigation into Hillary Clinton's private email server.

Andrew McCabe becomes acting FBI director.

May 11 – Trump says in an interview with NBC's Lester Holt that he was thinking of "this Russia thing" when he decided to fire Comey but that he would've fired him without the recommendation regardless. "He made a recommendation, but regardless of [the] recommendation I was going to fire Comey, knowing there was no good time to do it. And, in fact, when I decided to just do it, I said to myself, I said, 'You know, this Russia thing with Trump and Russia is a made-up story. It's an excuse by the Democrats for having lost an election that they should have won.'"

May 17 – Rosenstein appoints former FBI director Robert S. Mueller as special counsel to investigate any possible collusion between the Trump campaign and the Russian government's efforts to influence the 2016 presidential election. This is where the gap in Strzok and Page's missing text messages ends.

May 19 – Strzok sends a text to Page in which he debates whether he should join Mueller's team. "You and I both know the odds are nothing. If I thought it was likely, I'd be there no question," he says in regard to evidence of Russian collusion with the Trump campaign.

In it, he writes that he had "nine one-on-one conversations with President Trump in four months—three in person and six on the phone." He confirms that on three occasions he told Trump he was not personally under investigation.

June 7 – Comey submits written testimony to the Senate Intelligence Committee in advance of his appearance the next day.

June 8 – Comey testifies under oath before the Senate Intelligence Committee. Comey admits that he gave a copy of a memo about his meeting with the president on February 14 to a friend, with instructions that he share the contents of the memo with a reporter. He says he did so "because I thought that might prompt the appointment of a special counsel."

June 14 – The *Washington Post* reports that Mueller has widened his inquiry to include "an examination of whether President Trump attempted to obstruct justice."

June 15 – Trump tweets: "They made up a phony collusion with the Russians story, found zero proof, so now they go for obstruction of justice on the phony story. Nice."

June 29 – The FBI renews their wiretap of Carter Page for the third and final time, which lasts through September 2017. McCabe and Rosenstein sign the warrant renewal.

July 8 – *The New York Times* breaks the story of Trump Jr. agreeing to a June 9, 2016, meeting with Russian lawyer Natalia Veselnitskaya at Trump Tower.

July 9 – Trump Jr. says of Veselnitskaya, "the woman stated that she had information that individuals connected to Russia were funding the Democratic National Committee and supporting Clinton. Her statements were vague, ambiguous and made no sense. No details or supporting information was provided or even offered. It quickly became clear that she had no meaningful information."

July 11 – Trump Jr. tweets out all his emails about the meeting with Veselnitskaya.

July 14 – Alexandra Chalupa denies working with the Ukrainians to undermine Trump.

July 26 – The FBI raids the Virginia home of Paul Manafort, Trump's former campaign chairman.

July 27 – Papadopoulos is arrested at Dulles International Airport on charges that he lied to FBI agents.

Devin Nunes sends a letter to DNI Dan Coates alleging "hundreds of unmasking requests" made under suspicious circumstances during the Obama administration.

Bill Browder testifies before the Senate Judiciary Committee that Natalia Veselnitskaya "is definitely working for the Russians. No question about it."

August 2 – Christopher Wray is named FBI director.

August 16 – Peter Strzok is removed from the Mueller probe.

August 22 – Glenn Simpson testifies before the Senate Judiciary Committee. It's in this testimony (not released until January 2018) that Simpson speaks of a "source within the Trump administration," later identified as the Papadopoulos/ Downer relationship. He says this before the meetings between Papadopoulos and Downer were made public.

September 13 – Susan Rice reveals during questioning from Congress that she requested to see protected identities of Trump transition members that were "incidentally" captured by "unrelated" surveillance.

September 19 – CNN reports that federal investigators "wiretapped former Trump campaign chairman Paul Manafort under secret court orders before and after the election," citing unnamed sources. According to CNN, the FBI obtained two warrants to conduct surveillance of Manafort through a FISA court. The first warrant was issued in 2014 and expired before Manafort joined Trump's campaign, but it's unclear when the second was issued.

Late September – The FBI surveillance of Carter Page ends.

October 5 – Papadopoulos pleads guilty to lying to FBI agents. His guilty plea is not made public until October 30.

October 17 – Former Obama UN ambassador Samantha Power tells congressional investigators that the hundreds of "unmasking" requests made in her name during the election were not made by her.

October 24 – *The New York Times* reports that the Clinton campaign and the DNC financed research that led to Steele and Fusion's anti-Trump dossier.

October 29 – *The Federalist* breaks the news that, since April 2016, Obama for America had paid over 972,000 dollars to Perkins Coie, which was funding Fusion's research. All payments were classified as "legal payments."

October 30 – Mueller charges Manafort and Rick Gates with tax and money laundering crimes. The charges are not related to Trump.

November 2 – Carter Page testifies under oath to the House Intelligence Committee that he has never met with the Russian officials described in Steele's dossier.

December 1 – Flynn pleads guilty to making false statements to the FBI. He says in a statement, "my guilty plea and agreement to cooperate with the Special Counsel's Office reflect a decision I made in the best interests of my family and of our country."

December 4 – CNN reports that Strzok was removed from Mueller's investigation over his anti-Trump text messages.

2018

January 3 – Paul Manafort files a lawsuit against the DOJ that asks the court to set aside the criminal charges brought against him by the special counsel. He alleges that Mueller's investigation "is completely unmoored from the Special Counsel's original jurisdiction to investigate 'any links and/or coordination between the Russian government and individuals associated with the campaign of President Donald Trump.'" The charges brought against Manafort stem from "unrelated, decade-old business dealings" that had "no connection whatsoever to the 2016 presidential election or even to Donald Trump," the suit states.

January 4 – Senators Chuck Grassley and Lindsey Graham refer criminal charges against Christopher Steele to the FBI for investigation.

January 9 – Senator Dianne Feinstein bypasses Chuck Grassley and releases Glenn Simpson's Senate Judiciary Committee testimony.

January 19 – A letter from the Justice Department to the Senate Homeland Security and Government Affairs Committee admits that the FBI "failed to preserve" five months of text messages belonging to Peter Strzok, from the dates December 24, 2016, to May 17, 2017. The FBI blames a technical glitch. Nearly four hundred pages of new texts between Strzok and Page were turned over by the DOJ to Congress.

January 25 – The DOJ's inspector general Michael Horowitz says his office "succeeded in using forensic tools to recover text messages from FBI devices, including text messages between Mr. Strzok and Ms. Page that were sent or received between December 14, 2016, and May 17, 2017."

January 29 – McCabe steps down as deputy FBI director.

January 30 – It is reported that the Justice Department inspector general is inquiring into why McCabe appears to have waited three weeks before acting on new Clinton emails found on Anthony Weiner's laptop that were discovered before the election. The inspector general's report later revealed that it was delayed to prioritize the Trump-Russia investigation.

February 2 – The "Nunes Memo" is released, confirming that the Steele dossier was used to establish probable cause to justify surveillance of Carter Page, and that the FBI also relied on a Michael Isikoff report that "corroborated" the dossier, even though Isikoff's source was Steele, the author of the dossier. The memo also addresses the Fusion back channel through Bruce Ohr and the DOJ.

February 24 – House Intelligence Committee Democrats release their own "rebuttal memo."

March 12 – The House Intelligence Committee concludes their probe into Russian collusion, finding evidence of attempted Russian interference, but no evidence of collusion between the Trump campaign and the Russians.

March 28 – The DOJ inspector general launches an investigation into the FBI and DOJ over potential abuses of the FISA system, including the wiretapping of Carter Page.

April 27 – The House Intelligence Committee's Republicans and Democrats release separate final reports, with Republicans finding no evidence of collusion and Democrats arguing that a case exists.

Peter Strzok and Lisa Page's "missing" text messages are leaked to the press after being delivered to congressional investigators the day prior.

May 19 – Stefan Halper is outed as the FBI's "inside source" within the Trump campaign.

June 14 – The inspector general report is published, showing bias at the FBI, media leaks, and insubordination by Comey, concluding that political bias did not impact the Clinton investigation, though the OIG could not say the same about the Russia investigation, which was not in its purview. A text exchange between Page and Strzok that was erased from the submission of texts to Congress reveals bias against Trump. "[Trump's] never going to become president, right?" Page asks Strzok on August 9, 2016. "No. No he's not. We'll stop it," Strzok replied.

July 13 – Deputy Attorney General Rod Rosenstein announces the indictment of 12 Russian military intelligence officers on charges they hacked the DNC computers to interfere with the 2016 election. This is the first time Special Counsel Robert Mueller targets the Russian government. The Russian officers "covertly monitored the computers, implanted hundreds of files containing malicious computer code, and stole emails and other documents," Rosenstein says. "The goal of the conspirators was to have an impact on the election." No evidence of collusion with the Trump campaign is found.

APPENDIX II

MEDIA LEAKS

Date of Publication	Headline	Publication/Source	Byline
5/25/17	Jared Kushner now a focus in Russia investigation	*The Washington Post*	Matt Zapotosky, Sari Horwitz, Devlin Barrett, and Adam Entous
5/24/17	How a dubious Russian document influenced the FBI's handling of the Clinton probe	*The Washington Post*	Karoun Demirjian and Devlin Barrett
5/24/17	Found at the Scene in Manchester: Shrapnel, a Backpack and a Battery	*The New York Times*	C.J. Chivers
5/24/17	Top Russian Officials Discussed How to Influence Trump Aides Last Summer	*The New York Times*	Matthew Rosenberg, Adam Goldman, and Matt Apuzzo

Date of Publication	Headline	Publication/Source	Byline
5/23/17	Trump asked DNI, NSA to deny evidence of Russia collusion	CNN	Jim Sciutto, Stephen Collinson, and Eli Watkins
5/22/17	Mueller briefed on secret Comey memos, source says	CNN	Pamela Brown and Shimon Prokupecz
5/22/17	Trump asked intelligence chiefs to push back against FBI collusion probe after Comey revealed its existence	*The Washington Post*	Adam Entous and Ellen Nakashima
5/20/17	As Trump prepared for Riyadh visit, Saudis blocked U.S. on terrorist sanctions	*The Washington Post*	Joby Warrick
5/20/17	Killing C.I.A. Informants, China Crippled U.S. Spying Operations	*The New York Times*	Mark Mazzetti, Adam Goldman, Michael S. Schmidt and Matt Apuzzo
5/20/17	Russia Probe Looking at Official in Trump White House	NBC News	Andrew Rafferty, Pete Williams, and Ken Dilanian
5/20/17	Comey now believes Trump was trying to influence him, source says	CNN	Pamela Brown, Gloria Borger, and Eric Lichtblau
5/19/17	Russia probe reaches current White House official, people familiar with the case say	*The Washington Post*	Devlin Barrett and Matt Zapotosky
5/19/17	White House looking at ethics rule to weaken special investigation: sources	Reuters	Julia Edwards Ainsley

Date of Publication	Headline	Publication/Source	Byline
5/19/17	Trump Told Russians That Firing 'Nut Job' Comey Eased Pressure from Investigation	*The New York Times*	Matt Apuzzo, Maggie Haberman, and Matthew Rosenberg
5/19/17	Russians officials bragged they could use Flynn to influence Trump, sources say	CNN	Gloria Borger, Pamela Brown, Jim Sciutto, Marshall Cohen, and Eric Lichtblau
5/19/17	Israeli Intelligence Furious Over Trump's Loose Lips	Foreign Policy	Kavitha Surana, Dan De Luce, Robbie Gramer
5/19/17	Sources: White House lawyers research impeachment	CNN	Evan Perez
5/18/17	Trump Team Planning Possible Retaliation for Classified Leak Allegations	Foreign Policy	Jenna McLaughlin
5/18/17	Trump campaign had at least 18 undisclosed contacts with Russians: sources	Reuters	Ned Parker, Jonathan Landay and Warren Strobel
5/18/17	Comey, Unsettled by Trump, Is Said to Have Wanted Him Kept at a Distance	*The New York Times*	Michael S. Schmidt
5/18/17	Trump Transition Said to Know of Flynn Inquiry before Hiring	*The New York Times*	Matthew Rosenberg and Mark Mazzetti
5/17/17	Comey Wrote Memo Saying Trump Urged Him to Drop Flynn Investigation: Sources	NBC News	Ken Dilanian, Dafna Linzer, Alex Johnson and Peter Alexander

Date of Publication	Headline	Publication/Source	Byline
5/17/17	Besieged White House denies, defends as new bombshells hit	Associated Press	Eric Tucker, Catherine Lucey, and Julie Pace
5/17/17	NSA feared its hacking tool would get out. Then it did.	*The Washington Post*	Ellen Nakashima and Craig Timberg
5/17/17	National security officials put Trump's name in their briefings as much as possible so he will keep reading	Reuters	Steve Holland and Jeff Mason
5/17/17	House minority leader to colleagues in 2016: 'I think Putin pays' Trump	*The Washington Post*	Adam Entous
5/17/17	Trump Has to Decide: 50,000 Troops to Afghanistan?	Bloomberg	Eli Lake
5/17/17	Trump Team Knew Flynn Was Under Investigation Before He Came to White House	*The New York Times*	Matthew Rosenberg and Mark Mazzetti
5/17/17	Memo: Trump asked Comey to end Flynn investigation	CNN	Pamela Brown, Jake Tapper, and Stephen Collinson
5/17/17	Flynn never spoke to Trump about ending investigations, sources close to former adviser say	Fox News	Catherine Herridge

Date of Publication	Headline	Publication/Source	Byline
5/16/17	Sources: Trump shared classified info with Russians	CNN	Dan Merica, Jake Tapper, and Jim Sciutto
5/16/17	Trump's disclosure endangered spy placed inside ISIS by Israel, officials say	ABC News	Brian Ross, James Gordon Meek, and Randy Kreider
5/16/17	Trump Officials on Comey Memo: 'Don't See How Trump Isn't Completely F*cked'	*The Daily Beast*	Lachlan Markay, Asawin Suebsaeng, and Jana Winter
5/16/17	Intelligence Trump shared with Russians came from Israel	CBS News	N/A
5/16/17	U.S. officials 'warned Israel' not to share sensitive intel with Trump administration	*Newsweek*	Jack Moore
5/16/17	Notes made by FBI Director Comey say Trump pressured him to end Flynn probe	*The Washington Post*	Devlin Barrett, Ellen Nakashima, and Matt Zapotosky
5/16/17	Comey Memo Says Trump Asked Him to End Flynn Investigation	*The New York Times*	Michael S. Schmidt
5/16/17	Israel Was Source of Intelligence Trump Shared With Russia: Sources	NBC News	Dafna Linzer and Ken Dilanian
5/16/17	Israel Said to Be Source of Secret Intelligence Trump Gave to Russians	*The New York Times*	Adam Goldman, Eric Schmitt, and Peter Baker

Date of Publication	Headline	Publication/Source	Byline
5/15/17	Trump Revealed Highly Classified Information To Russians During White House Visit	*BuzzFeed News*	Jim Dalrymple II and Jason Leopold
5/15/17	Top US officials warn Trump against moving US embassy to Jerusalem	CNN	Jeremy Diamond and Elise Labott
5/15/17	Trump Revealed Highly Classified Intelligence to Russia, in Break With Ally, Officials Say	*The New York Times*	Matthew Rosenberg and Eric Schmitt
5/15/17	Trump revealed highly classified information to Russian foreign minister and ambassador	*The Washington Post*	Greg Miller and Greg Jaffe
5/12/17	Former Trump Adviser Paul Manafort's Bank Records Sought in Probe	*The Wall Street Journal*	Michael Rothfield, Mark Maremont and Rebecca Davis O'Brien
5/12/17	Cyber operation targeting ISIS divided Obama officials	*The Washington Post*	Ellen Nakashima
5/11/17	In a Private Dinner, Trump Demanded Loyalty. Comey Demurred.	*The New York Times*	Michael S. Schmidt
5/11/17	Before the ax, Comey was pushing Trump-Russia probe harder	*The Associated Press*	Julie Pace

Date of Publication	Headline	Publication/Source	Byline
5/10/17	Michael Flynn targeted by grand jury subpoenas, sources confirm	CBS News	N/A
5/10/17	Grand jury subpoenas issued in FBI's Russia investigation	CNN	Evan Perez, Shimon Prokupecz, and Pamela Brown
5/9/17	Trump Advisers Call for More Troops to Break Deadlock in Afghan War	*The New York Times*	Michael R. Gordon
5/8/17	U.S. poised to expand military effort against Taliban in Afghanistan	*The Washington Post*	Missy Ryan and Greg Jaffe
5/8/17	Obama Warned Trump Against Hiring Mike Flynn, say Officials	NBC News	Kristen Welker, Peter Alexander, Dafna Linzer and Ken Dilanian
5/1/17	Making Afghanistan Great Again	Bloomberg	Eli Lake
4/21/17	Putin-linked think tank drew up plan to sway 2016 US election	Reuters	Ned Parker, Jonathan Landay and John Walcott
4/21/17	Justice Dept. is Weighing Prosecution of Assange	*The New York Times*	Adam Goldman
4/21/17	Russia tried to use Trump advisers to infiltrate campaign	CNN	Pamela Brown, Shimon Prokupecz, Jim Sciutto and Marshall Cohen

Date of Publication	Headline	Publication/Source	Byline
4/20/17	Justice Dept. debating charges against WikiLeaks members in revelations of diplomatic, CIA materials	*The Washington Post*	Matt Zapotosky and Ellen Nakashima
4/19/17	Exxon Seeks U.S. Waiver to Resume Russia Oil Venture	*The Wall Street Journal*	Jay Solomon and Bradley Olson
4/19/17	Trump Adviser's Visit to Moscow Got the F.B.I.'s Attention	*The New York Times*	Scott Shane, Mark Mazzetti and Adam Goldman
4/18/17	FBI used dossier allegations to bolster Trump-Russia investigation	CNN	Evan Perez, Shimon Prokupecz and Manu Raju
4/16/17	Trump Is Willing to Consider a Sudden Strike on North Korea	Bloomberg	Jennifer Jacobs and Michelle Jamrisko
4/12/17	Court Approved Wiretap on Trump Campaign Aide over Russia Ties	*The New York Times*	Matthew Rosenberg and Matt Apuzzo
4/11/17	FBI obtained FISA warrant to monitor Trump adviser Carter Page	*The Washington Post*	Ellen Nakashima, Devlin Barrett and Adam Entous
4/7/17	C.I.A. Tracked Russian Prying in the Summer	*The New York Times*	Eric Lichtblau
4/6/17	Trump considering military action in Syria in retaliation for chemical attack	CNN	N/A

Date of Publication	Headline	Publication/Source	Byline
4/6/17	Trump considering military strike on Syria in response to poison gas attack	*Los Angeles Times*	W.J. Hennigan
4/6/17	Kushner Omitted Meeting with Russians on Security Clearance Forums	*The New York Times*	Jo Becker and Matthew Rosenberg
4/5/17	Trump Giving Military New Freedom, But With That Comes Danger	*The New York Times*	Helene Cooper
4/3/17	Top Obama Adviser Sought Names of Trump Associates in Intel	Bloomberg	Eli Lake
4/3/17	Susan Rice requested to unmask names of Trump transition officials, sources say	Fox News	Adam Housley
4/1/17	U.S. increasingly sees Iran's hand in the arming of Bahraini militants	*The Washington Post*	Souad Mekhennet and Joby Warrick
3/30/17	2 White House Officials Helped Give Nunes Intelligence Reports	*The New York Times*	Matthew Rosenberg, Maggie Haberman and Adam Goldman
3/30/17	Mike Flynn Offers to Testify in Exchange for Immunity	*The Wall Street Journal*	Shane Harris, Carol E. Lee and Julian E. Barnes
3/30/17	Three White House officials tied to files shared with House intelligence chairman	*The Washington Post*	Greg Miller and Karen DeYoung

Date of Publication	Headline	Publication/Source	Byline
3/28/17	Trump administration sought to block Sally Yates from testifying to Congress on Russia	*The Washington Post*	Devlin Barrett and Adam Entous
3/23/17	U.S. Officials: Info suggests Trump associates may have coordinated with Russians	CNN	Pamela Brown, Evan Perez, Shimon Prokupecz, and Jim Sciutto
3/22/17	Before Trump job, Manafort worked to aid Putin	*The Associated Press*	Jeff Horwitz and Chad Day
3/16/17	Internal Trump administration data undercuts travel ban	*The Washington Post*	Devlin Barrett, Abigail Hauslohner and David Nakamura
3/14/17	Trump wants to relax rules governing drone strikes	*The Washington Post*	Greg Jaffe and Karen DeYoung
3/12/17	Trump Administration Is Said to Be Working to Loosen Counterterrorism Rules	*The New York Times*	Charlie Savage and Eric Schmitt
3/10/17	FBI investigation continues into 'odd' computer link between Russian bank and Trump organization	CNN	Pamela Brown and Jose Pagliery
3/5/17	Comey Asks Justice Dept. to Reject Trump's Wiretapping claim	*The New York Times*	Michael S. Schmidt and Michael D. Shear

Date of Publication	Headline	Publication/Source	Byline
3/5/17	Comey Asks Justice Department to publicly reject Trump's wiretap claim	*Los Angeles Times*	Laura King and Del Quentin Wilber
3/4/17	More Trump advisers disclose meetings with Russia's ambassador	CNN	Sara Murray, Jim Acosta and Theodore Schleifer
3/2/17	White House staff told to preserve Russia-related materials	*The Associated Press*	Julie Pace and Vivian Salama
3/2/17	Chaotic Yemen raid still reverberates for president	*The Washington Post*	Missy Ryan and Thomas Gibbons-Neff
3/2/17	Investigations Probed Jeff Sessions' Contacts with Russian Officials	*The Wall Street Journal*	Carol E. Lee, Christopher S. Stewart, Rob Barry and Shane Harris
3/2/17	Top Trump Advisers Are Split on Paris Agreement on Climate Change	*The New York Times*	Coral Davenport
3/1/17	Sessions met with Russian envoy twice last year, encounters he later did not disclose	*The Washington Post*	Adam Entous, Ellen Nakashima and Greg Miller
3/1/17	Obama Administration Rushed to Preserve Intelligence of Russian Election Hacking	*The New York Times*	Matthew Rosenberg, Adam Goldman and Michael S. Schmidt

Date of Publication	Headline	Publication/Source	Byline
2/28/17	FBI once planned to pay former British spy who authored controversial Trump dossier	*The Washington Post*	Tom Hamburger and Rosalind S. Helderman
2/24/17	DHS report casts doubt on need for Trump travel ban	*The Washington Post*	Matt Zapotosky
2/24/17	State Department writes anti-leak memo, which promptly leaks	*The Washington Post*	Josh Rogin
2/24/17	Trump administration sought to enlist intelligence officials, key lawmakers to counter Russia stories	*The Washington Post*	Greg Miller and Adam Entous
2/24/17	FBI refused White House request to knock down recent Trump-Russia stories	CNN	Jim Sciutto, Evan Perez, Shimon Prokupecz, Manu Raju, and Pamela Brown
2/16/17	Flynn in FBI interview denied discussing sanctions with Russian ambassador	*The Washington Post*	Sari Horwitz and Adam Entous
2/16/17	Spies Keep Intelligence from Donald Trump on Leak Concerns	*The Wall Street Journal*	Shane Harris and Carol E. Lee
2/16/17	Classified Memo Tells Intelligence Analysts to Keep Trump's Daily Brief Short	*Mother Jones*	Ashley Dejean

Date of Publication	Headline	Publication/Source	Byline
2/15/17	Trump aides were in constant touch with senior Russian officials during campaign	CNN	Pamela Brown, Jim Sciutto and Evan Perez
2/14/17	Trump Campaign Aides Had Repeated Contacts with Russian Intelligence	*The New York Times*	Michael S. Schmidt and Matt Apuzzo
2/14/17	Flynn's Downfall Sprang From 'Eroding Level of Trust'	*The New York Times*	Peter Baker, Glenn Thrush, Maggie Haberman, Adam Goldman and Julie Hirschfeld Davis
2/13/17	Michael Flynn Resigns as National Security Adviser	*The New York Times*	Maggie Haberman, Matthew Rosenberg, Matt Apuzzo and Glenn Thrush
2/13/17	Justice Dept. warned Trump team about Flynn's contact with Russia	*The Associated Press*	N/A
2/13/17	Justice Department warned White House that Flynn could be vulnerable to Russian blackmail, officials say	*The Washington Post*	Adam Entous, Ellen Nakashima and Philip Rucker
2/12/17	Turmoil at the National Security Council, From the Top Down	*The New York Times*	David E. Sanger, Eric Schmitt and Peter Baker
2/10/17	US investigators corroborate some aspects of the Russia dossier	CNN	Jim Sciutto and Evan Perez

Date of Publication	Headline	Publication/Source	Byline
2/10/17	Flynn Said to Talk to Sanctions to Russians in 2016	*The New York Times*	Matthew Rosenberg and Matt Apuzzo
2/9/17	National security adviser Flynn discussed sanctions with Russian ambassador, despite denials, officials say	*The Washington Post*	Greg Miller, Adam Entous, and Ellen Nakashima
2/9/17	Caution urged on terror label for Iranian entity	*The Washington Post*	Karen DeYoung
2/9/17	In call with Putin, Trump denounced Obama-era nuclear arms treaty	Reuters	Jonathan Landay and David Rohde
2/8/17	Trump's faux-pas diplomacy	*Politico*	Tara Palmeri, Kenneth P. Vogel, Josh Dawsey and Nahal Toosi
2/8/17	U.S. Weighs Terror Label on Iran Revolutionary Guard, Muslim Brotherhood	*The Wall Street Journal*	Felicia Schwartz and Jay Solomon
2/3/17	Trump team ditches Obama's plan to take Raqqa	*The Washington Post*	Adam Entous, Greg Jaffe, and Missy Ryan
2/2/17	'This was the worst call for far': Trump badgered, bragged and abruptly ended phone call with Australian leader	*The Washington Post*	Greg Miller and Philip Rucker

Date of Publication	Headline	Publication/Source	Byline
2/2/17	Trump had heated exchange with Australian PM, talked 'tough hombres' with Mexican leader	CNN	Jake Tapper, Eli Watkins, Jim Acosta and Euan McKirdy
2/2/17	Trump to Mexico: take care of 'bad hombres' or US might	*The Associated Press*	Vivian Salama
2/1/17	More immigration measures weighted	*The Washington Post*	Abigail Hauslohner, Janell Ross
1/27/17	How Civilian Prosecution Gave the U.S. a Key Informant	*The New York Times*	Adam Goldman and Benjamin Weiser
1/27/17	President Is Said to Seek Plan for U.S. to Strike ISIS Harder	*The New York Times*	Michael R. Gordon, Helene Cooper and Eric Schmitt
1/26/17	Trump signals changes to US interrogation, detention policy	*The Associated Press*	Desmond Butler and Deb Riechmann
1/25/17	White House draft orders calls for review on use of CIA 'black site' prisons overseas	*The Washington Post*	Greg Miller
1/25/17	Leaked Draft of Executive Order Could Revive C.I.A. Prisons	*The New York Times*	Mark Mazzetti and Charlie Savage
1/22/17	U.S. Eyes Michael Flynn's Links to Russia	*The Wall Street Journal*	Carol E. Lee, Devlin Barrett and Shane Harris

Date of Publication	Headline	Publication/Source	Byline
1/20/17	U.S. counterintelligence officials are examining possible ties between Russia and Trump associates	*The Washington Post*	Ellen Nakashima and Greg Miller
1/20/17	Wiretapped Data Used in Inquiry of Trump Aides	*The New York Times*	Michael S. Schmidt, Matthew Rosenberg, Adam Goldman and Matt Apuzzo

Source of Tables: Johnson, Ron. Majority Staff Report of the Committee on Homeland Security and Governmental Affairs United States Senate. "State Secrets: How an Avalanche of Media Leaks is Harming National Security." 6 July 2017.

APPENDIX III

CHARTS OF CONNECTIONS

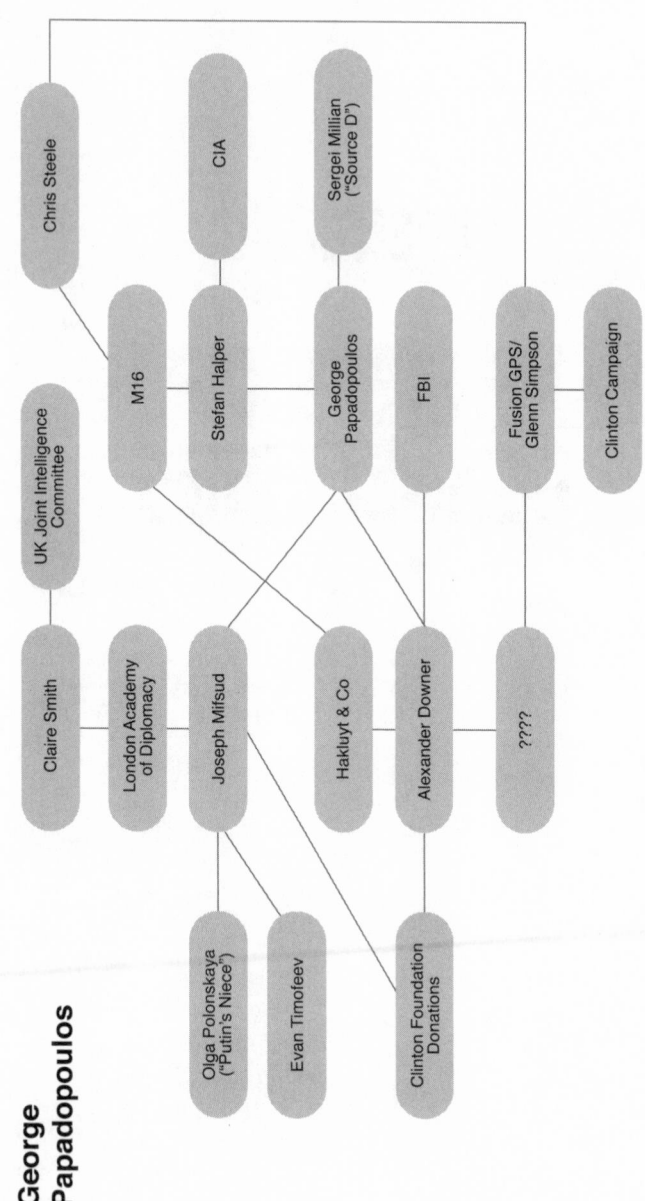

George Papadopoulos

Chris Steele / Fusion GPS

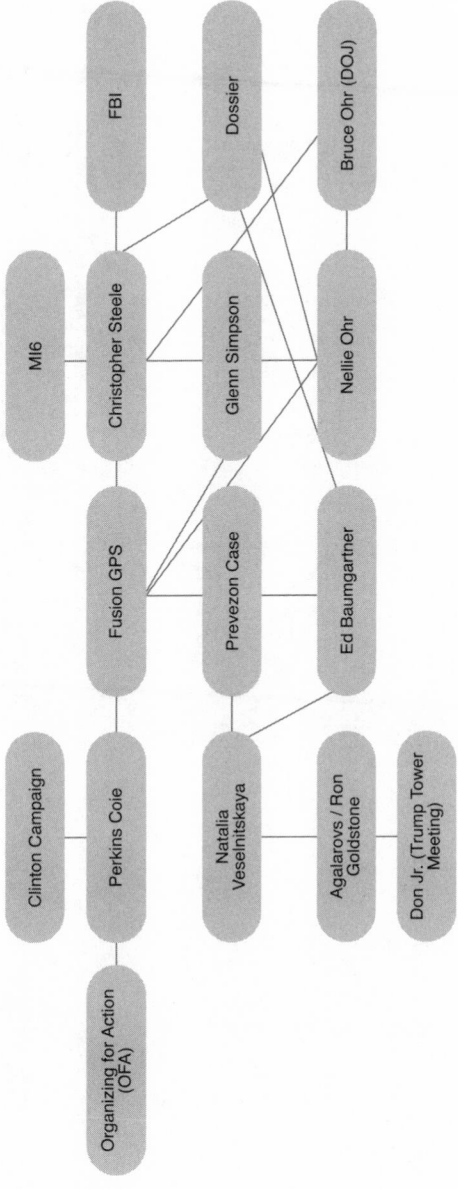

American and British Intelligence

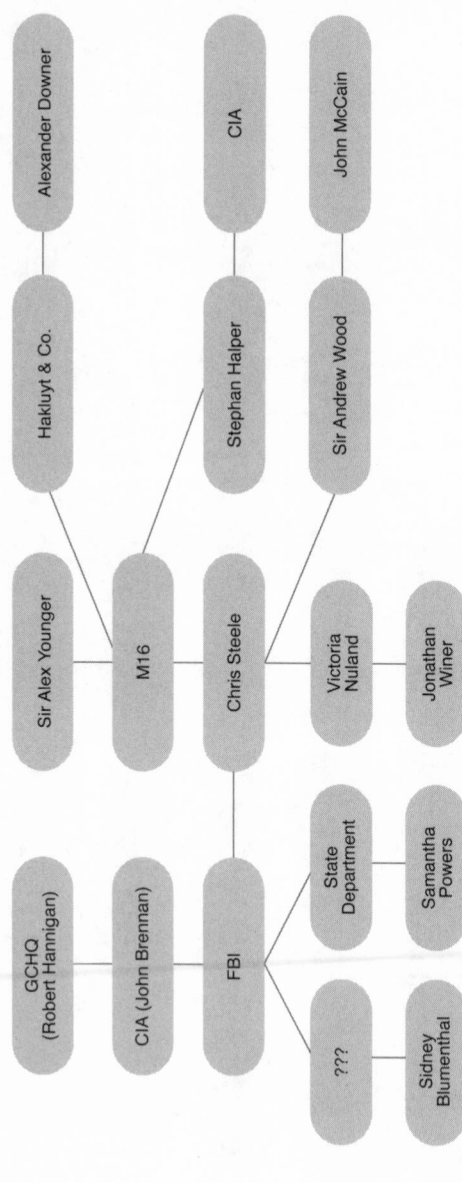

American and British Intelligence (Cont.)

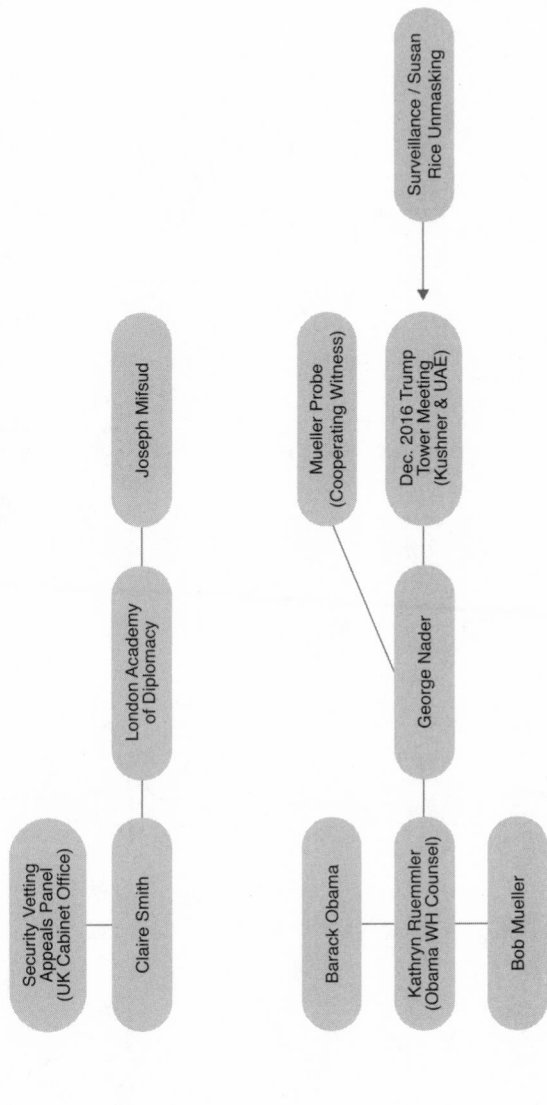

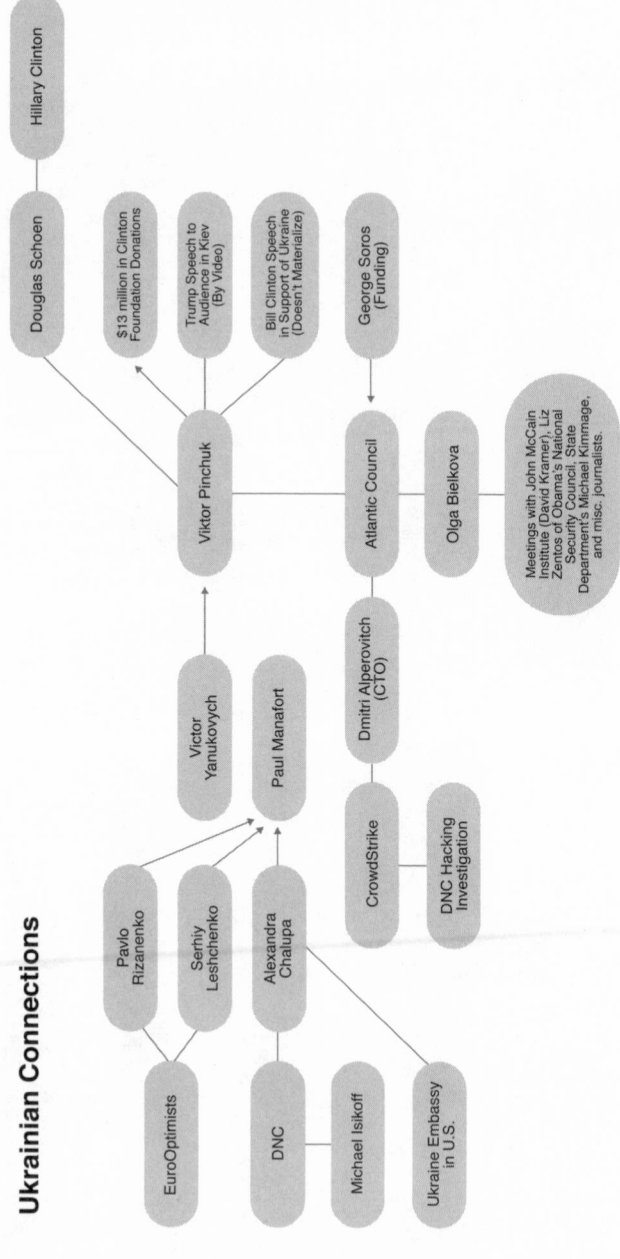

Ukrainian Connections

ENDNOTES

INTRODUCTION

1   Carter, Sara. "Collusion Delusion: New Documents Show Obama Officials, FBI Coordinated in Anti-Trump Probe." Sara A. Carter, 29 March 2018, https://saraacarter.com/new-documents-suggest-coordination-by-obama-white-house-cia-and-fbi-in-trump-investigation/.
2   Ibid.

PART 1

1   Press Release. "Judicial Watch Obtains Emails Showing Podesta Group's Work for Pro-Russia Ukrainian Political Party." Judicial Watch, 17 May 2018, https://www.judicialwatch.org/press-room/press-releases/judicial-watch-obtains-emails-showing-podesta-groups-work-pro-russia-ukrainian-political-party/?utm_source=t.co&utm_medium=social&utm_campaign=press%20release.
2   Ibid.
3   Ibid.
4   Ibid.
5   Ibid.
6   WikiLeaks. "Ukraine: Extreme Makeover for the Party of Regions?" Public Library of US Diplomacy, https://wikileaks.org/plusd/cables/06KIEV473_a.html. Accessed 14 April 2018.
7   Detrick, Hallie. "Former Trump Campaign Chair Paul Manafort Has Been Under FBI Surveillance for Years." *Fortune*, 19 September 2017, http://fortune.com/2017/09/19/paul-manafort-fbi-surveillance-donald-trump-russia/.
8   Thrush, Glenn. "To Charm Trump, Manafort Sold Himself as an Affordable Outsider." *The New York Times*, 8 April 2017, https://www.nytimes.com/2017/04/08/us/to-charm-trump-paul-manafort-sold-himself-as-an-affordable-outsider.html.
9   Ibid.
10 Ibid.
11 Winter, Tom, and Ken Dilanian. "Donald Trump Aide Paul Manafort Scrutinized for Russian Business Ties." NBC News, 18 August 2016, https://www.nbcnews.com/news/us-news/donald-trump-aide-paul-manafort-scrutinized-russian-business-ties-n631241.

12   "Trump Campaign Manager Manafort Has Shady Ukraine Ties." YouTube, uploaded by Hromadske International, 6 December 2017, https://www.youtube.com/watch?v=j4lOJQ8F19A.

13   Ibid.

14   Ioffe, Julia. "What Exactly Did Paul Manafort Do Wrong?" *The Atlantic*, 24 March 2017, https://www.theatlantic.com/international/archive/2017/03/much-ado-about-manafort/520743/.

15   Ibid.

16   Merica, Dan. "DNC denies working with Ukrainian government, but contractor floated anti-Trump material." CNN Politics, 12 July 2017, https://www.cnn.com/2017/07/12/politics/dnc-ukraine-trump-material/index.html.

17   Isikoff, Michael. "Top Trump Aide Lobbied for Pakistani Spy Front." Yahoo News, 18 April 2016, https://www.yahoo.com/news/top-trump-aide-lobbied-for-1409744144007222.html.

18   Isikoff, Michael. "Trump's Campaign Chief Is Questioned About Ties to Russian Billionaire." Yahoo News, 26 April 2016, https://www.yahoo.com/news/trumps-campaign-chief-ducks-questions-about-214020365.html.

19   WikiLeaks. "You saw this, right?" DNC emails, https://wikileaks.org/dnc-emails/emailid/3962. Accessed 14 April 2018.

20   Ibid.

21   Kramer, Andrew, et al. "Secret Ledger in Ukraine Lists Cash for Donald Trump's Campaign Chief." *The New York Times*, 14 August 2016, https://www.nytimes.com/2016/08/15/us/politics/paul-manafort-ukraine-donald-trump.html.

22   Ibid.

23   Greenwood, Max. "Report: Manafort Part of Intelligence Review of Intercepted Russian Communications." *The Hill*, 19 January 2017, http://thehill.com/policy/national-security/315213-us-intelligence-agencies-law-enforcement-will-examine-intercepted.

24   Schmidt, Michael, et al. "Intercepted Russian Communications Part of Inquiry Into Trump Associates." *The New York Times*, 19 January 2017, https://www.nytimes.com/2017/01/19/us/politics/trump-russia-associates-investigation.html.

25   Merica, Dan. "DNC Denies Working with Ukrainian Government, but Contractor Floated Anti-Trump Material." CNN Politics, 12 July 2017, https://www.cnn.com/2017/07/12/politics/dnc-ukraine-trump-material/index.html.

26   Vogel, Kenneth, and David Stern. "Ukrainian Efforts to Sabotage Trump Backfire." *Politico*, 11 January 2017, https://www.politico.com/story/2017/01/ukraine-sabotage-trump-backfire-233446.

27   Ibid.

28   Ibid.

29   Ibid.

30   Ibid.

31   *Foundation for Accountability & Civic Trust v. Democratic National Committee.* Before the Federal Election Commission complaint, https://docs.wixstatic.com/ugd/65db76_0f5023e8f1e84ade94fd538bb4c2b3a9.pdf. Accessed 15 April 2018.

32   Ibid.

33   "Grassley Raises Further Concerns Over Foreign Agent Registration." Senator Chuck Grassley, 24 July 2017, https://www.grassley.senate.gov/news/news-releases/grassley-raises-further-concerns-over-foreign-agent-registration.

34   Ibid.

35   "Grassley Statement on Indictments Filed by Special Counsel's Office." Senator Chuck Grassley, 30 October 2017, https://www.grassley.senate.gov/news/news-releases/grassley-statement-indictments-filed-special-counsel%E2%80%99s-office.

36 Ibid.

37 Bensinger, Ken. "These Reports Allege Trump Has Deep Ties to Russia." BuzzFeed, 10 January 2017, https://www.buzzfeed.com/kenbensinger/these-reports-allege-trump-has-deep-ties-to-russia?utm_term=.juN585y56#.cpqqPqlq2.

38 Smith, Lee. "Did President Obama Read the 'Steele Dossier' in the White House Last August?" Tablet magazine, 20 December 2017, https://www.tabletmag.com/jewish-news-and-politics/251897/obama-steele-dossier-russiagate.

39 Olearchyk, Roman. "Ukraine's Leaders Campaign Against 'Pro-Putin' Trump." *The Financial Times*, 28 August 2016, https://www.ft.com/content/c98078d0-6ae7-11e6-a0b1-d87a9fea034f.

40 Ibid.

41 Vogel, Kenneth, and David Stern. "Ukranian Efforts to Sabotage Trump Backfire." *Politico*, 11 January 2017, https://www.politico.com/story/2017/01/ukraine-sabotage-trump-backfire-233446.

42 Olearchyk, Roman. "Ukraine's Leaders Campaign Against 'Pro-Putin' Trump." *The Financial Times*, 28 August 2016, https://www.ft.com/content/c98078d0-6ae7-11e6-a0b1-d87a9fea034f.

43 Ibid.

44 Karatnycky, Adrian. "Why Trump Is Wrong about Ukrainian Interference in US Elections." Atlantic Council, 31 July 2017, http://www.atlanticcouncil.org/blogs/ukrainealert/why-trump-is-wrong-about-ukrainian-interference-in-us-elections.

45 Vogel, Kenneth, and David Stern. "Ukrainian Efforts to Sabotage Trump Backfire." *Politico*, 11 January 2017, https://www.politico.com/story/2017/01/ukraine-sabotage-trump-backfire-233446.

46 Supplemental Statement Pursuant to the Foreign Agents Registration Act of 1938, as amended. Registrant: Doug Schoen, 30 April 2016, https://www.fara.gov/docs/6071-Supplemental-Statement-20160517-10.pdf.

47 Zhuk, Alyona. "Poroshenko Bloc Denies Its Disobedient Member Seat on Investigative Commission." *Kyiv Post*, 18 May 2016, https://www.kyivpost.com/article/content/ukraine-politics/poroshenko-bloc-denies-its-disobedient-member-seat-on-investigative-commission-414006.html.

48 Ibid.

49 Gnap, Dmytro. "Ukrainian Billionaires Exchanged Luxury London Real Estate in Secret Settlement." The Organized Crime and Corruption Reporting Project, 15 December 2017, https://www.occrp.org/en/paradisepapers/ukrainian-billionaires-exchanged-luxury-london-real-estate-in-secret-settlement.

50 Sukhov, Oleg. "New Generations Come to Power, with Help from Pinchuk, One Way or Another: Do They Owe Him?" *Kyiv Post*, 14 October 2016, https://www.kyivpost.com/ukraine-politics/new-generations-come-power-help-pinchuk-one-way-another-owe.html.

51 Ibid.

52 Ibid.

53 Ibid.

54 Atlantic Council. "Ukraine in Europe Initiative," http://www.atlanticcouncil.org/ukraine.

55 "Prepared Remarks by Victoria Nuland on a Transatlantic Renaissance." Atlantic Council, 12 November 2013, http://www.atlanticcouncil.org/news/transcripts/prepared-remarks-by-victoria-nuland-on-a-transatlantic-renaissance. Accessed 12 April 2018.

56 "Dmitri Alperovitch." Atlantic Council, http://www.atlanticcouncil.org/about/experts/list/dmitri-alperovitch. Accessed 12 April 2018.

57 Lipton, Eric, et al. "Foreign Powers Buy Influence at Think Tanks." *The New York Times*, 6 September 2014, https://www.nytimes.com/2014/09/07/us/politics/foreign-powers-buy-influence-at-think-tanks.html.

58 Ibid.

59 Ibid.

60 Ibid.

61 Ibid.

62 Bielkova, Olga. "Helping Ukraine: How?" *Huffington Post*, 6 May 2014, https://www.huffingtonpost.com/entry/helping-ukraine-how_b_5268913.html.

63 Bielkova, Olga. "Ukraine: What We Have Learned This Winter." *Huffington Post*, 21 May 2014, https://www.huffingtonpost.com/entry/ukraine-what-we-have-learned-this-winter_b_5357847.html.

64 "Olga Bielkova." *Huffington Post*, https://www.huffingtonpost.com/author/olga-bielkova. Accessed 18 April 2018.

65 Grimaldi, James, and Rebecca Ballhaus. "Clinton Charity Tapped Foreign Friends." *The Wall Street Journal*, 19 March 2015, https://www.wsj.com/articles/clinton-charity-tapped-foreign-friends-1426818602.

66 Bogardus, Kevin. "Ukrainian Billionaire Hires Clinton Pollster." *The Hill*, 29 October 2011, http://thehill.com/business-a-lobbying/190553-ukrainian-billionaire-hires-clinton-pollster.

67 Chozick, Amy. "Trade Dispute Centers on Ukrainian Executive with Ties to Clintons." *The New York Times*, 12 February 2014, https://www.nytimes.com/2014/02/13/us/politics/trade-dispute-centers-on-ukrainian-executive-with-ties-to-clintons.html.

68 Ibid.

69 Ross, Rory. "Hillary Clinton's Big Benefactor Has Trade Links with Iran." *Newsweek*, 18 April 2015, http://www.newsweek.com/2015/04/24/hillary-clinton-runs-white-house-and-row-over-ukrainian-benefactors-trade-322253.html.

70 Helderman, Rosalind, et al. "Clintons' Foundation Has Raised Nearly $2 Billion—and Some Key Questions." *Washington Post*, 18 February 2015, https://www.washingtonpost.com/politics/clintons-raised-nearly-2-billion-for-foundation-since-2001/2015/02/18/b8425d88-a7cd-11e4-a7c2-03d37af98440_story.html?utm_term=.dad6a8fb49b6.

71 Ibid.

72 Danilova, Maria. "As Pro-European Protests Seize Ukraine, Jewish Oligarch Victor Pinchuk Is a Bridge to the West." *Tablet* magazine, 13 December 2013, http://www.tabletmag.com/jewish-news-and-politics/155976/ukraines-western-face.

73 Chozick, Amy, and Steve Eder. "Foundation Ties Bedevil Hillary Clinton's Presidential Campaign." *The New York Times*, 20 August 2016, https://www.nytimes.com/2016/08/21/us/politics/hillary-clinton-presidential-campaign-charity.html.

74 Soldak, Katya. "Ukraine's Victor Pinchuk: The Oligarch in the Middle of the Crisis." *Forbes*, 3 March 2014, https://www.forbes.com/sites/katyasoldak/2014/03/03/ukraines-victor-pinchuk-the-oligarch-in-the-middle-of-the-crisis/#58d36f735ece.

75 Clinton, William. "Remarks at the State Dinner for President Leonid Kuchma of Ukraine." American Presidency Project, 22 November 1994, http://www.presidency.ucsb.edu/ws/?pid=49519.

76 Soldak, Katya. "Ukraine's Victor Pinchuk: The Oligarch in the Middle of the Crisis." *Forbes*, 3 March 2014, https://www.forbes.com/sites/katyasoldak/2014/03/03/ukraines-victor-pinchuk-the-oligarch-in-the-middle-of-the-crisis/#58d36f735ece.

77 Ibid.

78 Ibid.

79 WikiLeaks. "Victor Pinchuk." Podesta emails, https://wikileaks.org/podesta-emails/emailid/18115. Accessed 15 April 2018.
80 Ibid.
81 Nardelli, Alberto. "The Professor at the Center of the Trump-Russia Probe Boasted to His Girlfriend In Ukraine That He Was Friends with Russian Foreign Minister Sergey Lavrov." BuzzFeed, 27 February 2018, https://www.buzzfeed.com/albertonardelli/the-mysterious-professor-at-the-center-of-the-russia-trump?utm_term=.rcyay9lwM#.srREWqow0.
82 Valdai Discussion Club, http://valdaiclub.com/about/valdai/. Accessed March 28, 2018.
83 Kirkpatrick, David. "The Professor Behind the Trump Campaign Adviser Charges." *The New York Times,* 31 October 2017, https://www.nytimes.com/2017/10/31/world/europe/russia-us-election-joseph-mifsud.html.
84 Amelina, Anna. "RIAC and CSIS Held a Seminar on Russia-US Cooperation on Building Regional Security." Russian Council, 26 April 2016, http://russiancouncil.ru/en/news/rsmd-i-csis-proveli-seminar-sotrudnichestvo-rossii-i-ssha-v-/?sphrase_id=12826817
85 Kortunov, Andrey, and Olga Oliker. "A Roadmap for US-Russia Relations." CSIS Russia and Eurasia Program and the Russian International Affairs Council, https://csis-prod.s3.amazonaws.com/s3fs-public/publication/170815_KortunovOliker_USRussiaRelations_Web.pdf.
86 Adam, Karla, et al. "Professor at Center of Russia Disclosures Claimed to Have Met with Putin." *Washington Post,* 31 October 2017, https://www.washingtonpost.com/world/professor-named-in-russia-disclosures-says-he-has-clean-conscious/2017/10/31/41a7a08e-be3b-11e7-959c-fe2b598d8c00_story.html?utm_term=.c29f75cc1ded.
87 Ibid.
88 Rogan, Tom. "Suspected Russian Spy, Joseph Mifsud, Visited D.C. in 2014, Promising to Dole Out Money to Students." *The Washington Examiner,* 2 November 2017, https://www.washingtonexaminer.com/suspected-russian-spy-joseph-mifsud-visited-dc-in-2014-promising-to-dole-out-money-to-students.
89 Brera, di Paolo G. "Russiagate, Mystery Professor Joseph Mifsud Speaks Out: 'Dirt on Hillary Clinton? Nonsense.'" *Repubblica,* 1 November 2017, http://www.repubblica.it/esteri/2017/11/01/news/russiagate_mystery_professor_joseph_mifsud_speaks_out_dirt_on_hillary_clinton_nonsense_-179948962/?refresh_ce.
90 "Executive Programmes & Short Courses." Geodiplomatics, http://geodiplomatics.com/short.htm. Accessed 5 April 2018.
91 "Claire Smith, Director at CH Smith Consulting Ltd." LinkedIn, https://www.linkedin.com/in/clairesmithuk/. Accessed 5 April 2018.
92 Smith, Lee. "The Maltese Phantom of Russiagate." RealClearInvestigations, 30 May 2018, https://www.realclearinvestigations.com/articles/2018/05/26/the_maltese_phantom_of_russiagate_.html.
93 Vos, Elizabeth Lea. "A Conversation with Chris Blackburn on the Contradictions Surrounding Mifsud." Zero Hedge, 23 April 2018, https://www.zerohedge.com/news/2018-04-23/conversation-chris-blackburn-contradictions-surrounding-mifsud.
94 Ibid.
95 Ibid.
96 Ibid.
97 Ignatius, David. "The CIA's Dissidents." *Washington Post,* 6 April 2004, http://archive.is/3srka#selection-231.1-247.517.
98 Ibid.

99   Vos, Elizabeth Lea. "A Conversation with Chris Blackburn on the Contra-
     dictions Surrounding Mifsud." Zero Hedge, 23 April 2018, https://
     www.zerohedge.com/news/2018-04-23/conversation-chris-blackburn-
     contradictions-surrounding-mifsud.
100 Ibid.
101 Ibid.
102 Brera,   di   Paolo   G.   "Russiagate,   Mystery   Professor   Joseph
     Mifsud   Speaks   Out: 'Dirt   On   Hillary   Clinton?   Nonsense.'"
     Repubblica,   1   November   2017,   http://www.repubblica.it/esteri
     /2017/11/01/news/russiagate_mystery_professor_joseph_mifsud_speaks_out_
     dirt_on_hillary_clinton_nonsense_-179948962/?refresh_ce.
103 Ibid.
104 Ibid.
105 Ross,   Chuck.   "Was   Joseph   Mifsud   a   Clinton   Foundation   Member?"
     Daily   Caller,   30   March   2018,   http://dailycaller.com/2018/03/30/
     joseph-mifsud-papadopoulos-clinton-foundation/.
106 Newton-Small,   Jay.   "An   Italian   Politician   Campaigns   for   Hillary
     Clinton   in   Philadelphia."   *Time*,   29   July   2016,   http://time.com/4429904/
     dnc-hillary-clinton-italian-europe/,
107 Harding,Luke,andSephanieKirchgaessner."TheBoss,theBoyfriendandtheFBI:The
     ItalianWomanintheEyeoftheTrump-RussiaInquiry."*TheGuardian*,18January2018,
     https://www.theguardian.com/us-news/2018/jan/18/
     simona-mangiante-trump-russia-joseph-mifsud-george-papadopoulos.
108 LaFraniere, Sharon, et al. "A London Meeting of an Unlikely Group: How a Trump
     Adviser Came to Learn of Clinton 'Dirt.'" *The New York Times*, 10 November 2017,
     https://www.nytimes.com/2017/11/10/us/russia-inquiry-trump.html.
109 Ibid.
110 Helderman, Rosalind. "Who's Who in the George Papadopoulos Court Docu-
     ments." *Washington Post*, 2 November 2017, https://www.washingtonpost.com/
     politics/whos-who-in-the-george-papadopoulos-court-documents/2017/10/30/
     e131158c-bdb3-11e7-97d9-bdab5a0ab381_story.html?noredirect=on&utm_
     term=.efd711a5f007.
111 Weill,   Kelly.   "'Putin's   Niece'   Catfished   Trump   Aide,   Offered   Kremlin
     Meeting." Daily Beast, 30 October 2017, https://www.thedailybeast.com/
     putins-niece-catfished-george-papadopoulos-offered-kremlin-meeting.
112 Helderman, Rosalind. "Who's Who in the George Papadopoulos Court Docu-
     ments." *Washington Post*, 2 November 2017, https://www.washingtonpost.com/
     politics/whos-who-in-the-george-papadopoulos-court-documents/2017/10/30/
     e131158c-bdb3-11e7-97d9-bdab5a0ab381_story.html?utm_term=.31be62818e77.
113 Ibid.
114 Ibid.
115 LaFraniere, Sharon, et al. "How the Russia Inquiry Began: A Campaign Aide,
     Drinks and Talk of Political Dirt." *The New York Times*, 30 December 2017, https://
     www.nytimes.com/2017/12/30/us/politics/how-fbi-russia-investigation-be-
     gan-george-papadopoulos.html.
116 House Permanent Select Committee on Intelligence. "Report on Russian Active
     Measures," 22 March 2018, https://intelligence.house.gov/uploadedfiles/final_
     russia_investigation_report.pdf.
117 Ibid.
118 Hall, Steven. "Russia's Outreach to George Papadopoulos Went Just How
     Spies Would Have Done It." *Washington Post*, 31 October 2017, https://www.
     washingtonpost.com/news/posteverything/wp/2017/10/31/russias-outreach-to-george-

papadopoulos-went-just-how-spies-would-have-done-it/?nid&utm_term=.
d2577d2bd070.

119 Ibid.

120 Ibid.

121 Magnay, Jacquelin. "Alexander Downer, Signing Off." *The Australian*, 28 April 2018, https://www.theaustralian.com.au/news/inquirer/alexander-downer-signing-off/news-story/02cd18d37828c8957bfb62b18e411595?memtype=anonymous.

122 LaFraniere, Sharon, et al. "How the Russia Inquiry Began: A Campaign Aide, Drinks and Talk of Political Dirt." *The New York Times*, 30 December 2017, https://www.nytimes.com/2017/12/30/us/politics/how-fbi-russia-investigation-began-george-papadopoulos.html.

123 Magnay, Jacquelin. "Alexander Downer, Signing Off." *The Australian*, 28 April 2018, https://www.theaustralian.com.au/news/inquirer/alexander-downer-signing-off/news-story/02cd18d37828c8957bfb62b18e411595?memtype=anonymous.

124 Ibid.

125 Ibid.

126 Ibid.

127 Ibid.

128 Ibid.

129 Strassel, Kimberley. "The Curious Case of Mr. Downer." *The Wall Street Journal*, 31 May 2018, https://www.wsj.com/articles/the-curious-case-of-mr-downer-1527809075?redirect=amp#click=https://t.co/QRnP4wEbkB.

130 Ibid.

131 Ibid.

132 Nicholson, Brendan, and Daniel Flitton. "Downer: Uranium Deal No Risk to Nuclear Pact." *The Age*, 18 August 2007, https://www.theage.com.au/national/downer-uranium-deal-no-risk-to-nuclear-pact/2007/08/17/1186857774716.html.

133 Bolt, Andrew. "Why Have We Donated to Clinton's Foundation?" *Herald Sun*, 20 October 2016, http://www.heraldsun.com.au/blogs/andrew-bolt/why-have-we-donated-to-clintons-foundation/news-story/96f87b9c4999e22cd3b022d267129896.

134 Tapscott, Mark. "Aussie Complaints Headed to FBI on Clinton Foundation's Dealings Down Under." LifeZette, 16 January 2018, https://www.lifezette.com/polizette/aussie-complaints-to-be-filed-with-fbi-on-clinton-foundations-dealing-down-under/.

135 Ibid.

136 Ibid.

137 "Business Intelligence Notes: UK," *Intelligence Newsletter*, No. 364, 26 August, 1999, p. 3.

138 D'Arcy, Janice. "Kissinger Still Wears Cloak of Secrecy." *Hartford Courant*, 29 March 2003, http://articles.courant.com/2003-03-29/news/0303292320_1_kissinger-associates-clients-firm/3.

139 Donovan, John. "Hakluyt & Company Spying for Shell." Royal Dutch Shell PLC, 19 March 2018, http://royaldutchshellplc.com/2018/03/19/hakluyt-company-spying-for-shell/.

140 Karel Komarek and Moravske Naftove Doly v. Ramco Energy PLC, Medusa Oil and Gas Limited, Medusa Czech Operations Limited, Michael Burchell, and Michael Denys Seymoure. England and Wales High Court Decision, 21 November 2002, http://www.bailii.org/ew/cases/EWHC/QB/2002/B2.html.

141 "Kissinger Associates, APCO Join in Strategic Alliance." APCO Worldwide, 12 October 2004.

142 Solomon, John, and Alison Spann. "Clintons Understated Support from Firm Hired by Russian Nuclear Company." *The Hill*, 28 November 2017, http://thehill.com/homenews/news/362234-clintons-understated-support-from-firm-hired-by-russian-nuclear-company.

143 Edgecliffe-Johnson, Andrew. "Survey—Corporate Security: The Top Players in Intelligence Industry." *The Financial Times*, 10 April 2001, https://www.smithbrandon.com/in-the-news/survey-corporate-security-the-top-players-in-intelligence-industry.

144 Overell, Stephen. "Masters of the Great Game Turn to Business." *The Financial Times*, 23 March 2000, http://shell2004.com/PDFs/FTandTheScotsmanHakluytarticles.pdf.

145 Ibid.

146 Tapscott, Mark. "Meet Hillary Clinton's Other, Much More Powerful and Shadowy Oppo Research Firm." LifeZette, 18 March 2018, https://www.lifezette.com/polizette/meet-hillary-clintons-other-more-powerful-shadowy-oppo-research-firm/.

147 Ibid.

148 Miranda, Charles. "Britain Is Concerned About Australia's Links to Hakluyt Security Firm Created by Former MI6 Agents." News.com.au, 18 January 2016, http://www.news.com.au/world/britain-is-concerned-about-australias-links-to-hakluyt-security-firm-created-by-former-mi6-agents/news-story/5d6a3c7ccbd5cd9992379aeecaa5e3dc.

149 Tapscott, Mark. "Meet Hillary Clinton's Other, Much More Powerful and Shadowy Oppo Research Firm." LifeZette, 18 March 2018, https://www.lifezette.com/polizette/meet-hillary-clintons-other-more-powerful-shadowy-oppo-research-firm/.

150 Miranda, Charles. "Britain Is Concerned About Australia's Links To Hakluyt Security Firm Created by Former MI6 Agents." News.com.au, 18 January 2016, http://www.news.com.au/world/britain-is-concerned-about-australias-links-to-hakluyt-security-firm-created-by-former-mi6-agents/news-story/5d6a3c7ccbd5cd9992379aeecaa5e3dc.

151 There is no Crown prosecutor of Russia. The correct title is "prosecutor general."

152 @DonaldJTrumpJr. "Obviously I'm the first person to ever take a meeting to hear info on an opponent...went nowhere but had to listen." 10 July 2017, 5:55 a.m., https://twitter.com/DonaldJTrumpJr/status/884395618784993280.

153 "Read the Emails on Donald Trump Jr.'s Russia Meeting." *The New York Times*, 11 July 2017, https://www.nytimes.com/interactive/2017/07/11/us/politics/donald-trump-jr-email-text.html.

154 Roth, Andrew. "The Man Who Drives Trump's Russia Connection." *Washington Post*, 22 July 2017, https://www.washingtonpost.com/world/europe/the-man-who-drives-trumps-russia-connection/2017/07/21/43485a0e-6c98-11e7-abbc-a53480672286_story.html?noredirect=on&utm_term=.b5d55cf608d8.

155 Ross, Chuck. "Report: Trump Bodyguard Testifies Russian Offered 'Five Women' to Trump, Was Rejected." Daily Caller, 9 November 2017, http://dailycaller.com/2017/11/09/report-trump-bodyguard-testifies-russian-offered-five-women-to-trump-was-rejected/.

156 Bertrand, Natasha. "Trump's Bodyguard's Testimony Raises New Questions About the Most Salacious Allegations In the Dossier." Business Insider, 10 November 2017, http://www.businessinsider.com/house-intelligence-asks-trump-bodyguard-about-moscow-prostitutes-allegation-2017-11.

157 Crilly, Rob. "British Publicist Rob Goldstone Breaks Silence Over Trump Tower Meeting to Deny Russian Plot." *The Telegraph*, 19 November 2017, https://www.telegraph.co.uk/news/2017/11/19/british-publicist-rob-goldstone-breaks-silence-trump-tower-meeting/.

158 "Bill Browder's Testimony to the Senate Judiciary Committee on Russia, Magnitsky Act: FULL TEXT." *The Washington Examiner*, 27 July 2017, https://www.washingtonexaminer.com/bill-browders-testimony-to-the-senate-judiciary-committee-on-russia-magnitsky-act-full-text.

159 Ibid.

160 Dilanian, Ken. "Trump Dossier Firm Also Supplied Info Used in Meeting of Russians, Trump Team." NBC News, 10 November 2017, https://www.nbcnews.com/news/us-news/trump-dossier-firm-also-supplied-info-used-meeting-russians-trump-n819526.

161 Forrest, Brett, and Paul Sonne. "Russian Lawyer Whom Trump Jr. Met Says She Was In Contact with a Top Russian Prosecutor." *The Wall Street Journal*, 14 July 2017, https://www.wsj.com/articles/russian-lawyer-who-trump-jr-met-says-she-was-in-contact-with-top-russian-prosecutor-1500063809.

162 Ibid.

163 Simmons, Keir, et al. "Russian Lawyer Veselnitskaya Says She Didn't Give Trump Jr. Info on Clinton." NBC News, 11 July 2017, https://www.nbcnews.com/news/world/russian-lawyer-who-met-trump-jr-i-didn-t-have-n781631.

164 Ibid.

165 Forrest, Brett, and Paul Sonne. "Russian Lawyer Whom Trump Jr. Met Says She Was In Contact with Top Russian Prosecutor." *The Wall Street Journal*, 14 July 2017, https://www.wsj.com/articles/russian-lawyer-who-trump-jr-met-says-she-was-in-contact-with-top-russian-prosecutor-1500063809.

166 Cohen, Kelly. "Paul Manafort Has Been On the FBI's Radar Since 2013." *The Washington Examiner*, 24 April 2018, https://www.washingtonexaminer.com/news/paul-manafort-has-been-on-the-fbis-radar-since-2013.

167 Dilanian, Ken. "Former Soviet Counterintelligence Officer at Meeting with Donald Trump Jr. and Russian Lawyer." NBC News, 14 July 2017, https://www.nbcnews.com/news/us-news/russian-lawyer-brought-ex-soviet-counterintelligence-officer-trump-team-n782851.

168 Ibid.

169 Ross, Chuck. "Exclusive: Oppo Researcher Behind Trump Dossier is Linked to Pro-Kremlin Lobbying Effort." Daily Caller, 13 January 2017, http://dailycaller.com/2017/01/13/exclusive-oppo-researcher-behind-trump-dossier-is-linked-to-pro-kremlin-lobbying-effort/.

170 Boylan, Dan. "Browder Stands By Claims That Russia Paid Firm Behind the Anti-Trump Dossier." *Washington Times*, 17 August 2017, https://www.washingtontimes.com/news/2017/aug/17/browder-stands-claims-russia-paid-firm-behind-anti/.

171 "Glenn Simpson Interview." Executive Session Permanent Select Committee, US House of Representatives, 14 November 2017, https://docs.house.gov/meetings/IG/IG00/20180118/106796/HMTG-115-IG00-20180118-SD002.pdf. Accessed April 15. Web.

172 Ibid.

173 Dilanian, Ken. "Trump Dossier Firm Also Supplied Info Use in Meeting of Russians, Trump Team." NBC News, 10 November 2017, https://www.nbcnews.com/news/us-news/trump-dossier-firm-also-supplied-info-used-meeting-russians-trump-n819526.

174 "Glenn Simpson Testimony." *Washington Post*, https://apps.washingtonpost.com/g/documents/politics/read-the-full-transcript-of-glenn-simpsons-senate-testimony/2700/. Accessed April 26, 2018.

175 Ibid.

176 Lynch, Collum. "McCain Solicits Russian U.N. Ambassador." *Washington Post*, 20 October 2008, http://voices.washingtonpost.com/44/2008/10/mccain-solicits-russian-un-amb.html.

177 Smith, Lee. "Did President Obama Read the 'Steele Dossier' in the White House Last August?" *Tablet* magazine, 20 December 2017, http://www.tabletmag.com/jewish-news-and-politics/251897/obama-steele-dossier-russiagate.

178 Smith, Lee. "Did Glenn Simpson Lie to Congress?" *Tablet* magazine, 12 January 2018, http://www.tabletmag.com/jewish-news-and-politics/253004/fusion-gps-donald-trump.

179 Ibid.

180 Ibid.

181 Ibid.

182 Ibid.

183 Ibid.

184 Ibid.

185 "Glenn Simpson Testimony." *Washington Post*, https://apps.washingtonpost.com/g/documents/politics/read-the-full-transcript-of-glenn-simpsons-senate-testimony/2700/. Accessed April 26, 2018.

186 Ibid.

187 LaFraniere, Sharon, et al. "Lobbyist at Trump Campaign Meeting Has a Web of Russian Connections." *The New York Times*, 21 August 2017, https://www.nytimes.com/2017/08/21/us/rinat-akhmetshin-russia-trump-meeting.html.

188 Ibid.

189 Ibid.

190 Ibid.

191 Ibid.

192 Grassley, Chuck. "Complaint: Firm Behind Dossier & Former Russian Intel Officer Joined Lobbying Effort to Kill Pro-Whistleblower Sanctions for Kremlin." Chuck Grassley, 31 March 2017, https://www.grassley.senate.gov/news/news-releases/complaint-firm-behind-dossier-former-russian-intel-officer-joined-lobbying-effort.

193 Ibid.

194 Ibid.

195 Herridge, Catherine, et al. "Inside the Trump Dossier Handoff: McCain's 'Go-Between' Speaks Out." Fox News, 11 December 2017, http://www.foxnews.com/politics/2017/12/11/inside-trump-dossier-handoff-mccains-go-between-speaks-out.html.

196 Schleifer, Theodore, et al. "Top Republican Billionaire Paul Singer Endorses Marco Rubio." CNN Politics, 31 October 2015, https://www.cnn.com/2015/10/30/politics/marco-rubio-paul-singer-endorsement/index.html.

197 "Glenn Simpson Testimony." *Washington Post*, https://apps.washingtonpost.com/g/documents/politics/read-the-full-transcript-of-glenn-simpsons-senate-testimony/2700/. Accessed April 26, 2018.

198 Ibid.

199 Ibid.

200 Ibid.

201 Ibid.

202 Isikoff, Michael, and David Corn. *Russian Roulette: The Inside Story of Putin's War on America and the Election of Donald Trump*. Grand Central Publishing, Kindle Edition, p. 173.

203 Hamburger, Tom, et al. "Manafort Offered to Give Russian Billionaire 'Private Briefings' on 2016 Campaign." *Washington Post*, 20 September 2017, https://

www.washingtonpost.com/politics/manafort-offered-to-give-russian-billionaire-private-briefings-on-2016-campaign/2017/09/20/399bba1a-9d48-11e7-8ea1-ed975285475e_story.html?utm_term=.14c65d5d46a4.

204 Ibid.

205 Ibid.

206 Lipton, Eric, et al. "The Perfect Weapon: How Russian Cyberpower Invaded the US." *The New York Times*, 13 December 2016, https://www.nytimes.com/2016/12/13/us/politics/russia-hack-election-dnc.html.

207 Miller, Ron. "Security Company CrowdStrike Scores $100M Led By Google Capital." TechCrunch, 13 July 2015, https://techcrunch.com/2015/07/13/security-company-crowdstrike-scores-100m-led-by-google-capital/.

208 Nicas, Jack. "Alphabet's Eric Schmidt Gave Advice to Clinton Campaign, Leaked Emails Show." *The Wall Street Journal*, 2 November 2016, https://www.wsj.com/articles/alphabets-eric-schmidt-gave-advice-to-clinton-campaign-leaked-emails-show-1478111270?mod=trending_now_7.

209 Daniel, Michael, et al. "Announcing the President's Commission on Enhancing National Cybersecurity." The White House, 13 April 2016, https://obamawhitehouse.archives.gov/blog/2016/04/13/announcing-presidents-commission-enhancing-national-cybersecurity.

210 "CrowdStrike General Counsel and Chief Risk Officer Appointed to the White House Commission." CrowdStrike, 18 April 2016.

211 Ibid.

212 Leopold, Jason. "He Solved the DNC Hack. Now He's Telling His Story for the First Time." BuzzFeed News, 8 November 2017, https://www.BuzzFeed.com/jasonleopold/he-solved-the-dnc-hack-now-hes-telling-his-story-for-the?utm_term=.shWv4lwPa2#.on8VazAE8B.

213 Ibid.

214 Frenkel, Sheera. "Meet Fancy Bear." BuzzFeed News, 15 October 2016, https://www.BuzzFeed.com/sheerafrenkel/meet-fancy-bear-the-russian-group-hacking-the-us-election?utm_term=.pyO56YDk89#.lmGO3LWeKq.

215 Lipton, Eric, et al. "The Perfect Weapon: How Russian Cyberpower Invaded the US." *The New York Times*, 13 December 2016, https://www.nytimes.com/2016/12/13/us/politics/russia-hack-election-dnc.html.

216 Ibid.

217 Kuzmenko, Oleksiy and Pete Cobus. "Think Tank: Cyber Firm at Center of Russian Hacking Charges Misread Data." VOA News, 23 March 2017, https://www.voanews.com/a/crowdstrike-comey-russia-hack-dnc-clinton-trump/3776067.html.

218 "Security Company Releases New Evidence of Russian Role in DNC Hack." *PBS NewsHour*, 22 December 2016, https://www.pbs.org/newshour/show/security-company-releases-new-evidence-russian-role-dnc-hack. Accessed May 3, 2018.

219 Leopold, Jason. "He Solved the DNC Hack. Now He's Telling His Story for the First Time." BuzzFeed News, 8 November 2017, https://www.BuzzFeed.com/jasonleopold/he-solved-the-dnc-hack-now-hes-telling-his-story-for-the?utm_term=.birqgPDKpd#.ytadQx94Y8.

220 McKirdy, Euan. "WikiLeaks' Assange: Russia Didn't Give Us Emails." CNN Politics, 4 January 2017, https://www.cnn.com/2017/01/04/politics/assange-wikileaks-hannity-intv/index.html.

221 Perez, Evan, and Daniella Diaz. "FBI: DNC Rebuffed Request to Examine Computer Servers." CNN Politics, 5 January 2017, https://www.cnn.com/2017/01/05/politics/fbi-russia-hacking-dnc-CrowdStrike/index.html.

222 Watkins, Ali. "The FBI Never Asked for Access to Hacked Computer Servers." *BuzzFeed*, 4 January 2017, https://www.buzzfeed.com/alimwatkins/the-fbi-never-asked-for-access-to-hacked-computer-servers?utm_term=.jkx828oBQe#.xn7z5zaJAr.

223 Williams, Katie Bo. "Comey: DNC Denied FBI's Requests for Access to Hacked Aervers." *The Hill*, 1 October 2017, http://thehill.com/policy/national-security/313555-comey-fbi-did-request-access-to-hacked-dnc-servers.

224 Ibid.

225 Williams, Katie Bo. "FBI Never Examined Hacked DNC Servers Itself: Report." *The Hill*, 4 January 2017, http://thehill.com/policy/national-security/312767-fbi-never-examined-hacked-dnc-servers-report.

226 Ross, Chuck. "DNC Refused to Comply with Dossier-Related Subpoena, so BuzzFeed Sued." Daily Caller, 13 February 2018, http://dailycaller.com/2018/02/13/BuzzFeed-sues-dnc/.

227 Wright, Austin. "Jeh Johnson: DNC Did Not Want DHS Help Following Election Hack." *Politico*, 21 June 2017, https://www.politico.com/story/2017/06/21/dnc-no-help-homeland-security-hacks-239800.

228 Ibid.

229 Ibid.

230 Ibid.

231 Ibid.

232 McCarthy, Andrew. "When Scandals Collide." *National Review*, 25 October 2017, https://www.nationalreview.com/corner/scandals-collide-dossier-dnc-server-perkins-coie/.

233 Krever, Mick. "US administration '100% certain' about Russian hacking." CNN Politics, 4 January 2017, https://www.cnn.com/2017/01/03/politics/russia-trump-hacking-john-kirby-amanpour/index.html.

234 Sheth, Sonam. "Susan Rice Reportedly Told the White House Cyber Team to 'Knock It Off' When They Floated Options to Combat Russian Meddling." Business Insider, 9 March 2018, http://www.businessinsider.com/susan-rice-told-white-house-cyber-team-to-knock-it-off-on-combatting-russian-meddling-2018-3.

235 Ibid.

236 Miller, Greg, et al. "Obama's Secret Struggle to Punish Russia for Putin's Election Assault." *Washington Post*, 23 June 2017, https://www.washingtonpost.com/graphics/2017/world/national-security/obama-putin-election-hacking/?utm_term=.3c13d40fcbbb.

237 Nakashima, Ellen. "Russian Government Hackers Penetrated DNC, Stole Opposition Research on Trump." *Washington Post*, 14 June 2016, https://www.washingtonpost.com/world/national-security/russian-government-hackers-penetrated-dnc-stole-opposition-research-on-trump/2016/06/14/cf006cb4-316e-11e6-8ff7-7b6c1998b7a0_story.html?utm_term=.e5d1ba479943.

238 Ibid.

239 Hamburger, Tom, et al. "Inside Trump's Financial Ties to Russia and His Unusual Flattery of Vladimir Putin." *Washington Post*, 17 June 2016, https://www.washingtonpost.com/politics/inside-trumps-financial-ties-to-russia-and-his-unusual-flattery-of-vladimir-putin/2016/06/17/dbdcaac8-31a6-11e6-8ff7-7b6c1998b7a0_story.html?noredirect=on&utm_term=.4686c6acda7d.

240 Haberman, Maggie. "House Inquiry Turns Attention to Trump Campaign Worker With Russia Ties." *The New York Times*, 20 May 2017, https://www.nytimes.com/2017/05/20/us/politics/michael-caputo-house-committee-russia-trump.html.

241 Johnson, Kevin and Erin Kelly. "Russia Hacks Democratic National Committee, Trump Info Compromised." *USA Today*, 14 June 2016, https://www.usatoday.com/story/news/politics/elections/2016/06/14/russia-hack-democratic-national-committee-trump/85867116/.

242 Davis, Sean. "Obama's Campaign Paid $972,000 to Law Firm That Secretly Paid Fusion GPS In 2016." *The Federalist*, 29 October 2017, http://thefederalist.com/2017/10/29/obamas-campaign-gave-972000-law-firm-funneled-money-fusion-gps/.

243 Ibid.

244 Isikoff, Michael, and David Corn. *Russian Roulette: The Inside Story of Putin's War on America and the Election of Donald Trump*. Grand Central Publishing, Kindle Edition, p. 144.

245 Ibid.

246 Davis, Sean. "Obama's Campaign Paid $972,000 to Law Firm That Secretly Paid Fusion GPS In 2016." *The Federalist*, 29 October 2017, http://thefederalist.com/2017/10/29/obamas-campaign-gave-972000-law-firm-funneled-money-fusion-gps/.

247 Ibid.

248 Ibid.

249 Vogel, Kenneth. "Litigators." *Politico*, 28 July 2011, https://www.politico.com/story/2011/07/litigators-059939.

250 Isikoff, Michael, and David Corn. *Russian Roulette: The Inside Story of Putin's War on America and the Election of Donald Trump*. Grand Central Publishing, Kindle Edition, p. 145.

251 "Glenn Simpson Testimony." *Washington Post*, https://apps.washingtonpost.com/g/documents/politics/read-the-full-transcript-of-glenn-simpsons-senate-testimony/2700/. Accessed April 26, 2018.

252 Ibid.

253 Ibid.

254 Ross, Chuck. "Here's How Clinton Campaign Cash Could Have Ended Up in the Hands of Russian Operatives." Daily Caller, 25 October 2017, http://dailycaller.com/2017/10/25/heres-how-clinton-campaign-cash-could-have-ended-up-in-the-hands-of-russian-operatives/.

255 Mayer, Jane. "Christopher Steele, The Man Behind the Trump Dossier." *The New Yorker*, 12 March 2018, https://www.newyorker.com/magazine/2018/03/12/christopher-steele-the-man-behind-the-trump-dossier.

256 Ibid.

257 Ibid.

258 Ibid.

259 Grassley, Charles. "To Paul E. Hauser." 9 February 2018, https://www.judiciary.senate.gov/imo/media/doc/2018-02-09%20CEG%20to%20Hauser%20(business%20with%20Mr.%20Steele%20and%20Mr.%20Deripaska).pdf. Accessed May 4, 2018.

260 Ibid.

261 "Live Coverage of Former CIA Director John Brennan's Testimony Before Congress." CNN, 23 May 2017, http://www.cnn.com/TRANSCRIPTS/1705/23/cnr.04.html. Accessed May 3, 2018. Web.

262 Smith, Lee. "Was Christopher Steele Paid by Russian Oligarch and Putin Ally Oleg Deripaska?" *Tablet* magazine, 12 February 2018, http://www.tabletmag.com/jewish-news-and-politics/255290/christopher-steele-putin-oleg-deripaska.

263 Ibid.

264 Ross, Chuck. "Photos: Trump Dossier Source Met with Kremlin Crony at Russian Expo." Daily Caller, 17 March 2017, http://dailycaller.com/2017/03/17/photos-trump-dossier-source-met-with-kremlin-crony-at-russian-expo/.

265 Mayer, Jane. "Christopher Steele, The Man Behind the Trump Dossier." *The New Yorker*, 12 March 2018, https://www.newyorker.com/magazine/2018/03/12/christopher-steele-the-man-behind-the-trump-dossier.

266 "Report on Russian Active Measures." House Permanent Select Committee on Intelligence, 22 March 2018, https://docs.house.gov/meetings/IG/IG00/20180322/108023/HRPT-115-1.pdf. Accessed May 1, 2018.

267 Ibid.

268 Ibid.

269 Bershidsky, Leonid. "It Appears Kremlin Was Playing Both Sides Against Each Other." *Chicago Tribune*, 31 October 2017, http://www.chicagotribune.com/news/opinion/commentary/ct-perspec-kremlin-steele-dossier-russia-1101-20171031-story.html.

270 Felton, Lena. "The Full Text of the Nunes Memo." *The Atlantic*, 2 February 2018, https://www.theatlantic.com/politics/archive/2018/02/read-the-full-text-of-the-nunes-memo/552191/.

271 Ibid.

272 Gregory, Paul Roderick. "The Trump Dossier Is Fake—And Here's Why." *Forbes*, 13 January 2017, https://www.forbes.com/sites/paulroderickgregory/2017/01/13/the-trump-dossier-is-false-news-and-heres-why/#49829da68674.

273 Ibid.

274 Ibid.

275 Ibid.

276 Gregory, Paul Roderick. "Forbes contributor." Email, 2018.

277 "Glenn Simpson Testimony." *Washington Post*, https://apps.washingtonpost.com/g/documents/politics/read-the-full-transcript-of-glenn-simpsons-senate-testimony/2700/. Accessed April 26, 2018.

278 Gregory, Paul Roderick. "The Trump Dossier Is Fake—And Here's Why." *Forbes*, 13 January 2017, https://www.forbes.com/sites/paulroderickgregory/2017/01/13/the-trump-dossier-is-false-news-and-heres-why/#49829da68674.

279 Ibid.

280 Besinger, Ken, et al. "These Reports Allege Trump Has Deep Ties to Russia." BuzzFeed News, 10 January 2017, https://www.BuzzFeed.com/kenbensinger/these-reports-allege-trump-has-deep-ties-to-russia?utm_term=.simpMpgpO#.roOabaMaJ.

281 Ibid.

282 Ibid.

283 Gregory, Paul Roderick. "The Trump Dossier Is Fake—And Here's Why." *Forbes*, 13 January 2017, https://www.forbes.com/sites/paulroderickgregory/2017/01/13/the-trump-dossier-is-false-news-and-heres-why/#49829da68674.

284 Ibid.

285 Scarborough, Rowan. "Obama Aide Started Christopher Steele-FBI Alliance." *Washington Times*, 13 March 2018, https://m.washingtontimes.com/news/2018/mar/13/obama-aide-started-christopher-steele-fbi-alliance/.

286 "Glenn Simpson Testimony." *Washington Post*, https://apps.washingtonpost.com/g/documents/politics/read-the-full-transcript-of-glenn-simpsons-senate-testimony/2700/. Accessed April 26, 2018.

287 Ibid.

288 Ibid.

289 Isikoff, Michael, and David Corn. *Russian Roulette: The Inside Story of Putin's War on America and the Election of Donald Trump*. Grand Central Publishing, Kindle Edition, pp. 153-154.

290 Ibid.

291 Tillett, Emily. "Victoria Nuland Says Obama State Dept. Informed FBI of Reporting from Steele Dossier." CBS News, 4 February 2018, https://www.cbsnews.com/news/victoria-nuland-says-obama-state-dept-informed-fbi-of-reporting-from-steele-dossier/.

292 Winer, Jonathan. "Devin Nunes Is Investigating Me. Here's the Truth." *Washington Post*, 8 February 2018, https://www.washingtonpost.com/opinions/devin-nunes-is-investigating-me-heres-the-truth/2018/02/08/cc621170-0cf4-11e8-8b0d-891602206fb7_story.html.

293 Bordelon, Brendan. "Meet Cody Shearer, the Strangest Character in Hillary's Vast Left-Wing Conspiracy." *National Review*, 1 June 2015, https://www.nationalreview.com/2015/06/meet-cody-shearer-strangest-character-hillarys-vast-left-wing-conspiracy-brendan/.

294 Baker, Peter and Jeff Zeleny. "Emanuel Wields Power Freely, and Faces the Risks." *The New York Times*, 15 August 2009, https://www.nytimes.com/2009/08/16/us/politics/16emanuel.html?pagewanted=all&mtrref=www.google.com.

295 Asher-Schapiro, Avi. "Libyan Oil, Gold, and Qaddafi: The Strange Email Sidney Blumenthal Sent Hillary Clinton in 2011." Vice News, 12 January 2016, https://news.vice.com/article/libyan-oil-gold-and-qaddafi-the-strange-email-sidney-blumenthal-sent-hillary-clinton-in-2011.

296 WikiLeaks. "H: Crucial Contact. Sid." Hillary Clinton Email Archive, https://wikileaks.org/clinton-emails/emailid/24444. Accessed April 21, 2018.

297 Ibid.

298 "Grassley Pursues America's Biggest Scandal." Powerline, 26 January 2018, https://www.powerlineblog.com/archives/2018/01/grassley-pursues-americas-biggest-scandal.php.

299 Strassel, Kimberley. "Who Is Christopher Steele?" *The Wall Street Journal*, 8 February 2018, https://www.wsj.com/articles/who-is-christopher-steele-1518135346/.

300 Ibid.

301 Harding, Luke, et al. "British Spies Were First to Spot Trump Team's Links with Russia." *The Guardian*, 13 April 2017, https://www.theguardian.com/uk-news/2017/apr/13/british-spies-first-to-spot-trump-team-links-russia.

302 Ibid.

303 Neumayr, George. "Confirmed: John Brennan Colluded with Foreign Spies to Defeat Trump." *American Spectator*, 19 April 2017, https://spectator.org/confirmed-john-brennan-colluded-with-foreign-spies-to-defeat-trump/.

304 Ibid.

305 Ibid.

306 Harding, Luke, et al. "British Spies Were First to Spot Trump Team's Links with Russia." *The Guardian*, 13 April 2017, https://www.theguardian.com/uk-news/2017/apr/13/british-spies-first-to-spot-trump-team-links-russia.

307 Ibid.

308 Wood, Paul. "Trump 'Compromising' Claims: How and Why Did We Get Here?" BBC News, 12 January 2017, http://www.bbc.com/news/world-us-canada-38589427.

309 Schulberg, Jessica. "Former CIA Chief Says Intelligence Warrants FBI's Trump-Russia Investigation." *HuffPost*, 23 May 2017, https://www.huffingtonpost.com/entry/john-brennan-cia-intelligence-trump-associates-russia-fbi-investigation_us_59245a35e4b094cdba57f744.

310 Bertrand, Natasha. "Former CIA Director: I Was Concerned about 'Interaction' between Russians and the Trump Campaign." Business Insider, 23 May 2017, http://www.businessinsider.com/john-brennan-russia-trump-collusion-testimony-2017-5.

311 Schulberg, Jessica. "Former CIA Chief Says Intelligence Warrants FBI's Trump-Russia Investigation." *HuffPost*, 23 May 2017, https://www.huffingtonpost.com/entry/john-brennan-cia-intelligence-trump-associates-russia-fbi-investigation_us_59245a35e4b094cdba57f744.

312 Smith, Lee. "How CIA Director John Brennan Targeted James Comey." *Tablet* magazine, 9 February 2018, http://www.tabletmag.com/jewish-news-and-politics/255020/how-cia-director-john-brennan-targeted-james-comey.

313 *Meet the Press.* "Transcript." NBC News, 4 February 2018, https://www.nbcnews.com/meet-the-press/meet-press-february-4-2018-n844541. Accessed May 3, 2018.

314 Smith, Lee. "How CIA Director John Brennan Targeted James Comey." *Tablet* magazine, 9 February 2018, http://www.tabletmag.com/jewish-news-and-politics/255020/how-cia-director-john-brennan-targeted-james-comey.

315 Frost, Mike, and Michel Gratton. *Spyworld: How C.S.E. Spies on Canadians and the World.* McClelland-Bantam, 1995, pp. 224–227.

316 Ibid.

317 Ibid.

318 Smith, Lee. "How CIA Director John Brennan Targeted James Comey." *Tablet* magazine, 9 February 2018, http://www.tabletmag.com/jewish-news-and-politics/255020/how-cia-director-john-brennan-targeted-james-comey.

319 *Meet the Press.* "Transcript." NBC News, 4 February 2018, https://www.nbcnews.com/meet-the-press/meet-press-february-4-2018-n844541. Accessed May 3, 2018.

320 Transcript. "Rep. Devin Nunes: DNC Lawsuit 'Must Be a Joke.'" Fox News, 22 April 2018, http://www.foxnews.com/transcript/2018/04/22/rep-devin-nunes-dnc-lawsuit-must-be-joke.html.

321 Isikoff, Michael, and David Corn. *Russian Roulette: The Inside Story of Putin's War on America and the Election of Donald Trump.* Grand Central Publishing, Kindle Edition, pp. 171–172.

322 Ibid.

323 Tapper, Jake. "Mook on DNC E-mail Leak." CNN Press Room, 24 July 2016, http://cnnpressroom.blogs.cnn.com/2016/07/24/mook-on-dnc-e-mail-leak-experts-are-now-saying-that-the-russians-are-releasing-these-e-mails-for-the-purpose-of-actually-helping-donald-trump/.

324 Isikoff, Michael, and David Corn. *Russian Roulette: The Inside Story of Putin's War on America and the Election of Donald Trump.* Grand Central Publishing, Kindle Edition, p. 175.

325 Ibid.

326 Ibid, p. 176–178.

327 Klein, Aaron. "Exclusive: Carter Page: Russian Investigation Will Unearth Obama Admin's 'Falsified' FISA Warrants Against Me." Breitbart, 10 May 2017, http://www.breitbart.com/big-government/2017/05/30/exclusive-carter-page-russia-investigation-will-unearth-falsified-fisa-warrants-against-me-from-obama-admin/.

328 Foreign Intelligence Surveillance Court application, Re: Cater W. Page. October 2016, pp 15-16.

329 "Judicial Watch Obtains Carter Page FISA Court Documents." Judicial Watch, 21 July 2018, https://www.judicialwatch.org/press-room/press-releases/judicial-watch-obtains-carter-page-fisa-court-documents/.

PART 2

1 Domestic Investigations and Operations Guide. Federal Bureau of Investigation, 16 October 2013, reviewed 16 October 2016, https://vault.fbi.gov/.

2   Ibid.
3   Ibid.
4   Singman, Brooke. "Grassley Rips Strzok-Page Amid Mystery Text: Obama White House Is Running This." Fox News, 23 May 2018, http://www.foxnews.com/politics/2018/05/23/grassley-rips-strzok-page-redactions-amid-mystery-text-obama-white-house-is-running-this.html.
5   Domestic Investigations and Operations Guide. Federal Bureau of Investigation, 16 October 2013, reviewed 16 October 2016, https://vault.fbi.gov/.
6   Ibid.
7   Ibid.
8   Ibid.
9   Ibid.
10 Heine, Debra. "Strzok-Page Texts Refer to 'Oconus Lures' (Spies) in December 2015." PJ Media, 6 June 2018, https://pjmedia.com/trending/strzok-page-texts-refer-to-oconus-lures-spies-in-december-of-2015/.
11 "Former C.I.A. Chief Tells of Concern Over Possible Russia Ties to Trump Campaign." *The New York Times*, 23 May 2017, https://www.nytimes.com/2017/05/23/us/politics/congress-testimony-john-brennan-russia-budget.html.
12 Report on Russian Active Measures. House Permanent Select Committee on Intelligence, 22 March 2018, https://intelligence.house.gov/uploadedfiles/final_russia_investigation_report.pdf.
13 Ibid.
14 Rep. Elise Stefanik asks questions at Comey hearing. YouTube, 20 March 2017, https://www.youtube.com/watch?v=HlXXZQgh72Y&feature=youtu.be.
15 Domestic Investigations and Operations Guide. Federal Bureau of Investigation, 16 October 2013, reviewed 16 October 2016, https://vault.fbi.gov/.
16 Ibid.
17 Koenig, Kailani. "James Clapper on Trump-Russia Ties: 'My Dashboard Warning Light Was Clearly On.'" NBC News, 28 May 2017, https://www.nbcnews.com/politics/politics-news/james-clapper-trump-russia-ties-my-dashboard-warning-light-was-n765601.
18 Domestic Investigations and Operations Guide. Federal Bureau of Investigation, 16 October 2013, reviewed 16 October 2016, https://vault.fbi.gov/.
19 Diaz, Daniella. "James Clapper on Collusion between Russia, Trump Aides: There Could Be Evidence." CNN, 13 May 2017, https://www.cnn.com/2017/05/12/politics/james-clapper-james-comey-donald-trump-russia/index.html.
20 Kazin, Matthew. "No Official Intel Used to Start FBI Probe Into Trump Campaign-Russia Collusion: Rep. Nunes." Fox Business, 22 April 2018, https://www.foxbusiness.com/politics/no-official-intel-used-to-start-fbi-probe-into-trump-campaign-russia-collusion-rep-nunes.
21 Ibid.
22 Ibid.
23 Ibid.
24 Wroe, David. "Joe Hockey Discussed Alexander Downer Revelations with FBI." *Sydney Morning Herald*, 2 January 2018, https://www.smh.com.au/politics/federal/joe-hockey-discussed-downers-russia-revelations-with-fbi-20180101-h0c58c.html.
25 Ross, Chuck. "Exclusive: In Private, Trump Aide George Papadopoulos Denies Collusion." Daily Caller, 23 April 2018, http://dailycaller.com/2018/04/22/george-papadopoulos-trump-collusion/.
26 Wroe, David. "Joe Hockey Discussed Alexander Downer Revelations with FBI." *Sydney Morning Herald*, 2 January 2018, https://www.smh.com.au/politics/

federal/joe-hockey-discussed-downers-russia-revelations-with-fbi-20180101-h0c58c.html.

27 Shabad, Rebecca. "Former CIA Chief Says There Were Contacts between Russia and Trump Aides." CBS News, 23 May 2017, https://www.cbsnews.com/news/former-cia-director-john-brennan-testifies-on-russia-live-updates/.

28 Ibid.

29 Neumayr, George and R. Emmett Tyrrell, Jr. "John Brennan, Obama's Head of the Innuendo Community." American Spectator, 23 March 2018, https://spectator.org/john-brennan-obamas-head-of-the-innuendo-community/.

30 Hopkins, Nick, and Julian Borger. "Exclusive: NSA Pays £100m In Secret Funding for GCHQ." The Guardian, 1 August 2013, https://www.theguardian.com/uk-news/2013/aug/01/nsa-paid-gchq-spying-edward-snowden.

31 Hopkins, Nick, and Luke Harding. "GCHQ Accused of Selling Its Services After Revelations of Funding by NSA." The Guardian, 2 August 2013, https://www.theguardian.com/uk-news/2013/aug/02/gchq-accused-selling-services-nsa.

32 Hopkins, Nick, and Julian Borger. "Exclusive: NSA Pays £100m In Secret Funding for GCHQ." The Guardian, 1 August 2013, https://www.theguardian.com/uk-news/2013/aug/01/nsa-paid-gchq-spying-edward-snowden.

33 Ibid.

34 Harding, Luke, et al. "British Spies Were First to Spot Trump Team's Links with Russia." The Guardian, 13 April 2017, https://www.theguardian.com/uk-news/2017/apr/13/british-spies-first-to-spot-trump-team-links-russia.

35 Carter, Sara. "Collusion Delusion: New Documents Show Obama Officials, FBI Coordinated in Anti-Trump Probe." Sara A. Carter, 29 March 2018. https://saraacarter.com/new-documents-suggest-coordination-by-obama-white-house-cia-and-fbi-in-trump-investigation/.

36 Ibid.

37 Apuzzo, Matt, et al. "FBI Is Investigating Trump's Russia Ties, Comey Confirms." The New York Times, 20 March 2017, https://www.nytimes.com/2017/03/20/us/politics/fbi-investigation-trump-russia-comey.html.

38 Ross, Chuck. "Exclusive: A London Meeting Before the Election Aroused George Papadopolos's Suspicions." Daily Caller, 26 March 2018, http://dailycaller.com/2018/03/25/george-papadopoulos-london-emails/.

39 Ross, Chuck. "Exclusive: Cambridge Prof with CIA, MI6 Ties Met with Trump Adviser During Campaign, Beyond." Daily Caller, 17 May 2018, http://dailycaller.com/2018/05/17/halper-trump-page-papadopoulos/.

40 Ross, Chuck. "Papadopoulos Was Approached by 'Highly Suspicious' Businessmen, His Wife Claims." Daily Caller, 7 June 2018, http://dailycaller.com/2018/06/06/george-papadopoulos-millian-suspicious/.

41 Ibid.

42 Ibid.

43 Ibid.

44 Zwirz, Elizabeth. "Former Trump Campaign Co-Chair Describes Meeting with Alleged FBI Informant." Fox News, 22 May 2018, http://www.foxnews.com/politics/2018/05/22/former-trump-campaign-co-chair-describes-meeting-with-alleged-fbi-informant.html.

45 Bloom, Dan. "ISIS Threat Has Been Exaggerated, Says Former MI6 Chief: Sir Richard Dearlove Thinks 'Pathetic' Britons Spreading Messages On Internet Should Be Ignored." Daily Mail, 7 July 2014, http://www.dailymail.co.uk/news/article-2684077/ISIS-threat-exaggerated-says-former-MI6-chief-Sir-Richard-Dearlove-thinks-pathetic-Britons-spreading-messages-internet-ignored.html.

46 @carterwpage. "Reporters keep asking me about my interactions with Prof. Halper. I found all our interactions to be cordial. Like this email I received about a year after I first met him. He never seemed suspicious. Just a few scholars exchanging ideas. He had interests in policy, and politics." Twitter, 20 May 2018, 2:20 a.m.

47 Herb, Jeremy, et al. "Fusion Co-founder: Dossier Author Feared Trump Was Being Blackmailed." CNN, 10 January 2018, https://www.cnn.com/2018/01/09/politics/feinstein-releases-glenn-simpson-transcript/index.html.

48 Levy, Joshua. Letter to Hon. Charles E. Grassley, Chairman, US Senate Committee on the Judiciary, 18 January 2018, https://www.judiciary.senate.gov/imo/media/doc/2018-01-18%20Fusion%20GPS%20to%20CEG%20(accuracy%20of%20testimony).pdf.

49 Goldman, Adam, et al. "FBI Used Informant to Investigate Russia Ties to Campaign, Not to Spy, as Trump Claims." *The New York Times*, 18 May 2018, https://www.nytimes.com/2018/05/18/us/politics/trump-fbi-informant-russia-investigation.html.

50 Drum, Kevin. "In Huge Disappoint, the FBI's Super-Secret Trump Informant Looks to Be . . . Stefan Halper." *Mother Jones*, 19 May 2018, https://www.motherjones.com/kevin-drum/2018/05/in-huge-disappointment-the-fbis-super-secret-trump-informant-turns-out-to-be-stefan-halper/.

51 *United States of America v. Evgeny Buryakov, Igor Sporyshev, and Victor Prodobnyy*. US Southern District of New York, 23 January 2015, http://online.wsj.com/public/resources/documents/2015_0126_spyring2.pdf.

52 Lichtblau, Eric and Steven Lee Myers. "Investigating Donald Trump, FBI Sees No Clear Link to Russia." *The New York Times*, 31 October 2016, https://www.nytimes.com/2016/11/01/us/politics/fbi-russia-election-donald-trump.html.

53 Sperry, Paul. "Carter Page: The FBI Ruined My Life." *New York Post*, 26 May 2018, https://nypost.com/2018/05/26/carter-page-the-fbi-ruined-my-life/.

54 Domestic Investigations and Operations Guide. Federal Bureau of Investigation, 16 October 2013, reviewed 16 October 2016, https://vault.fbi.gov/.

55 "James Clapper Tries to Clear Obama's Name of Likely FBI Informant Trump Campaign." Daily Headlines, 27 May 2018, https://www.dailyheadlinesnow.com/2018/05/27/james-clapper-tries-to-clear-obamas-name-of-likely-fbi-informant-in-trump-campaign/.

56 Domestic Investigations and Operations Guide. Federal Bureau of Investigation, 16 October 2013, reviewed 16 October 2016, https://vault.fbi.gov/.

57 Ibid.

58 Lichtblau, Eric and Steven Lee Myers. "Investigating Donald Trump, FBI Sees No Clear Link to Russia." *The New York Times*, 31 October 2016, https://www.nytimes.com/2016/11/01/us/politics/fbi-russia-election-donald-trump.html.

59 Ibid.

60 Weber, Peter. "Famously agreeable FISA court reportedly turned down FBI request to monitor Trump officials." The Week, 11 January 2017, http://theweek.com/speedreads/672504/famously-agreeable-fisa-court-reportedly-turned-down-fbi-request-monitor-trump-officials.

61 Domestic Investigations and Operations Guide. Federal Bureau of Investigation, 16 October 2013, reviewed 16 October 2016, https://vault.fbi.gov/.

62 General Services Administration website, https://www.fpds.gov/ezsearch/fpds portal?q=HALPER%2C+STEFAN+PRINCIPAL_NAICS_CODE%3A%225 41720%22&s=FPDS&templateName=1.4&indexName=awardfull&x=0&y=0. Accessed May 24, 2018.

63 Peterson, Bill. "Coming In from the Cold, Going Out to the Bush Campaign." *Washington Post*, 1 March 1980, https://www.washingtonpost.com/archive/

politics/1980/03/01/coming-in-from-the-cold-going-out-to-the-bush-campaign/3758ff60-0d13-43a6-9a6f-c692e20d5378/?utm_term=.50fc7237a276.

64 Werner, Leslie. "Baker Is Backed on Carter Papers." *The New York Times*, 24 May 1984, https://www.nytimes.com/1984/05/24/us/baker-is-backed-on-carter-papers.html.

65 Lesar, Jack. "A Former Ronald Reagan Campaign Official Charged Thursday." UPI, 7 July 1983, https://www.upi.com/Archives/1983/07/07/A-former-Ronald-Reagan-campaign-official-charged-Thursday-administration/4669426398400/.

66 "Clinton Best Option for US-UK 'Special Relationship'-Ex-White House Official." Sputnik, 3 November 2016, https://sputniknews.com/politics/201611031047032702-clinton-us-uk-cooperation/.

67 Cheney, Kyle. "Warner: Identifying FBI Source to Undermine Russia Probe Could Be a Crime." *Politico*, 18 May 2018, https://www.politico.com/story/2018/05/18/warner-russia-probe-source-fbi-crime-598042.

68 Goldman, Adam, et al. "FBI Used Informant to Investigate Russia Ties to Campaign, Not to Spy, as Trump Claims." *The New York Times*, 18 May 2018, https://www.nytimes.com/2018/05/18/us/politics/trump-fbi-informant-russia-investigation.html.

69 Ross, Chuck. "FBI Informant Stefan Halper Accused of Making 'False' and 'Absurd' Allegations About Russia Infiltration at Cambridge." Daily Caller, 23 May 2018, http://dailycaller.com/2018/05/23/halper-false-russia-claims/.

70 Corera, Gordon. "A Russian Honeytrap for Gen Flynn? Not Me..." BBC, 12 May 2017, http://www.bbc.com/news/magazine-39863781.

71 Ibid.

72 "Cambridge Spy Journal Shuts Down After Row Over Links to Russia." *The Telegraph*, 28 December 2016, https://www.telegraph.co.uk/news/2016/12/28/cambridge-spy-journal-shuts-row-links-russia/.

73 Ibid.

74 Willigress, Lydia, and Luke Heighton. "Cambridge Spy Seminars Hit By Whispers of Russian Links As Three Intelligence Experts Resign." *The Telegraph*, 17 December 2016, https://www.telegraph.co.uk/news/2016/12/16/intelligence-experts-cut-ties-cambridge-spy-seminars-amid-claims/.

75 Lichtblau, Eric. "C.I.A. Had Evidence of Russian Effort to Help Trump Earlier Than Believed." *The New York Times*, 6 April 2017, https://www.nytimes.com/2017/04/06/us/trump-russia-cia-john-brennan.html.

76 Carter, Sara. "Collusion Delusion: New Documents Show Obama Officials, FBI Coordinated in Anti-Trump Probe." Sara A. Carter, 31 March 2018, https://saraacarter.com/new-documents-suggest-coordination-by-obama-white-house-cia-and-fbi-in-trump-investigation/.

77 Ibid.

78 Singman, Brooke. "Documents Suggest Coordination Between CIA, FBI, Obama WH and Dem Officials Early In Trump-Russia Probe: Investigators." Fox News, 28 March 2018, http://www.foxnews.com/politics/2018/03/28/documents-suggest-possible-coordination-between-cia-fbi-obama-wh-and-dem-officials-early-in-trump-russia-probe-investigators.html.

79 Bensinger, Ken, et al. "These Reports Allege Trump Has Deep Ties to Russia." BuzzFeed, 10 January 2017, https://www.buzzfeed.com/kenbensinger/these-reports-allege-trump-has-deep-ties-to-russia?utm_term=.jtyL743ll#.mxNDe2Jww.

80 Singman, Brooke. "Republicans Turn Focus to FBI's Mccabe Over Texts On 'Insurance' Against Trump." Fox News, 14 December 2017, http://www.foxnews.com/politics/2017/12/14/republicans-turn-focus-to-fbis-mccabe-over-texts-on-insurance-against-trump.html.

81 Wilber, Del Quentin. "In FBI Agent's Account, 'Insurance Policy' Text Referred to Russia Probe," *The Wall Street Journal*, 18 December 2017, https://www.wsj.com/articles/in-fbi-agents-account-insurance-policy-text-referred-to-russia-probe-1513624580.

82 Inspector General Report. Report on the Special Study of NSA Controls to Comply with the FISA Amendments Act 704 and 705(b) Targeting and Minimization Procedures. National Security Agency/Central Security Service, 7 January 2016, https://www.dni.gov/files/documents/icotr/51117/NSA_IG_Report_1_7_16_ST-15-0002.pdf. Note, the report was made public on May 10, 2017.

83 diGenova, Joseph. "The Politicization of the FBI." *Imprimis*, vol. 47, no. 2, February 2018, https://imprimis.hillsdale.edu/the-politicization-of-the-fbi/.

84 Ibid.

85 Ibid.

86 Singman, Brooke. "Documents Suggest Coordination Between CIA, FBI, Obama WH and Dem Officials Early In Trump-Russia Probe: Investigators." Fox News, 28 March 2018, http://www.foxnews.com/politics/2018/03/28/documents-suggest-possible-coordination-between-cia-fbi-obama-wh-and-dem-officials-early-in-trump-russia-probe-investigators.html.

87 A Review of Various Actions by the Federal Bureau of Investigation and the Department of Justice in Advance of the 2016 Election. Office of the Inspector General, US Department of Justice, June 2018, https://www.justice.gov/file/1071991/download.

88 Kranish, Michael. "Inside the Day That Set In Motion Michael Flynn's Guilty Plea." *Washington Post*, 8 December 2017, https://www.washingtonpost.com/politics/inside-the-day-that-set-in-motion-michael-flynns-guilty-plea/2017/12/08/f5c477a0-da9b-11e7-b1a8-62589434a581_story.html?utm_term=.8be5f47cf58f.

89 Carter, Sara. "What Happened During the FBI Interview with Flynn." Sara Carter, 24 May 2018, https://saraacarter.com/what-happened-during-the-fbi-interview-with-flynn/.

90 Ibid.

91 Ibid.

92 *Politico* staff. "Full Text: Michael Flynn Criminal Information." *Politico*, 1 December 2017, https://www.politico.com/story/2017/12/01/michael-flynn-federal-charges-full-text-274421.

93 York, Byron. "Comey Told Congress FBI Agents Didn't Think Michael Flynn Lied." *The Washington Examiner*, 12 February 2018, https://www.washingtonexaminer.com/byron-york-comey-told-congress-fbi-agents-didnt-think-michael-flynn-lied.

94 Ibid.

95 Ibid.

96 Entous, Adam, et al. "Justice Department Warned White House That Flynn Could Be Vulnerable to Russian Blackmail, Officials Say." *Washington Post*, 13 February 2017, https://www.washingtonpost.com/world/national-security/justice-department-warned-white-house-that-flynn-could-be-vulnerable-to-russian-blackmail-officials-say/2017/02/13/fc5dab88-f228-11e6-8d72-263470bf0401_story.html?utm_term=.497f26a5df7b.

97 "To James Madison from George Logan, [19 January] 1810," https://founders.archives.gov/documents/Madison/03-02-02-0227.

98 Ignatius, David. "Why Did Obama Dawdle on Russia's Hacking?" *Washington Post*, 12 January 2017, https://www.washingtonpost.com/opinions/why-did-obama-dawdle-on-russias-hacking/2017/01/12/75f878a0-d90c-11e6-9a36-1d296534b31e_story.html?utm_term=.d54f27d48669.

99 Ibid.

100 Savage, Charlie. "N.S.A. Gets More Latitude to Share Intercepted Communications." *The New York Times*, 12 June 2017, https://www.nytimes.com/2017/01/12/us/politics/nsa-gets-more-latitude-to-share-intercepted-communications.html.

101 Ibid.

102 ACLU Comment on Expansion of NSA Information Sharing. ACLU, 12 January 2017, https://www.aclu.org/news/aclu-comment-expansion-nsa-information-sharing.

103 Inspector General Report. Report on the Special Study of NSA Controls to Comply with the FISA Amendments Act 704 and 705(b) Targeting and Minimization Procedures. National Security Agency/Central Security Service, 7 January 2016, https://www.dni.gov/files/documents/icotr/51117/NSA_IG_Report_1_7_16_ST-15-0002.pdf. Note, the report was made public on May 10, 2017.

104 FISA Section 702 Debate. US House of Representatives Permanent Select Committee on Intelligence, https://intelligence.house.gov/uploadedfiles/2017_section_702_fact_sheet.pdf.

105 Ibid.

106 The report was published April 26, 2017, but not made public until 2018. https://www.scribd.com/document/349261099/2016-Cert-FISC-Memo-Opin-Order-Apr-2017-4#from_embed.

107 Payton, Bre. "Bombshell: Intelligence Reports Show Trump Was Monitored by the Obama Admin Post-Election." *The Federalist*, 22 March 2017, http://thefederalist.com/2017/03/22/bombshell-intelligence-reports-show-trump-monitored-obama-admin-post-election/.

108 Ibid.

109 Transcript. "Susan Rice: The World Wonders and Worries If the White House Can Be Trusted." PBS, 22 March 2017, https://www.pbs.org/newshour/show/susan-rice-world-wonders-worries-white-house-can-trusted.

110 Raju, Manu. "Exclusive: Rice Told House Investigators Why She Unmasked Senior Trump Officials." CNN, 18 September 2017, https://www.cnn.com/2017/09/13/politics/susan-rice-house-investigators-unmasked-trump-officials/index.html.

111 Ibid.

112 Lord, Debbie. "Read Transcripts of Rep. Devin Nunes' News Conference about Trump Surveillance." AJC, 23 March 2017, https://www.ajc.com/news/national/read-transcripts-rep-devin-nunes-news-conferences-about-trump-surveillance/NdZ4qQv7uBnjcH9E3HSRPJ/.

113 Kredo, Adam. "Fmr. U.N. Amb. Power Emerges As Central Figure In Obama Unmasking Investigation." *The Washington Free Beacon*, 19 July 2017, http://freebeacon.com/national-security/fmr-u-n-amb-power-emerges-central-figure-obama-unmasking-investigation/.

114 "Gowdy: Former UN Ambassador Samantha Power Claims Others Unmasked In Her Name." Fox News, 18 October 2017, http://www.foxnews.com/politics/2017/10/18/gowdy-former-un-ambassador-samantha-power-claims-others-unmasked-in-her-name.html.

115 "Grassley, Graham Uncover 'Unusual Email' Sent by Susan Rice to Herself on Trump's Inauguration Day." Chuck Grassley, 12 February 2018, https://www.grassley.senate.gov/news/news-releases/grassley-graham-uncover-unusual-email-sent-susan-rice-herself-president-trump-s.

116 Shear, Michael and Matt Apuzzo. "FBI Director James Comey Is Fired by Trump." *The New York Times*, 9 May 2017, https://www.nytimes.com/2017/05/09/us/politics/james-comey-fired-fbi.html.

117 Keneally, Meghan. "Why James Comey Says President Trump Is 'Unfit' for Office." ABC News, 16 April 2018, https://abcnews.go.com/Politics/james-comey-president-trump-unfit-office/story?id=54499156.

118 *Politico* Staff. "Full Text: James Comey Testimony Transcript on Trump and Russia." *Politico*, 8 June 2017, https://www.politico.com/story/2017/06/08/full-text-james-comey-trump-russia-testimony-239295.

119 A Review of Various Actions by the Federal Bureau of Investigation and the Department of Justice in Advance of the 2016 Election. Office of the Inspector General, US Department of Justice, June 2018, https://www.justice.gov/file/1071991/download.

120 Schmidt, Michael. "Comey Memo Says Trump Asked Him to End Flynn Investigation." *The New York Times*, 16 May 2017, https://www.nytimes.com/2017/05/16/us/politics/james-comey-trump-flynn-russia-investigation.html?smid=tw-share&_r=1.

121 28 CFR 600.1-Grounds for Appointing a Special Counsel. US Government Publishing Office, https://www.gpo.gov/fdsys/granule/CFR-2010-title28-vol2/CFR-2010-title28-vol2-sec600-1. Accessed May 15, 2018.

122 Press release. "Appointment of Special Counsel." DOJ, 17 May 2017, https://www.justice.gov/opa/pr/appointment-special-counsel.

123 Ibid.

124 *Politico* Staff. "Full Text: James Comey Testimony Transcript on Trump and Russia." *Politico*, 8 June 2017, https://www.politico.com/story/2017/06/08/full-text-james-comey-trump-russia-testimony-239295.

125 Zapotosky, Matt. "Trump Said Mueller's Team Has '13 hardened Democrats.' Here Are the Facts." *Washington Post*, 18 March 2018, https://www.washingtonpost.com/news/post-politics/wp/2018/03/18/trump-said-muellers-team-has-13-hardened-democrats-here-are-the-facts/?utm_term=.7459a7cdd6c6.

126 Ibid.

127 Gerstein, Josh. "Judge Halts Depositions for Bill and Hillary Clinton and Ex-aides." *Politico*, 21 July 2015, https://www.politico.com/blogs/under-the-radar/2015/07/judge-halts-depositions-for-bill-and-hillary-clinton-and-ex-aides-210968.

128 Heine, Debra. "Another One! Mueller Deputy Was Personal Attorney of Ben Rhodes, Represented Clinton Foundation." PJ Media, 5 December 2017, https://pjmedia.com/trending/another-one-mueller-deputy-personal-attorney-ben-rhodes-represented-clinton-foundation/.

129 "Hume: Mueller Deputy's Email to Sally Yates Raises 'Impartiality' Questions." *Fox News Insider*, 5 December 2017, http://insider.foxnews.com/2017/12/05/andrew-weissmann-sends-email-sally-yates-ripping-travel-ban-hume-responds.

130 Muller, Derek. "Ranking the Most Liberal and Conservative Lawfirms." *Excess of Democracy*, 16 July 2013, http://excessofdemocracy.com/blog/2013/7/ranking-the-most-liberal-and-conservative-law-firms.

131 Savage, Charlie. "Departing White House Counsel Held Powerful Sway." *The New York Times*, 6 April 2014, https://www.nytimes.com/2014/04/07/us/politics/departing-white-house-counsel-held-powerful-sway.html.

132 Hastings, Michael, and Evan McMorris-Santoro. "Advisers Urged Obama Early On to Release Comprehensive Benghazi Timeline." BuzzFeed, 21 May 2013, https://www.buzzfeed.com/mhastings/advisers-urged-obama-early-on-to-release-comprehensive-bengh?utm_term=.iaKKxgpJz#.upMQ5kwgb.

133 Powell, Sidney. "Swamp Reunion: Obama's Three Muses Reappear in Mueller's Trump Investigation." Daily Caller, 1 March 2018, http://dailycaller.com/2018/03/01/reunited-and-it-feels-so-swampy-obamas-three-muses-reappear-in-muellers-trump-investigation/.

134 Ibid.

135 Kwong, Jessica. "Mueller Protected Obama and Clinton, So He Should Be Fired, Republican Resolution Claims." *Newsweek*, 3 November 2017, http://www.newsweek.com/gop-using-muellers-role-uranium-deal-call-his-resignation-russia-probe-701673.

136 Fandos, Nicholas, et al. "Secret Memo Hints at a New Republican Target: Rod Rosenstein." *The New York Times*, 28 January 2018, https://www.nytimes.com/2018/01/28/us/politics/rod-rosenstein-carter-page-secret-memo.html?smid=tw-share.

137 A Review of Various Actions by the Federal Bureau of Investigation and the Department of Justice in Advance of the 2016 Election. Office of the Inspector General, US Department of Justice, June 2018, https://www.justice.gov/file/1071991/download.

138 Ibid.

139 Ibid.

140 Ibid.

141 Johnson, Ron. Majority Staff Report of the Committee on Homeland Security and Governmental Affairs United States Senate. "State Secrets: How an Avalanche of Media Leaks Is Harming National Security," 6 July 2017.

142 Ibid.

143 Ibid.

144 Ibid.

145 Ibid.

146 Ibid.

147 *Freedom Watch, Inc. v. The Honorable Jeff B. Sessions, et al.* Case 1:17-cv-02459, US District Court for the District of Columbia, 15 November 2017, https://www.freedomwatchusa.org/freedom-watch-files-complaint-to-force-doj-investigation-int.

148 Ainsley, Julia and Tom Winter. "Mueller Team Asking If Trump Tried to Hide Purpose of Trump Tower Meeting." NBC News, 28 August 2017, https://www.nbcnews.com/news/usnews/mueller-team-asking-if-trump-tried-hide-purpose-trump-tower-n796746.

149 Harris, Shane. "Special Counsel Examines Possible Role Flynn Played in Seeking Clinton Emails from Hackers." *The Wall Street Journal*, 25 August 2017, https://www.wsj.com/articles/special-counsel-examines-possible-role-flynn-played-in-seekingclinton-emails-from-hackers-1503694304.

150 "Sources: Russians Bragged About Using Flynn," CNN, undated video of news broadcast, available at http://www.cnn.com/videos/politics/2017/05/20/russia-michael-flynn-donaldtrump-influence-brown-borger-ac.cnn/video/playlists/michael-flynn/.

151 *Freedom Watch, Inc. v. Jefferson B. Sessions, et al.* Memorandum Opinion, Case 1:17-cv-02459-ABJ, US District Court for the District of Columbia, 20 December 2017, https://assets.documentcloud.org/documents/4334309/document-22000529.pdf.

152 "Trump Administration Rips Leaks Surrounding Mueller Probe." Fox News, 16 June 2017, http://www.foxnews.com/politics/2017/06/16/trump-administration-rips-leaks-surrounding-mueller-probe.html.

153 Gerstein, Josh. "Manafort Seeks Court Hearing On Leaks." *Politico*, 30 April 2018, https://www.politico.com/story/2018/04/30/manafort-court-leaks-rights-561674.

154 *United States v. Paul J. Manafort Jr.* "Memorandum of law in support of motion to require a hearing regarding improper disclosures relating to confidential Grand Jury information and potentially classified materials."

155 Ibid.

156 Ibid.

157 House Permanent Select Committee on Intelligence. "Report on Russian Active Measures." House Intelligence, 22 March 2018, https://intelligence.house.gov/uploadedfiles/final_russia_investigation_report.pdf. Accessed May 20, 2018.

158 Entous, Adam, et al. "Secret CIA Assessment Says Russia Was Trying to Help Trump Win White House." *Washington Post*, 9 December 2016, https://www.washingtonpost.com/world/national-security/obama-orders-review-of-russian-hacking-during-presidential-campaign/2016/12/09/31d6b300-be2a-11e6-94ac-3d324840106c_story.html?utm_term=.5723d1a03ea8.

159 Sanger, David and Scott Shane. "Russian Hackers Acted to Aid Trump in Election, US Says." *The New York Times*, 9 December 2016, https://www.nytimes.com/2016/12/09/us/obama-russia-election-hack.html.

160 Arkin, William. "US Officials: Putin Personally Involved in US Election Hack." NBC News, 14 December 2016, https://www.nbcnews.com/news/us-news/u-s-officials-putin-personally-involved-u-s-election-hack-n696146.

161 Starr, Barbara, et al. "Intel Analysis Shows Putin Approved Hacking." CNN, 15 December 2016, https://www.cnn.com/2016/12/15/politics/russian-hacking-vladimir-putin-donald-trump/index.html.

162 House Permanent Select Committee on Intelligence. "Report on Russian Active Measures." House Intelligence, 22 March 2018, https://intelligence.house.gov/uploadedfiles/final_russia_investigation_report.pdf. Accessed May 20, 2018.

163 York, Byron. "Comey Told Congress FBI Agents Didn't Think Michael Flynn Lied." *Washington Examiner*, 12 February 2018, https://www.washingtonexaminer.com/byron-york-comey-told-congress-fbi-agents-didnt-think-michael-flynn-lied/article/2648896.

164 Barrett, Devlin. "FBI Has Questioned Trump Campaign Adviser Carter Page at Length In Russia Probe." *Washington Post*, 26 June 2017, https://www.washingtonpost.com/world/national-security/fbi-has-questioned-trump-campaign-adviser-carter-page-at-length-in-russia-probe/2017/06/26/1a271dcc-5aa5-11e7-a9f6-7c3296387341_story.html?utm_term=.637bc86fa3b6.

165 Rucker, Philip. "Trump Adviser: 'I Would Not Be Concerned' About a Russia Back Channel, Irrespective of Kushner." *Washington Post*, 27 May 2017, https://www.washingtonpost.com/news/post-politics/wp/2017/05/27/trump-adviser-i-would-not-be-concerned-about-a-russia-back-channel-irre-spective-of-kushner/?utm_term=.8810efcd31ff.

166 "'This Week' Transcript 6-18-17: Newt Gingrich, Rep. Adam Schiff, and Douglas Lute." ABC News, 18 June 2017, https://abcnews.go.com/Politics/week-transcript-18-17-newt-gingrich-rep-adam/story?id=48105960

167 Cohen, Marshall. "Special Counsel Team Members Donated to Dems, FEC Records Show." CNN Politics, 13 June 2017, https://www.cnn.com/2017/06/12/politics/robert-mueller-donations-democrats-fec/index.html.

168 Barrett, Devlin, et al. "Special Counsel Is Investigating Trump for Possible Obstruction of Justice, Officials Say." *Washington Post*, 14 June 2017, https://www.washingtonpost.com/world/national-security/special-counsel-is-investigating-trump-for-possible-obstruction-of-justice/2017/06/14/9ce02506-5131-11e7-b064-828ba60fbb98_story.html?utm_term=.4c2c2c3a14df.

169 Ibid.

170 @realDonald Trump. "They made up a phony collusion with the Russians story, found zero proof, so now they go for obstruction of justice on the phony story. Nice" Twitter, 15 June 2017, 3:55 a.m.

171 Lynch, Sarah. "FBI Chief Sees No Evidence of White House Interference In Russia Probe." Reuters, 7 September 2017, https://www.reuters.com/article/

us-usa-fbi-russia/fbi-director-sees-no-evidence-of-interference-in-russia-probe-idUSKCN1BI2JN.

172 House Permanent Select Committee on Intelligence. Russia Investigation, Majority Summary, https://intelligence.house.gov/uploadedfiles/hpsci_russia_investigation_one_page_summary.pdf. Accessed May 19, 2018.

173 Ibid.

174 House Permanent Select Committee on Intelligence. Russia Investigation Minority Views, https://democrats-intelligence.house.gov/uploadedfiles/20180411_-_final_-_hpsci_minority_views_on_majority_report.pdf. Accessed May 19, 2018.

175 Ibid.

176 Ibid.

PART 3

1   Solomon, John, and Alison Spann. "Clintons Understated Support from Firm Hired by Russian Nuclear Company." *The Hill*, 18 November 2017, http://thehill.com/homenews/news/362234-clintons-understated-support-from-firm-hired-by-russian-nuclear-company.

2   Williams, Katie. "Dems: Uranium One Informant Provided 'No Evidence of Clinton 'Quid Pro Quo.'" *The Hill*, 8 March 2018, http://thehill.com/policy/national-security/377404-dems-uranium-one-informant-provided-no-evidence-of-wrongdoing-by.

3   Solomon, John, and Alison Spann. "Clintons Understated Support from Firm Hired by Russian Nuclear Company." *The Hill*, 18 November 2017, http://thehill.com/homenews/news/362234-clintons-understated-support-from-firm-hired-by-russian-nuclear-company.

4   Ibid.

5   Ibid.

6   Scannell, Kara, et al. "Mueller Indicts 13 Russian Nationals Over 2016 Election Interference." CNN, 17 February 2018, https://www.cnn.com/2018/02/16/politics/mueller-russia-indictments-election-interference/index.html.

7   Manfred, R. "How Moscow Meddles in the West's Elections." Heritage Foundation, 24 July 1984, https://www.heritage.org/election-integrity/report/how-moscow-meddles-the-wests-elections.

8   @realDonaldTrump. "The single greatest Witch Hunt in American history continues. There was no collusion, everybody including the Dems knows there was no collusion, & yet on and on it goes. Russia & the world is laughing at the stupidity they are witnessing. Republicans should finally take control!" 10 January 2018, 7:14 a.m., https://twitter.com/realDonaldTrump/status/951109942685126656.

9   McCarthy, Andrew. "Mueller Investigation: Politics, Not Law Enforcement or Counterintelligence. *National Review*, 2 December 2017, https://www.nationalreview.com/2017/12/robert-mueller-trump-russia-investigation-michael-flynn-obama-administration-foreign-policy-israel/.

10 Corn, David, and Michael Isikoff. "Why the Hell Are We Standing Down?" *Mother Jones*, 9 March 2018, https://www.motherjones.com/politics/2018/03/why-the-hell-are-we-standing-down/.

11 McCarthy, Andrew. "Clinton-Obama Emails: The Key to Understanding Why Hillary Wasn't Indicted." *National Review*, 23 January 2018, https://www.nationalreview.com/2018/01/hillary-clinton-barack-obama-emails-key-decision-not-indict-hillary/.

12 A Review of Various Actions by the Federal Bureau of Investigation and the Department of Justice in Advance of the 2016 Election. Office of the Inspector General,

US Department of Justice, June 2018, https://www.justice.gov/file/1071991/download.

13 Jones, Susan. "WikiLeaks: Podesta Asks Clinton's Lawyer, 'Think We Should Hold Emails To and From (Obama)?'" CNS News, 14 October 2016, https://www.cnsnews.com/news/article/susan-jones/wikileaks-podesta-asks-clintons-lawyer-think-we-should-hold-emails-and.

14 Staff. "BleachBit?!...Gowdy Says Hillary Deleted Emails, 'So Even God Couldn't Read Them.'" Fox News, 25 August 2016, http://insider.foxnews.com/2016/08/25/trey-gowdy-clinton-deleted-emails-so-even-god-couldnt-read-them.

15 Breitman, Kendall. "'Earnest' Obama, Hillary Corresponded Via Her Personal Email." *Politico*, 9 March 2015, https://www.politico.com/story/2015/03/obama-hillary-clinton-personal-email-115899.

16 Flores, Reena. "Obama Weighs In On Hillary Clinton's Private Emails." CBS News, 7 March 2015, https://www.cbsnews.com/news/obama-weighs-in-on-hillary-clinton-private-emails/.

17 McCarthy, Andrew. "Clinton-Obama Emails: The Key to Understanding Why Hillary Wasn't Indicted." *National Review*, 23 January 2018, https://www.nationalreview.com/2018/01/hillary-clinton-barack-obama-emails-key-decision-not-indict-hillary/.

18 Gerstein, Josh and Nolan D. McCaskill. "Obama Used a Pseudonym in Emails with Clinton, FBI Documents Reveal." *Politico*, 23 August 2016, https://www.politico.com/story/2016/09/hillary-clinton-emails-fbi-228607.

19 McCarthy, Andrew. "Clinton-Obama Emails: The Key to Understanding Why Hillary Wasn't Indicted." *National Review*, 23 January 2018, https://www.nationalreview.com/2018/01/hillary-clinton-barack-obama-emails-key-decision-not-indict-hillary/.

20 Shear, Michael. "Obama Tells 60 Minutes Hillary Clinton Made Email 'Mistake.'" *The New York Times*, 11 October 2015, https://www.nytimes.com/2015/10/12/us/politics/obama-tells-60-minutes-hillary-clinton-made-email-mistake.html.

21 A Review of Various Actions by the Federal Bureau of Investigation and the Department of Justice in Advance of the 2016 Election. Office of the Inspector General, US Department of Justice, June 2018, https://www.justice.gov/file/1071991/download.

22 Wolfgang, Ben. "Obama Says Hillary Clinton's Private Server Did Not Endanger National Security." *Washington Times*, 10 April 2016, https://www.washingtontimes.com/news/2016/apr/10/obama-says-hillary-clinton-emails-did-not-endanger/.

23 Easley, Jonathan. "Republicans Demand New Special Counsel Over Lost FBI Text Messages." *The Hill*, 22 January 2018, http://thehill.com/policy/national-security/370097-republicans-demand-new-special-counsel-over-lost-fbi-text-messages.

24 Statement by FBI Director James Comey. FBI.gov, 5 July 2016, https://www.fbi.gov/news/pressrel/press-releases/statement-by-fbi-director-james-b-comey-on-the-investigation-of-secretary-hillary-clinton2019s-use-of-a-personal-e-mail-system. Accessed April 3, 2018.

25 Corn, David, and Michael Isikoff. "Why the Hell Are We Standing Down?" *Mother Jones*, 9 March 2018, https://www.motherjones.com/politics/2018/03/why-the-hell-are-we-standing-down/.

26 Solomon, John, and Alison Spann. "Informant Provided FBI Evidence Russia Aided Iran Nuclear Program During Obama Years." *The Hill*, 26 March 2018, http://thehill.com/video/in-the-news/380366-informant-provided-fbi-evidence-russia-aided-iran-nuclear-program-during.

27 Ibid.

28 Ibid.

29　Ibid.

30　Ibid.

31　Grigorii Zinoviev, "Declaration of Zinoviev on the Alleged 'Red Plot,'" *The Communist Review,* vol. 5, no. 8 (December 1924), pp. 365–366.

32　Ibid.

33　Norton-Taylor, Richard. "Zinoviev Letter Was Dirty Trick by MI6." *The Guardian,* 3 February 1999, https://www.theguardian.com/politics/1999/feb/04/uk.political news6.

34　Ibid.

35　Ibid.

36　Jury, Louise. "Official: Zinoviev Letter Was Forged." *Independent,* 4 February 1999, https://www.independent.co.uk/news/official-zinoviev-letter-was-forged-1068600.html.

37　Johnson, Jenna. "Donald Trump on Waterboarding: 'If It Doesn't Work, They Deserve It Anyway.'" *Washington Post,* 23 November 2015, https://www.washingtonpost.com/news/post-politics/wp/2015/11/23/donald-trump-on-waterboarding-if-it-doesnt-work-they-deserve-it-anyway/?utm_term=.77db59b51470.

38　Sceats, Sonya. "British Complicity In Torture Still Needs to Be Smoked Out, for the Victims' Sake." *The Guardian,* 9 June 2016, https://www.theguardian.com/commentisfree/2016/jun/09/british-complicity-torture-mi6-rendition-decision-not-to-charge-uk-example.

39　Ibid.

40　Ibid.

41　McCarthy, Tom. "Donald Trump: I'd Bring Back 'A Hell of a Lot Worse Than Waterboarding.'" *The Guardian,* 7 February 2016, https://www.theguardian.com/us-news/2016/feb/06/donald-trump-waterboarding-republican-debate-torture.

42　Pengelly, Martin. "CIA Chief Brennan Would Not Carry Out Waterboarding Torture for Trump or Cruz." *The Guardian,* 10 April 2016, https://www.theguardian.com/law/2016/apr/11/cia-john-brennan-waterboarding-republican-president-trump-cruz.

43　Timm, Trevor. "Donald Trump's Anti-Terror Policies Sound a Lot Like War Crimes." *The Guardian,* 1 July 2016, https://www.theguardian.com/commentisfree/2016/jul/01/donald-trump-anti-terror-policies-war-crimes-waterboarding-torture.

44　Intelligence and Security Committee of Parliament. Annual Report 2016–2017. 20 December 2017, http://isc.independent.gov.uk/news-archive/20december2017. Accessed 7 April 2018.

45　Ibid.

46　Ibid.

47　Parkinson, Justin. "What Does a Donald Trump Win Mean for UK Politics?" BBC News, 9 November 2016, http://www.bbc.com/news/uk-politics-37851551.

48　Martin, Alexander. "Trump's Torture Support Could Mean the End of the GCHQ-NSA Relationship." *The Register,* 9 November 2016, https://www.theregister.co.uk/2016/11/09/trumps_torture_support_means_end_of_gchq_nsa_relationship/.

49　Ibid.

50　Ibid.

51　MacAskill, Ewen. "'Extreme Surveillance' Becomes UK Law with Barely a Whimper." *The Guardian,* 19 November 2016, https://www.theguardian.com/world/2016/nov/19/extreme-surveillance-becomes-uk-law-with-barely-a-whimper

52　Ibid.

53 Travis, Alan. "UK Security Agencies Unlawfully Collected Data for 17 Years, Court Rules." *The Guardian,* 17 October 2016, https://www.theguardian.com/world/2016/oct/17/uk-security-agencies-unlawfully-collected-data-for-decade.

54 @realDonaldTrump. "Ukrainian efforts to sabotage Trump campaign – 'quietly working to boost Clinton.' So where is the investigation A.G." 25 July 2017, 3:03 a.m. https://twitter.com/realDonaldTrump/status/889788202172780544.

55 Karatnycky, Adrian. "Why Trump Is Wrong about Ukrainian Interference in US Elections." Atlantic Council, 31 July 2017, http://www.atlanticcouncil.org/blogs/ukrainealert/why-trump-is-wrong-about-ukrainian-interference-in-us-elections.

56 Olearchyk, Roman. "Ukraine's Leaders Campaign Against 'Pro-Putin' Trump." *Financial Times,* 28 August 2016, https://www.ft.com/content/c98078d0-6ae7-11e6-a0b1-d87a9fea034f.

57 Vogel, Kenneth, and David Stern. "Ukrainian Efforts to Sabotage Trump Backfire." *Politico,* 11 January 2017, https://www.politico.com/story/2017/01/ukraine-sabotage-trump-backfire-233446.

58 Karatnycky, Adrian. "Why Trump Is Wrong about Ukrainian Interference in US Elections." Atlantic Council, 31 July 2017, http://www.atlanticcouncil.org/blogs/ukrainealert/why-trump-is-wrong-about-ukrainian-interference-in-us-elections.

59 Vogel, Kenneth, and David Stern. "Ukrainian Efforts to Sabotage Trump Backfire." *Politico,* 11 January 2017, https://www.politico.com/story/2017/01/ukraine-sabotage-trump-backfire-233446.

60 @realDonald Trump. "Terrible! Just found out that Obama had my "wires tapped" in Trump Tower just before the victory. Nothing found. This is McCarthyism!" 4 March 2017, 3:35 a.m., https://twitter.com/realDonaldTrump/status/837989835818287106.

61 @realDonaldTrump. "Is it legal for a sitting President to be 'wire tapping' a race for president prior to an election? Turned down by court earlier. A NEW LOW!" 4 March 2017, 3:49 a.m., https://twitter.com/realDonaldTrump/status/837993273679560704.

62 @realDonaldTrump. "Why did the Obama Administration start an investigation into the Trump Campaign (with zero proof of wrongdoing) long before the Election in November? Wanted to discredit so Crooked H would win. Unprecedented. Bigger than Watergate! Plus, Obama did NOTHING about Russian meddling." 5 March 2018, 5:22 a.m., https://twitter.com/realDonaldTrump/status/970650759091163137.

63 Kelly, Erin. "Trump Blocks Release of Dem Memo Rebutting GOP Claims of FBI Surveillance Abuse." *USA Today,* 9 February 2018, https://www.usatoday.com/story/news/politics/2018/02/09/trump-agrees-trump-authorizes-release-democratic-memo-rebutting-republican-claims-fbi-surveillance/317476002/.

64 Robbins, James. "Nunes Memo Exposes Abuse of Power." *USA Today,* 2 February 2018, https://www.usatoday.com/story/opinion/2018/02/02/nunes-memo-exposes-abuse-power/1088772001/.

ABOUT THE AUTHORS

 Dan Bongino is a former Secret Service agent, NYPD police officer, and a former Republican nominee for the U.S. Senate and the House. He is a multiple-time *New York Times* bestselling author and he is the host of the top-ranked podcast *The Dan Bongino Show*.

D.C. McAllister is a journalist, author, and political commentator whose work can be found at *The Daily Wire*, *PJ Media*, and *The Federalist*. She is the author of *A Burning and Shining Light: The Life and Ministry of David Brainerd* and *What Men Want to Say to Women (But Can't)*

 Matt Palumbo is *The Dan Bongino Show*'s "resident fact checker" and author of *The Conscience of a Young Conservative* and *Debunk This!* He is also the co-founder of Unbiased America.

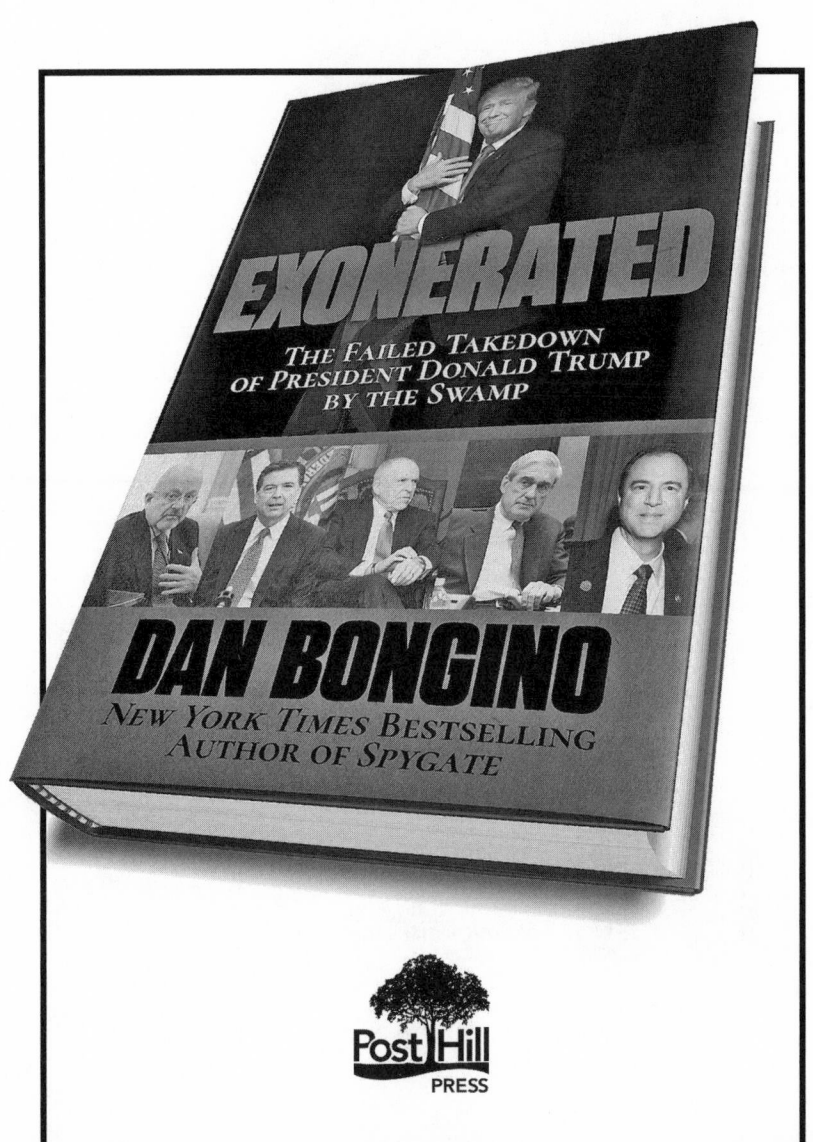